AUBURN & CORD

Lee Beck & Josh B. Malks

Motorbooks International
Publishers & Wholesalers

First published in 1996 by Motorbooks International Publishers & Wholesalers, 729 Prospect Avenue, PO Box 1, Osceola, WI 54020-0001 USA

Library of Congress Cataloging-in-Publication Data
Beck, Lee, 1960
    Auburn & Cord / Lee Beck, Josh B. Malks.
      p. cm.
    Includes index.
    ISBN 0-7603-0172-7 (casebound : alk. paper)
    1. Auburn automobile--History. 2. Cord
    automobile--History.
    I. Malks, Josh B., 1935- II. Title.
    TL215.A77B43 1996
    338.7'629222'0973--dc20   96-10496

On the front cover: Cord's elegant 1930 L-29 convertible sedan. From its inception, the L-29, and later the 810 and 812, were embraced by celebrities and the well heeled. Frank Lloyd Wright owned an L-29 from new and held onto it for some 30 years. This immaculate example is owned by Leonard Urlick. *Randy Leffingwell*

On the title page: The 810 Westchester sedan showcar. This body style was always Buehrig's favorite, an opinion shared by many enthusiasts. *Josh B. Malks collection*

On the back cover: Upper image: Two models pose at a Chicago-area golf course with a new 1935 Auburn cabriolet. *Ralph W. Dwight collection* Center image: Auto touring when men were men. It took a certain amount of dedication and determination to travel in the dead of the Indiana winter in this 1908 Auburn Model G. Lower image: The L-29's drive unit was a lengthy proposition. Inboard brakes meant costly service when it was time for new brake shoes.

Printed in Hong Kong

CONTENTS

Acknowledgments   **6**

Introduction   **7**

1   The Most for the Money   **9**
The Early Days to 1915

2   The Chicago Gang   **25**
1916-1923

3   The Cord that Binds   **39**
1924-1926

4   Explosive Growth   **57**
1927-1931

5   The Horse Pulls the Cart: The Cord L-29   **81**
1927-1932

6   The Sun Sets on Auburn   **103**
1932-1936

7   Grace Under Pressure: A New Cord   **119**
1933-1935

8   Kinetic Sculpture: The Cord 810 and 812   **135**
1935-1937

9   The Dismantling of Auburn   **153**
1937 Through the End

Index   **160**

Acknowledgments

I was most fortunate to have served for three years as archivist at the Auburn-Cord-Duesenberg Museum in the late 1980s. It was during my tenure there that I discovered that a book dedicated solely to the history of the Auburn Automobile Company (AAC), and its Auburn and Cord products, had never been published up to that time. With that in mind, and facing a massive restructuring of the archives, I began collecting the necessary information—taking copious notes from the materials at hand—in hopes of someday writing that book on the AAC. These notes remained in a file box until I knew the Auburn and Cord book would become a reality.

After I left the museum, I always feared someone would beat me to the punch of writing a book on Auburns and Cords. That never happened. Instead, the collective interest of the old car hobby shifted from prewar to postwar automobiles. In retrospect, that ensured my place in line to do the Auburn/Cord book. It also made my story difficult to sell, as conventional wisdom said that the market for prewar books (or prewar anything for that matter) had dried up. I didn't subscribe to that notion, and I believed the Auburn and Cord stories too interesting to neglect.

Thankfully, Senior Editor Zack Miller and the folks at Motorbooks International believed as I did and gave me the chance to write the book. I agreed to do so, however, only with the involvement of Cord historian Josh Malks. Ever since my tenure at the ACD museum, I have followed new developments as they related to Auburns. I could not match Josh's depth on Cords, however, as he diligently dug for every scrap of new information that could be turned up on that marque.

While the story of Errett Lobban Cord and his ventures with the Auburn Automobile Company has been told time and again, the tellings were frequently filled with inaccuracies. This was mostly due to the lack of proper background materials. Fortunately, I found the museum's archives rich with the information needed to fill the gaps as accurately as a 60-year time span allows. Histories studying the period prior to Cord's involvement with the company and after his departure from it are almost nonexistent. One could almost conclude the AAC never existed without Cord. But it did, and the company had a rich and interesting history both before and after Cord.

I would like to thank Gregg Buttermore and his assistant, John Emery, for their patience and cooperation in assisting me with this project. Gregg served as archivist at the Auburn-Cord-Duesenberg Museum before my tenure and is back at the helm doing a wonderful job. Inevitably, after getting involved with the research for this book, I found notes still lacking. Without Gregg and John's invaluable help and the museum's cooperation, I would have been dead in the water. All photos excepting those in chapters five, seven, and eight are from the Auburn-Cord-Duesenberg Museum, including those denoted from the Alan H. Leamy, Ralph Dwight, and McIntyre collections, unless noted otherwise. Patent drawings courtesy the U.S. Patent Office, unless noted otherwise.

Appreciation also goes to Henry Blommel for his priceless input. Over the years Henry fed information to me from his vast archives of Auburn and Cord materials. Bill Dreist, of Saginaw, Michigan, proved an invaluable source for documenting the origins of the original Auburn speedster design. Thanks also to Kerrie Romero of the University of Dayton archives, who provided me with a number of important documents that allowed me to flesh out the story of Victor Emanuel, a key player in the hostile takeover of the Cord Corporation. Moody's Investor Service also deserves recognition for its assistance in sending me all of its old research on the AAC. It was nice to have a reliable source of financial figures on the company after it went public in 1919.

Finally, I would like to express my gratitude to the hundreds of contributors to the Auburn-Cord-Duesenberg Club's newsletter. For more than 40 years, the miscellaneous tidbits of information that have appeared within the pages of the newsletter has provided a chronicle of Auburn history like no other source.

I am glad to see all of these various efforts finally come to fruition.

—Lee Beck, Piqua, Ohio

Most books, no matter how meticulously researched, fall short of perfection. Authors grit their teeth, hope no one notices, and vow to do even better if given the chance.

Zack Miller, my editor at Motorbooks International, had worked with me on two previous publishing efforts. When Zack offered the opportunity to collaborate with Lee Beck on the sections of *Auburn and Cord* that dealt with the two series of Cord automobiles, I jumped at the chance.

Readers of my previous book, *Cord 810/812: The Timeless Classic*, may find some variations in fact from that work to this. Even in the short time that elapsed between the two, fresh facts came to light

Dedication

Dedicated to my wife, Lora, and my daughter, Taylor Anne, who lost a husband and a father, respectively, for the year-plus that I labored on this manuscript.

—Lee Beck

Dedicated to my mom, who read to me from the day I was born, hoping I'd someday be able to write.

—Josh B. Malks

and new interpretations were put on old ones. While the story of the Cord marque in this book is considerably condensed, it has the benefit of additional time for reflection and analysis.

In addition to those acknowledged by Lee Beck, several other scholars helped add new data. Bob Fabris served as the first Cord L-29 Historian for the Auburn-Cord-Duesenberg Club. Over the decades he had personal contact with many of the principals in the story, including Cornelius Van Ranst, John Oswald, Alfred H. Rzeppa, Philip Wright, Rudy Creteur, Alexis deSakhnoffsky, Leo Goossen, and Fred Miller. Bob's extensive writings have incorporated, with permission, the research of Jerry Gebby, Strother MacMinn, Griffith Borgeson, Warren Fitzgerald, and Karl Ludvigsen. It was Bob who first obtained the diary and records of Herb Snow and made them available to researchers.

Paul J. Bryant is the Cord L-29 Historian of the Auburn-Cord-Duesenberg Club at this writing. He shared his interviews with Eddie Offutt and Myron Stevens and his statistical records. Paul also provided some unique and important photographs. Thanks also to Jim Brockman, for filling in the history of the L-29 speedster.

As in my earlier volume, Ronald B. Irwin, Cord 810-812 Historian of the Auburn-Cord-Duesenberg Club, hovered protectively over the material. Additional assistance was provided by Stan Gilliland, R. Oliger, D. Sherman, Stan Shirley, and Chuck Marsh.

Photographs and illustrations in chapters five, seven, and eight were borrowed from many sources; they're credited after each caption. (As Lee indicates, those not otherwise attributed came from the files and collections of the Auburn-Cord-Duesenberg Museum.) Patent drawings were reproduced at the archives maintained at Sy³ in Sunnyvale, California. I thank Don Howell for his meticulous searches of those patent records.

Some of the photographs in chapter eight previously existed only in obscure dealer literature or in old newspapers, unreproducible in their original state. The same was true of the dynomometer chart of the supercharged Cord engine, with its pencilled notations by August Rickenbach. We have the artistry of Douglas Graham and his magic computer to thank for their reappearance in this book in a quality that does them justice. Doug's talented contribution is much appreciated.

—Josh B. Malks, San Jose, California

Introduction

No less than 10 automotive manufacturers' nameplates have emerged from the town of Auburn, Indiana. This is rather startling when one considers the population of the town was only some 5,000 at the turn of the century. Most of the carmakers lived and died before World War I. The last company to go, the Auburn Automobile Company (AAC or Auburn), manufactured cars until 1937.

Indiana held many of the right ingredients for a lucrative automotive market to spawn within the state. The numerous German immigrants who moved there brought their woodworking skills to the carriage industry. Such skills were also important in the early days of automobile production. The state also benefitted from numerous rivers and canals, crucial to early and middle 19th century commerce. This, in turn, led the railroads to Indiana. The state offered any number of open doors through which raw materials might enter, with finished goods leaving on the same tracks. Still, these seeming advantages do not completely explain such a plethora of automakers. Reason tells us the manufacturers from a small burg in northeastern Indiana should have become nothing more than footnotes in the annals of automotive lore. Instead, the products of the AAC—namely, Auburn and Cord—refuse to go away. As of 1996, nearly 60 years had passed since the last Auburn left the assembly line, 59 years since the final Cord. Yet these nameplates remain the objects of intense interest. Auburns and Cords are cherished, actively collected, extensively sought. The question that comes to mind is, "Why does the interest in Auburns and Cords persist?" The answers lie in the history of the company that brought forth these marques. It is a history as fascinating and as complex as the cars themselves.

The AAC had a personality of its own, almost transcending the individual personalities that made the company tick. Only a chronological telling of the AAC's history can sort out this complicated and sometimes tangled tale. Even then, we are left wanting for the details that died with the men who designed and built these fascinating marques.

It is time, after some 60 years, that the story of Auburn and Cord be told as clearly as the historical record will allow its recounting.

An aerial view of Auburn, Indiana, circa 1931, looking north. In the foreground is the Auburn Automobile Company's complex. The smokestack of the powerplant almost points directly to the DeKalb County Courthouse, situated in the heart of downtown Auburn.

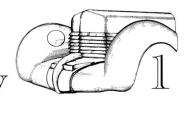

The Most for the Money

The Early Days to 1915

The Auburn Automobile Company (AAC) stopped manufacturing cars in 1937, some six decades ago. More than a decade before that a group of Chicago investors bought out the original owners. And nearly a century has passed since a family of carriage makers filed the papers of incorporation for the AAC. We can even look back further if we wish, some 150 years in fact (see sidebar), to see the earliest roots of the AAC.

The AAC company had its beginnings at the dawn of the 20th century. Although the automobile as an industry was still in its infancy, particularly in the United States, it was growing fast. Many automakers developed from carriage manufacturers, a natural progression considering that early inventors and tinkerers installed internal-combustion engines in, on, and under carriages. The Eckhart Carriage Company (ECC) of Auburn, Indiana, was no exception. Charles Eckhart and two of his three sons, Frank and Morris, became involved in trying to bring an automobile to fruition, one which would bear their hometown's name. The answer to the question, "Which of the Eckharts initiated the idea of building an automobile?" is elusive. There is apparently some controversy as to whether Frank or Morris built the first Auburn. Most of the controversy, however, has never been between automotive historians, but rather among family members. Within the archives of the Auburn-Cord-Duesenberg Museum reside the recollections of George B. Eckhart, grandson of Charles and son of Frank Eckhart. Not surprisingly, his writings give the credit to his father. Due to a lack of a traceable history supporting Morris' side of the story, George's

THE MOST *for* THE MONEY

history will have to suffice. Ignoring the conflicting stories, the chronology evidently remains the same; only the names change to fit whoever is championing the cause.

A Prototype Emerges

Frank Eckhart, in his capacity of selling carriages to the wholesale trade, traveled extensively. One can only presume that somewhere, be it New York, Chicago, or elsewhere, Frank caught a glimpse of his first horseless carriage at a trade show, chugging down a street, or perhaps side-by-side, with an Eckhart carriage in a loyal dealer's showroom. Frank decided to buy a curved-dash Oldsmobile in 1900 and traveled to Lansing, Michigan, to buy it. One could assume that this is the automobile referred to in the November 21, 1900, issue of *The Horseless Age*, where it was reported that "[Charles] Eckhert [sic], candidate for governor of Indiana on the Prohibition ticket, made his canvass during the recent campaign in an automobile. Mr. Eckhert [sic]

Charles Eckhart was born in 1841, the third son of German immigrants. Charles' parents migrated to Germantown, Pennsylvania, in 1838. His father, John Eckhardt, was a weaver, and as a boy Charles helped spool yarn. As was customary for the day, Charles' education was brief, lasting only 18 months.

Charles left home at the age of 16. The young Eckhart served a wheelwright's apprenticeship at a Hilltown, Pennsylvania, carriage shop. He left for a time to seek better employment, then returned to find the shop had been purchased by D. R. Moyer. This arrangement was more agreeable to Eckhart. In 1859, Charles bought out his employer—then in financial trouble—with his savings and an $800 note.

Eckhart's work consisted mostly of repairs to carriages and wagons. He sold the carriage business at the outbreak of the Civil War and served in the Union Army. It was around this time that Charles dropped the letter "d" from the spelling of his family name, preferring Eckhart.

After the war, Charles returned to his home state for a short time, entering the Bryant and Stratton Business College in Philadelphia. His funds soon ran out, and he returned to the carriage trade, this time self-employed in Norristown, Pennsylvania. By 1866, his immediate prospects looked gloomy, and Charles traveled to Indiana to visit an uncle (or two uncles, by some accounts) who resided on a farm near Waterloo, Indiana, just north of Auburn. He stayed on in Waterloo, marrying Barbara Ellen Ashelman in the fall of 1866. Family accounts have him working for the Studebaker

Charles Eckhart, family patriarch and automotive manufacturer.

brothers in South Bend at this time. This seems unlikely, as the commuting distance from Waterloo to South Bend would have been prohibitive in the days of horse-powered transportation. More trustworthy is an account printed in a 1914 abstract of DeKalb County, Indiana, which states Charles "secured a position at his trade in Kendallville," Kendallville being but a short distance from Waterloo. Who this Kendallville carriage maker was who employed Charles remains unknown. The abstract has Charles moving to Auburn for the first, and for a short time, in 1867.

In the fall of 1867, Charles moved back to Pennsylvania, where he went into the carriage business with his former employer, D. R. Moyer. Moyer pulled out of the carriage business after a year, and Charles labored on until the fall of 1874, when he quit and returned with his family to Auburn. All of his children—three sons and a daughter—were born during his time in Pennsylvania.

Barbara traded her inheritance of 80 acres of farmland to her brother Moses for a brick house and a five-acre plot (today located on East Seventh Street in Auburn). Unable to find employment when the Panic of 1874 hit, Charles undertook repairing carriages out of his home. Though it was a humble beginning, the five acres surrounding the Eckhart homestead served Charles well. Small buildings began to dot the grounds. "He built a small shop nearby, a structure 18 by 24 feet, two stories high, and in that building, in March 1875, started what is the Eckhart Carriage Company of today," the DeKalb County Abstract reported. Eventually, a full-fledged factory sprouted up, and the ECC offered a complete line of carriages. Charles incorporated the business in 1885 (and re-incorporated in 1903). In 1888, it was capitalized at $20,000. The Auburn Weekly Courier reviewed several local businesses around 1900, and reported that the company "sold 195 carriages last year . . . and . . . sales thus far . . . indicate that this year they will sell 250 buggies."

"From the start he always insisted on the best of workmanship and strict honesty in his business," the DeKalb County Abstract recorded. Details were heeded. An Eckhart carriage included double-collar steel axles, tempered steel springs, steel tires, and hickory running gears. Bodies were framed in white ash; only glue and screws fastened an Eckhart buggy, no nails. Tops used steel-bow sockets, rubberized cloth, and solid-forged Norway iron rails. The beauty of such features is lost on those of us living in the late 20th century, but to customers of 100 years ago, they meant everything.

Charles was a religious and civic-minded man. The DeKalb County Abstract pointed out that although Charles "succeeded so well with such meager schooling as he had, one might expect him

An Eckhart carriage, as illustrated by a turn-of-the-century brochure.

to esteem school but lightly, but he does not do so. He believes every child is better off with schooling." As a member of the Advent Christian Church, he gave liberally to its institution of higher learning, Aurora College in Aurora, Illinois (at the time, it was known as the Advent Christian College). Eckhart Hall is still a part of its campus. It was Charles who provided the needed funds ($20,000 to be exact) to establish Auburn's local library named, appropriately, Eckhart Library. He also played a key role in creating Eckhart Park, which now hosts the judging of Auburns, Cords, and Duesenbergs every Labor Day weekend. Charles was also instrumental in establishing the Auburn YMCA, a charity in which the Eckhart family remained active even after they moved to the Los Angeles area. Charles' letterhead reflected his philanthropy: "I claim no privilege for myself or for my children that I am not doing my utmost to secure for all others on equal terms."

Charles was also a teetotaler. In 1900, he ran unsuccessfully for governor of Indiana on the Prohibition Party ticket. His personal letters were always concerned with business or philanthropic matters and offer little insight regarding Eckhart's personality. Only once was the veil surrounding this man dropped. Family historian George B. Eckhart wrote, "Charles was the disciplinarian of the family, demanding obedience from all, and getting it. He ruled the home with an iron hand." That Charles looked after the interest of others in the community, there is no question. And the same concern rings true for his own children. As each boy reached eight years of age, Charles insisted that he learn the carriage trade. This, however, was never allowed to interfere with the boys' schooling. Each of the boys learned different aspects of the carriage trade. Frank, his oldest, mastered painting. Next was Morris, who learned the blacksmith trade, and then William, who was coached in upholstering. In 1893, Charles retired from the company's day-to-day business affairs, and his sons took over. Frank had already been on the road selling Eckhart carriages for six years when he became president of the company. Morris took over the sales position vacated by his older brother. And Frank was president of the ECC for only a short time before the Eckharts decided to pursue the idea of manufacturing their own automobile.

This photo shows the Eckhart family around the time Charles' sons became seriously involved with the Eckhart Carriage Company. Standing: Anne, William, Frank, and Morris. Seated: Charles and Barbara.

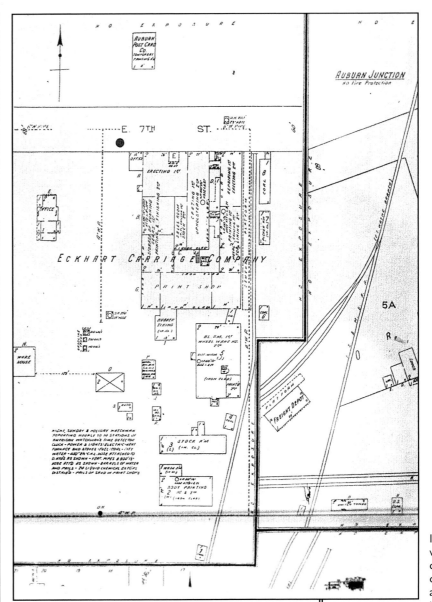

Insurance plats were commonly drawn at the turn of the century and acted as an inventory of towns in case a fire wiped out all traces of buildings. Shown here is the Eckhart Carriage Company's complex at its height in 1914.

is a carriage manufacturer, and proposes manufacturing automobiles in the near future." This last statement indicates that as early as 1900, Charles Eckhart wanted to pursue automotive manufacturing in earnest. This calls into question George's narrative when he talks of Frank's lone support for manufacturing automobiles.

The curved-dash Olds, sporting a one-cylinder engine, seating for two, tiller steering, and no top, left something to be desired for roadability and weather protection. In 1902, a doctor in Auburn purchased a 15-horsepower, two-cylinder Winton detachable tonneau that carried five passengers, used a standard steering wheel, and also had a windshield and lights. The Oldsmobile withered in comparison. Frank Eckhart desired something ". . . bigger and better than the Oldsmobile," according

This photograph has typically been credited as depicting the first Auburn prototype. It most certainly reflects the Auburn as it was manufactured for the 1903 model year.

One of the earliest known Auburn ads, showing its 1903 model. *National Automotive Historical collection*

to George. That same year, a Winton dealer in Chicago advertised a model similar to the doctor's model. The dealer listed it for $2,700, and Frank decided to pursue the purchase. Upon arrival in Chicago, Frank found the price of the Winton had risen to $3,000, and this was without windshield or lights. Frank balked at the price and retired to his hotel to ponder the wisdom of the purchase. While there, the story goes, Frank ran into a sales representative who sold goods to the ECC. Frank relayed his story to the rep, then added that he knew where to obtain an engine if only he could lay his hands on a transmission and differential. The rep replied that he knew of a gentleman in Springfield, Illinois, from whom Frank could purchase those items. Frank traveled to Springfield and purchased the mechanical goods, then proceeded to Logansport, Indiana, to obtain a two-cylinder engine. Enlisting the ". . . help of a blacksmith"—likely an employee of the ECC—the duo assembled the first prototype. This early Auburn held a single-cylinder, 95-cubic-inch engine, good for six horsepower. It employed tiller steering, much like the Olds. Clearly, an automobile exactly like that of the Winton was not critical.

Although no recorded history remains regarding from whom Frank purchased his drivetrain, some educated speculation is not out of order. Logansport was home to Rutenber, maker of automobile engines in the early part of this century. The company moved to the small central-Indiana town in mid-1902. AAC would later rely on Rutenber to supply a good many of its engines to the company. As for the source of the transmission and drivetrain in Springfield,

Illinois, another future Auburn supplier lends itself as a possibility. Charles Rayfield invented and built automotive carburetors in that town; his sons Bill and John would later manufacture automobiles under the family name. In light of their combined interests, it's reasonable to expect the family to have had a transmission or two in domestic stock, even a few years before the Rayfields entered the automotive manufacturing field. That Auburn would use Rayfield carburetors in the years ahead is no secret.

Frank's prototype must have been a success, or at least it convinced the Eckharts that they were capable of manufacturing a like automobile. According to *Moody's Manual of Investments*, the Eckharts incorporated their new operation in 1903 as the Auburn Automobile Company. In hindsight, it seems a bit premature to establish a company based on one prototype. Automotive history is littered with those who did the same with nothing more than the prototype coming of it. The Eckharts, however, were not a brash family, and once the company was established, sheer determination to succeed took over. Financially secure from their success in the carriage trade, the Eckharts were also fiscally conservative. Knowing their character, it's little surprise the Eckharts built the AAC into a viable, albeit small, automotive manufacturer.

Auburn Initiates Production

In its April 29, 1903, issue, *The Horseless Age* reported, "The Auburn Automobile Company has one automobile being tested." This must have referred to the Auburn model the company displayed at its inaugural outing, the 1903 Chicago Automobile Show, held February 11 to 21. The March 1, 1903, issue of *Cycle and Automobile Trade Journal* describes this late arrival to the show in detail. The new Auburn was a four-stroke, 142.6-cubic-inch, single-cylinder model, producing 10 horsepower at 900 rpm. The engine was mounted

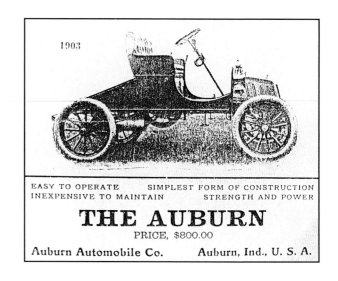

1903

EASY TO OPERATE   SIMPLEST FORM OF CONSTRUCTION
INEXPENSIVE TO MAINTAIN   STRENGTH AND POWER

THE AUBURN
PRICE, $800.00

Auburn Automobile Co.   Auburn, Ind., U. S. A.

amidships, with the copper-pipe radiator mounted in front and beneath the frame. A float-feed carburetor supplied fuel, fired by a jump-spark ignition. The transmission was of the planetary gear variety, with two forward speeds and a reverse. Twenty-eight-inch artillery-style wheels, made of "second-growth hickory," allowed the Auburn to roll on three-inch clincher tires. The rear axle utilized a Brown-Lipe differential. The body sported a maroon coat of paint with black moldings. The seats were trimmed in leather. The two-passenger body featured a sloping "torpedo deck," as it was later dubbed. It was very similar to what Winton created in 1902. The Auburn's wheelbase was set at 78 inches and the track width at 56 inches in deference to standard carriage widths. Thus, an Auburn could follow the ruts in the road during dry season. It was reported that the "body can be removed by taking out four nuts. . . . All adjustments of the motor and transmission can be made without detaching any other parts." Four years later, the AAC was still using these bragging rights in its sales literature. Simplicity in design was a valued asset.

Folklore tells us the company produced 25 automobiles, some accounts report 50, by the end of its first year of manufacturing, 1903. The paper trail following the early Auburn models can become confusing. As early as the April 1, 1903, issue of *Cycle and Automobile Trade Journal* one can find a description of a 12-horsepower, two-cylinder Auburn riding on 30-inch artillery wheels and showing a rear-entrance tonneau attached to the torpedo deck. Listed at $1,400 with side lamps and tool kit, this two-cylinder Auburn weighed in at 1,250 pounds. The summary goes on to say that the company was "also putting out a runabout with detachable tonneau, of similar construction (to the model shown); price, $900; with tonneau, $1,000; weight, 1,050 and 1,150 pounds." This latter runabout accurately describes the single-cylinder Auburn, but what of the two-cylinder model? Only a drawing depicts the two-cylinder Auburn, and although the Eckharts may have already been planning to up the cylinder ante on their cars in 1903, this likely did not occur until 1905. The earliest known sales brochure, produced by the AAC in 1904, only describes a single-cylinder model, dubbed the Model A. Cost was listed at $1,250 by that year, but the remainder of the specifications match those of the Auburn displayed at the 1903 Chicago Auto Show. *Motor Age* mentioned in its February 11, 1904, issue that the AAC "displayed at the 1904 Chicago Automobile Show," setting up across the aisle from the Ford Motor Company. "Representing the Auburn Automobile Company," the magazine went on to say, "were Morris Eckhart, Frank Eckhart, Frank Shugar [sic], George Shugar [sic], Sam Brink, [and] Milton Stewart [of] Auburn, Indiana."

Auburn Expands

By 1904, sales of Auburns justified the expansion of production facilities. Auburns built before this date were somehow manufactured between the ECC's carriages. Now, the company erected a two-story 60x100-foot building behind the ECC complex, solely for the purpose of manufacturing the new automobile. Yet, even with all this forward momentum, George Eckhart reports that there was "considerable concern in the minds of . . . family [members] as to whether [continued manufacture of automobiles] should be given up or continued." George recorded that discussions revolved around the horseless carriage as being a "fad and its future . . . as very indefinite. It was a good many years before the banks considered loans to car builders as safe and desirable investments. It was only [at] the insistence of Frank that the car business [should continue]. . . . [The] fortune that was to come to the family through the Auburn Automobile Company (was due) to his foresight." This is an interesting insight into the Eckhart family, but one has to wonder how it all fits. For instance, Charles was rather progressive in 1900 by campaigning in an automobile. The indirect quote in *The Horseless Age*, mentioning the possibility of becoming an automobile manufacturer "in the near future," is attributed to Charles. Does this sound like a cynical, paternal authority within a family-owned company? Curious, too, is the knowledge that it was Morris, not Frank, who headed the new automotive operations. Frank remained in active management at the ECC. Morris receives little due from his nephew. "In later years, Uncle Morris tried to take credit for this, but I have the true story from my dad," George recorded. George did give his uncle some recognition. After the company moved to its final destination on the south end of Auburn, "Morris took [to] more active management of the car factory and developed the

The Auburn, Model A 1904—Front View

In 1904, Auburn used a model designation for its vehicle for the first time, in this case the Model A. It used a single headlamp and had pronounced catwalks around its "hood."

The Auburn, Model B, 1905

For 1905, Auburn's Model B grew in stature on the front end and used dual headlamps.

business into [a sizable] investment. Good profits were made each year and some years very phenomenal earnings." Many employees of the ECC started to move over to the Auburn line.

By 1905, the two-cylinder Auburn was reality. Its 196.4-cubic-inch, horizontally opposed engine developed 18 horsepower at 800 rpm. Peripheral details between the Model B and the single-cylinder Model A remained essentially the same. The Model B's wheelbase, however, stretched to 92 inches. Sales literature claimed a top speed of 35 miles per hour. The AAC also ventured into building station wagons, such as they were. Actually, these wagons were placed on stretched Auburn chassis, with three bench seats capable of holding nine adults. They are reminiscent of the early sightseeing buses used at Yellowstone Park. No top covered the passengers. Reportedly, AAC built only a couple, and the station wagons were not shown in sales literature.

The *Auburn Weekly Courier* noted in its July 5, 1906, edition that the AAC "has increased its facilities until they can turn out 100 per year of which is now celebrated as the Auburn vehicle." Such production figures hardly sound like a reason for celebration, even in 1906, but the Eckharts pushed on. The 1906 model offerings were unchanged from the previous year. A solitary, two-cylinder model—dubbed the Model C—carried the Auburn nameplate. The displacement of the two-banger increased to 216.5 cubic inches, and it developed 24 horsepower. This engine would not

undergo any further refinements until its demise after the 1911 model year.

It is thought the AAC purchased the 24-horsepower two-cylinder from the Model Gas and Gasoline Engine Company, whose factory was located on Auburn's south side. Auburn lawyer E. A. Myers started the company in 1902. In 1904, a number of local banks closed in Auburn, and Myers found his company in receivership. Myers reorganized in 1906 and moved his company to Peru, Indiana. It was then that Myers split his company into two segments: the Model Automobile Company, responsible for automobile production, and the Model Gas Engine Works, which produced engines, clutches, and transmissions. In 1912, Myers sold his Model Gas Engine Works to business interests in Pittsburgh. By 1913, his automotive business was floundering. Trying to stave off the inevitable, Myers contracted with the Rayfields of Springfield, Illinois, (whom we previously met) to build the Rayfield car for that family. Apparently Myers never bothered to tell the Rayfields that his company was in receivership. Rayfield sued for breach of contract, but could not collect. In a ghastly domino effect, the Rayfield automotive manufacturing assets (but not the carburetor business) were sold at public auction in February 1916 to cover the company's disastrous foray with Myer's automotive venture. Ironically, one of the Eckharts, perhaps aware of Model's financial woes but not necessarily its receivership, may have instigated a meeting between Myers and the Rayfield family. It's all postulation, but the connections between the three companies were there.

Auburn started to expand its offerings in 1907. No less than three different models—all using the 216.5-cubic-inch, 24-horsepower, two-cylinder engine—could be found in the company's sales brochure. The Model D was decidedly different from previous Auburns in that it had a five-passenger, side-entrance touring body ($1,250). The Model E (price unknown) was a Model D with the additions of a top, gas headlights, and Prest-o-lite tank (carried gas for the headlights). The Model F shared the same chassis as the Models D and E, but used a two-passenger runabout body ($1,150). They all used 32-inch artillery wheels and Raymond drum brakes at the rear wheels. The wheelbase grew to 100 inches. The brochures announced the chain-driven Auburn as capable of 40 miles per hour.

Beginning in 1907, the AAC started to use the slogan, "The Most for the Money." It remained in Auburn brochures throughout the Eckhart's ownership of the company. Also touted in sales literature was "Established 1902," in reference to the first Auburn prototype built that year. Before the Eckharts sold Auburn, the start date had slid back to 1901. When Errett Lobban Cord gained control of the company in the late 1920s, his advertising people simply rounded the date off to 1900.

MODEL-C

Auburn introduced its first four-cylinder models in 1909, moving the company away from its single- and two-cylinder roots.

Although hood profiles and molding curves changed on the 1908 Auburns, little else differed. In fact, the Model G was almost a direct carryover from the Model D, and the Model H a carryover from the Model E. The sole exception was the elimination of the Model F runabout in favor of a much more exciting Model K. Although dubbed a runabout, it was closer to a roadster in body style. Customers could specify single or dual rumble seats. The fenders swooped more dramatically, connected by the running board. The carburetor of choice was a Schebler. Prices rose $100 for equivalent models, the Model G selling for $1,350, the Model K runabout for $1,250. It was around this time that the Eckharts apparently called upon the services of an advertising agency for production of AAC brochures. Printing suddenly switched from Chicago to Grand Rapids, Michigan, and the sales prose and verbiage took on a different tone, robust at times.

For 1909, Models G, H, and K carried over intact from the previous year. This was the first time the AAC used the same designations in two consecutive years. The bigger news came with the introduction of the four-cylinder models. Auburn mounted the L-head fours up front, using a fan behind a radiator to pull cooling air through the core. The Rutenber engine displaced 201 cubic inches, with the cylinders cast separately. The drop-forged crankshaft rode on five main bearings mounted in an aluminum alloy crankcase. Valves were all the same size and interchangeable. The sliding-gear transmission now gave three speeds forward and one for reverse. For the first time, an Auburn used a driveshaft for transferring horsepower to the wheels. Now two sets of brakes worked on the rear drums. External contracting bands pinched the outside of the drum when a driver pushed the pedal. Internal, expanding shoes—an early ancestor of drum brakes—were used only in conjunction with the emergency brake lever. Auburn used this braking arrangement for many years to come. All four-cylinder models rode on 106-inch wheelbases and were later referred to as the 30 series. The Model B ($1,400 and not to be confused with the 1905 Model B), a touring car, was similar to the two-cylinder Model G in body concept. The Model C ($1,350), although listed as a double-rumble roadster, was more conventional in style than the Model K. Auburn listed the Model D ($1,300) as a single-rumble roadster. The AAC had grown sufficiently to warrant moving its operations off the ECC complex entirely. The Eckharts moved their company to the south end of Auburn along a trestle then known as the Vandalia tracks.

A New Factory

The AAC occupied a factory complex originally built by the Auburn Foundry and Machine Company in 1885, then later used by the Model Gas and Gasoline Engine Company. Model Gas had

Melvin E. Leasure, factory superintendent of Auburn at the time this photo was taken in 1910, is in the driver's seat of this 1910 Auburn 40 chassis. Leasure won the 40-horsepower-class stock car race with this car at the Oklahoma state fairgrounds' half-mile dirt track on April 22, 1910, covering 5 miles in seven minutes, five seconds, for an average of 42.34 miles per hour.

vacated the premises three years earlier, and the Auburn Commercial Club arranged the sale of the complex to the AAC. The company erected a new two-story building, which served as its administration building until 1930. In the years after the AAC's demise in 1937, the top story was shaved off, but the bottom floor still remains in active use by the City of Auburn's street department. It stands just north of the present-day Auburn-Cord-Duesenberg Museum.

For 1910, Auburn created a new series, designated the Auburn 40. That numbering, however, was not used in identifying individual models; instead, the alphabet soup continued. Auburn introduced the Auburn 40 "to meet the demand for longer wheelbases, higher wheels, more room, and consequently, more power." The buyer did indeed receive all of these improvements. In this series, the wheelbase grew to 116 inches, with 36-inch wheels. A 35- to 40-horsepower Rutenber 318-cubic-inch four-cylinder powered the 40, and its Remy magneto ignition was standard. Production body color was dark blue with gold pinstriping. The Model X, in the 40 series, was of the touring variety. On this model, the top was part of the price ($1,650). The Model R, a Baby Tonneau, listed for the same price. The Model S (also $1,650) combined the body attributes of the Model C and D and let the buyer designate either a single or double rumble. The remaining Auburn models for 1910 simply carried over from the previous year. On April 22, 1910, the AAC's factory superintendent, Melvin E. Leasure, raced an Auburn 40 over a one-mile dirt track in a five-mile event at the Oklahoma State Fair. Leasure won the 40- to 60-horsepower class by beating a Knox and an Interstate.

Despite growing success, the Eckharts discussed the sale of the AAC to various interests as early as July 1911 (perhaps earlier, but this is the earliest verifiable date). Frank Eckhart wrote to his father at this time, "The sale of the automobile business is off from the best information which I can get. . . . I am not sorry that [the] deal fell through, if Morris does not get it into his head to throw it all over, . . ." which was a rare display of emotion in an Eckhart letter. Frank went on

to write, ". . . if [Morris] insists on [being] dissatisfied it might be better if we sell out." Simon Straus, of the Straus Brothers, had been the interested party; little more is known of this potential buyer.

Increasingly, the Eckhart family spent their time in Los Angeles. The carriage business remained reasonably profitable in 1911. According to Frank, "We are invoicing at the carriage factory; will sell about 4,100 jobs this year and so far as I can see ought to make some money." For 1911, the Auburn 40 series remained mostly unchanged from the previous year. The Model X touring became the Model Y touring ($1,700). The Model R baby tonneau turned into the Model T baby tonneau ($1,700), and the Model S roadster with single or double rumble begat the Model M roadster with single or double rumble ($1,700).

The letter change does denote a few alterations. The new models used three-quarter elliptical springs at the rear instead of the former full elliptical springs. Gas headlights were standard fare. Both the 40 and 30 series Auburns now used leather-faced cone clutches. The wheelbase on the Model Y and T was lengthened to 120 inches. The Model S retained the previous year's 116-inch wheelbase. These models were offered with dark blue livery and white pinstriping. One new addition to the 40 series was the Model N ($1,750), simply listed as a "fore[sic]-door car," and painted in Battleship Gray (later known as Auburn Gray). In the 30 series, the company dubbed the fore-door the Model L ($1,400) and the touring the Model F ($1,400 and similar to the previous Model B). Both sported Royal Blue paint. The roadster dropped out of sight in Auburn 30 guise, but was retained in the 24 (two-cylinder) series. The Model G touring and Model K roadster two-cylinders made their last appearance. Emory Oscar Penry, more commonly known as E. O. Penry, joined the AAC in 1911, starting as a road tester on February 1. Penry rose through the ranks of the company, eventually obtaining the position of vice president of manufacturing.

No sooner than the new year, 1912, turned over, the Eckharts suffered a loss. Back at the ECC complex, still actively running after the AAC had moved out three years earlier, the "body filling rooms" burned to the ground. These rooms, where workers rendered final touches to the wooden carriage bodies before painting, represented the building in which the AAC had its roots. The *Auburn Courier* for January 18, 1912, covered the story with: "ECKHART WAREROOMS BURNED! Fire Which Started From An Unknown Source Tuesday Morning Completely Destroyed the Filling Rooms of Carriage Company—$25,000 DAMAGES—Several thousand carriage bodies were burned and practically a year's stock destroyed." And that was just the headlines. The story continued in grandiose form:

"The body filling rooms, or in other words, the birthplace of the Auburn automobile, was totally destroyed by fire Tuesday morning, and in spite of heroic efforts of the city fire department, which arrived upon the scene within a very few minutes after the alarm was sounded. The main factory was temporarily shut down as a result of the fire, and twelve employees of the finishing rooms lost their jobs overnight. There was nothing saved from the building. A bicycle belonging to one of the employees, which cost $35 last season, was included in the ruins."

Frank Eckhart was indirectly quoted by the newspaper as saying "$25,000 would be a conservative figure of the loss sustained, which was fully covered by insurance." The report also noted that if no temporary quarters could be found for the filling rooms, "room . . . will be made in the main factory building."

Symbolically, the fire represented a separation of the AAC from its beginnings: ". . . all that remains of the former home of the Auburn automobile factory . . . are the tottering chimneys of four in number and the smoldering ruins." The carriage business, however, continued for another six years.

In correspondence to his father, Frank announced intentions for the 1912 model year. "The [company has] plans for [1912], which include a 30–35 horsepower [model], [a] 40 horsepower four-

Auburn entered the six-cylinder market in 1912. This later example, a 1914 Auburn 6-46, is parked in front of a canvas sheet. This was a common practice of the day as it helped advertising retouchers airbrush the background a solid white. In fact, this photo was the basis for the 6-46's illustration in Auburn's 1914 catalog.

cylinder, and a 50–60 [horsepower], six-cyl[inder], seven-passenger car. The two-cyl[inders] are all sold except one." As predicted, a six-cylinder Auburn emerged for the first time, a touring car known as the Six-50. It utilized a 421-cubic-inch Rutenber, producing some 50 horsepower, with the engine's cylinders individually cast. The pistons wore five rings, one of which was positioned over the wrist pin bore to prevent the pin from working out and scoring the cylinder wall. There was a three-point engine suspension used, and a Bosch magneto. The Six-50 was the biggest Auburn to date, with a 135-inch wheelbase riding on 37-inch wheels. The price tag was rather large, too: $3,000. Painted in Purple Lake with nickel trim, it was a majestic-looking machine. The external/internal brakes of lower-priced Auburns gave way to double internal brakes on the Six-50 (the Model 40-N had also used this system in 1911).

Auburn's model designations became increasingly maddening. In addition to the Six-50, the 40 series started to use the number "40" in model nomenclature. Still, the company couldn't quite bring itself to drop its lettering system. Hence, there was now the Model 40-N touring ($1,750), the fore-door designation being dropped. Next was the Model 40-H, also a touring model similar to the 40-N but bedecked with more trim, pinstriping, and a top despite the lower cost ($1,650). The 40-N only had the double internal brakes and Royal Blue paint in its favor. The 40-H came in dark blue. Finally, the new model in the series was a wonderful roadster, the Model 40-M ($1,750). Unlike the previous year's roadster, the Model 40-M featured a vestibuled body with a round gas tank immediately behind the seat. Gone were the

stuffy-looking single or dual rumbles. The design featured long, sweeping fenders, leaving little in the way of a running board for such a long car.

Yet another series included the Model 35-L touring ($1,400), using a Rutenber 280.6-cubic-inch four. This engine was basically a 421-cubic-inch six with two fewer cylinders. Wheelbase for the 35-L was 115 inches, with 34-inch wheels. To finish the line, Auburn offered in its 30 series two models: the Model 30-L ($1,100) and the Model 30-L ($1,100). No, that's not a typo; the company used the same designation. Or did the printers commit a huge error? At any rate, one was a touring, the other a vestibuled roadster similar to the 40-M. Both 30-L models utilized 112-inch wheelbases and Royal Blue paint. Battleship Gray was optional. The engines now featured oil filters. The 30-L roadster used an oval gas tank instead of the round tank found on the 40-M.

Along the way, Auburn's promotional booklets became wonderful pieces of literature. Full-color artwork with art nouveau graphics and muted tones adorned the covers. Inside the 1912 edition, photographs were tied in with renderings of the models. According to the catalog, "pleasure-seekers" shot the photographs, which depicted a way of life now long gone. Tall redwoods surrounding a large Victorian retreat home; Auburns driving along narrow, dusty country roads or parked along broad boulevards in front of ornate inns; meeting with farmers hauling hay with ox-drawn wagons. Imagine, just lazily touring the roads of America photographing whatever scenes one happens upon.

The best way to sum up Auburn's 1913 model line-up is to say it was out of control—a model line gone mad. The AAC offered no less than 14 distinct models that year. This doubles the number of models offered in 1912. In addition, some 1913 models were offered with option packages. The Auburn line-up for 1913 looked like this: Model 6-50 touring ($3,000), Model 6-45 touring ($2,000), Model 6-45 limousine ($3,200), Model 6-45 coupe ($2,600), Model 6-45-B roadster ($2,000), Model 40-L touring ($1,650), Model 40-A roadster ($1,650), Model 40 town car ($2,500), Model 37-L touring ($1,400), Model 35-L touring ($1,400), Model 33-L touring ($1,150), Model 33-M roadster ($1,150), Model 30-L touring ($1,150), and Model 30-M roadster ($1,150).

This list represents no less than eight new models and three new engine offerings. The 6-50 and 6-45 are the first models that the AAC used with hyphenated designations where the first number referred to the engine's cylinder count and the second to the model number. Auburn would use this nomenclature through 1933.

Auburn engineers designed the 6-45 around a 130-inch wheelbase and 36-inch wheels. The 6-45-B represents the apogee of brass-era Auburn roadsters. The 6-45 was a lower-priced six-cylinder

Auburn's line of vestibuled roadsters were probably the most dashing models offered by the company under Eckhart management. Most certainly the six-cylinder roadsters were the desired models.

Model 6-45-B
Six Cylinder Two Passenger Roadster—45 Horse Power

Specifications

Auburn (although the limousine—at $3,200— would be the most expensive Auburn would ever produce). The 348-cubic-inch six shared the same stroke as the 421-cubic-inch six of the 6-50, but the bore was reduced. The 348 was not a Rutenber but rather a Continental. This signified a shift for Auburn's pricing, as the company could purchase Continental engines at a lower price than Rutenber engines. Economy of manufacturing was apparent in the Continental engines. For instance, cylinders were cast in pairs on the 348, instead of separately as on the 421. An option package for the 6-45 touring and 6-45-B roadster included a windshield, speedometer, foot rail, and top for an additional $150. On the 40-L and 40-A, the option package included a Prest-O-Lite tank, windshield, speedometer, electric side and taillights, battery, and top for an additional $150. For the 37, 35-L, 33-L, 33-M, 30-L, and 30-M, the package included a Prest-O-Lite tank, speedometer, windshield, and top for an additional $100 to $125.

Although the Model 40 Auburns carried over from 1912, the town car was a new body offering. Formal in appearance, it offered seating for five. The 37-L touring shared the same price, wheelbase, and body as the 35-L touring and differed only in the engine. The 37-L utilized a 269.5-cubic-inch four versus the 280.6-cubic-inch four of the 35-L. The 33-L offered a lower price than the 35-L. Its 122-inch wheelbase measured three inches shorter than the 35-L's, although wheel size remained the same. The 33-L's 232-cubic-inch block was cast *en bloc* for monetary savings, while the 35 series still used separately cast cylinders. The 30 series was continued, although its pricing equaled that of the 33 series.

This plethora of models apparently didn't work for Auburn in 1913, and the company quickly retreated from this scenario. For 1914, the model line shrank to seven models divided between two lines: the Auburn Six and the 4-40. The Auburn Six was the 6-45 of the previous year, although touted as the "new Auburn Six"; pricing remained the same for the touring and roadster models. Auburn no longer offered a limousine, and the coupe shifted to the 40 series. However, the equipment of the previous year's $150 option package was now included in the advertised $2,000. Only the six-passenger touring model was new within the six-cylinder range ($2,100). AAC's sales pitch in the 1914 catalog is rather confusing. It mentions the 40 series as previously selling for $1,975, which does not agree with the 1913 catalog. Also, the 1914 catalog describes the 1913 40 models as being "electrically cranked," though no mention is made of the feature in the 1913 catalog (a gross oversight if Auburns had electric starters). Perhaps Auburn introduced electric starters late in the model year.

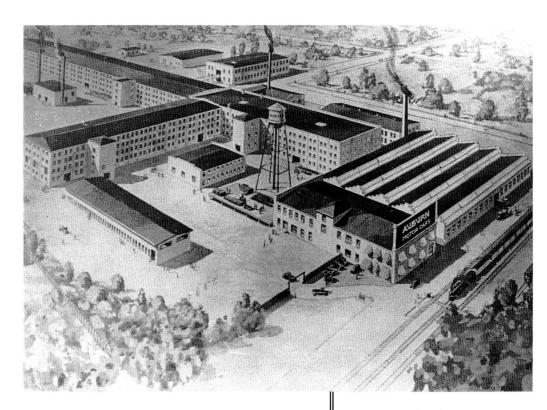

An overview of the Auburn complex during the Eckhart era. Once the Eckharts moved to this site, on the south side of Auburn, the company remained there until most operations moved to Connersville, Indiana, in 1933.

This could account for the $325 discrepancy between prices in the 1913 catalog and those quoted from 1913 in the 1914 catalog. The catalog also emphasized how inexpensively one could buy the 4-40 Auburn at $1,490 (five-passenger touring and roadster), and with the $1,150 30 series Auburns gone, a higher-priced base Auburn needed all the help it could get. Although the 4-40 again used a 318-cubic-inch four, it was not the same engine as the previous year. Reflecting a change in engine sources (the company used is unknown), the new four used a T-head configuration instead of an L-head. The 40 series wheelbase dropped to 120 inches. The six-passenger touring was captioned as a 4-41 ($1,590), and the coupe of the 40 series was very similar to the 1913 6-45 coupe.

The DeKalb County Abstract of 1914 noted that the Eckharts had capitalized the AAC at $20,000 at its inception and that it was now capitalized at $500,000. The review of the AAC remarked that the company did not "advertise extensively . . . [yet] business has reached about 2 million dollars a year, and Auburn automobiles are sold in about one-half the states of the Union, every car being a good advertisement for the factory." The abstract listed Charles as president, Frank as vice president, and Morris as secretary-treasurer and general manager. This was how the papers of incorporation listed these positions. Charles supposedly had retired some 20 years earlier; in fact, he remained active in business matters, though not on a day-to-day basis (Morris took care of the daily concerns). The

continued on page 22

Like the Eckharts, the Zimmerman family was engaged in the manufacture of carriages and other horse-drawn vehicles at the turn of the century, with Auburn serving as home base for their factories. The Zimmermans announced their entry into the automotive market in 1907, and proceeded to manufacture vehicles the following year. Early Zimmermans used an air-cooled, two-cylinder engine attached to a buggy chassis, an idea most of the automotive market had moved beyond some years earlier. However, instead of slinging the engine under the buggy, the Zimmermans mounted their engines up front, under a hood. Although not long on technology, the least expensive Zimmerman could be had for $650, far less than the lowest priced Auburn at $1,250. By 1910, the Zimmermans added a more standard four-cylinder model to their model line which, in fact, was built by Auburn. The company moved aggressively forward. In 1913, a 44-horsepower six-cylinder was introduced, selling for $1,950.

The Zimmermans also formed a subsidiary, known as the de Soto Motor Car Company, some 16 years before Walter Chrysler introduced a model of the same name. The inaugural de Soto was a 55-horsepower, five-passenger touring model, priced higher ($2,180) than the Zimmerman six. That price also included electric lights and a compressed-air starter. Apparently the Zimmermans never saw the de Soto as an upscale line, as the next year the company introduced its cheapest model—a $385, 10-horsepower, two-cylinder cyclecar—under the de Soto name as well.

For 1915, the only Zimmerman was a 38-horsepower, six-cylinder touring model selling for $1,750. The company had planned to move the de Soto manufacturing facilities to Fort Wayne and rename it the Motorette, but the move never came to pass. In 1910, Franklin Zimmerman died at the age of 37. His father, Elias Zimmerman, passed on in 1914 at 85. This left Elias' other son, John, to carry on alone, which he did for another year before selling out to the Eckharts.

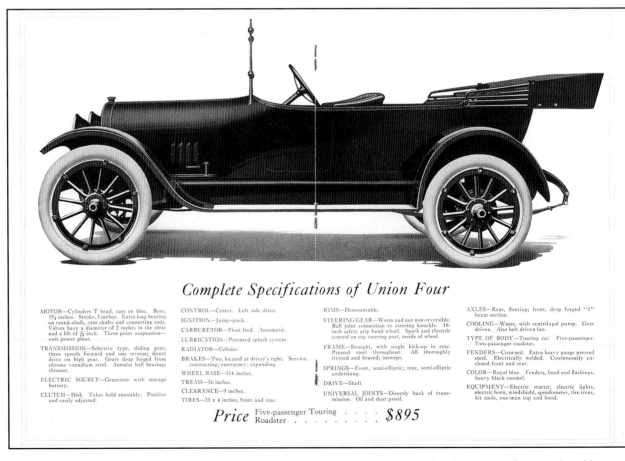

Complete Specifications of Union Four

MOTOR—Cylinders T head, cast en bloc. Bore, 3¾ inches. Stroke, 5 inches. Extra long bearing on crank-shaft, cam shafts and connecting rods. Valves have a diameter of 2 inches in the clear and a lift of ⁷⁄₁₆-inch. Three point suspension—unit power plant.

TRANSMISSION—Selective type, sliding gear; three speeds forward and one reverse; direct drive on high gear. Gears drop forged from chrome vanadium steel. Annular ball bearings thruout.

ELECTRIC SOURCE—Generator with storage battery.

CLUTCH—Disk. Takes hold smoothly. Positive and easily adjusted.

CONTROL.—Center. Left side drive.

IGNITION—Jump-spark.

CARBURETOR—Float feed. Automatic.

LUBRICATION—Patented splash system.

RADIATOR—Cellular.

BRAKES—Two, located at driver's right. Service, contracting; emergency, expanding.

WHEEL BASE—114 inches.

TREAD—56 inches.

CLEARANCE—9 inches.

TIRES—33 x 4 inches, front and rear.

RIMS—Demountable.

STEERING GEAR—Worm and nut non-reversible. Ball joint connection to steering knuckle. 18-inch safety grip hand wheel. Spark and throttle control on top steering post, inside of wheel.

FRAME—Straight, with single kick-up in rear. Pressed steel throughout. All thoroughly riveted and braced; inswept.

SPRINGS—Front, semi-elliptic; rear, semi-elliptic underslung.

DRIVE—Shaft.

UNIVERSAL JOINTS—Directly back of transmission. Oil and dust proof.

AXLES—Rear, floating; front, drop forged "I" beam section.

COOLING—Water, with centrifugal pump. Gear driven. Also belt driven fan.

TYPE OF BODY—Touring car. Five-passenger. Two-passenger roadster.

FENDERS—Crowned. Extra heavy gauge pressed steel. Electrically welded. Continuously enclosed front and rear.

COLOR—Royal blue. Fenders, hood and flashings, heavy black enamel.

EQUIPMENT—Electric starter, electric lights, electric horn, windshield, speedometer, tire irons, kit tools, one-man top and hood.

Price Five-passenger Touring *$895*
　　　　Roadster . . . .

After the Zimmerman Manufacturing Company closed its doors, the AAC attempted to keep its workers employed by producing the Union in the former Zimmerman factory. The venture lasted only a year.

The 1911 Model Z was one of the more sophisticated Zimmermans.

E. A. Johnson and Frank Eckhart take a leisure car camping in a western state with a 1915 Auburn.

continued from page 19

abstract listed William Eckhart as being in Los Angeles "with the Shugers Manufacturing Company, makers of automobile tops." (The Shugers name belonged to George W. Shugers, who had married Anne Eckhart, Charles' daughter.) One interesting note from the DeKalb abstract reads: "The manufacture and assembly of automobiles is the sole business of this concern, although the company at one time manufactured buggies." Already the ECC was spoken of in past tense, though in fact, the company produced carriages until the Eckharts dissolved it in 1918. However, the Eckhart family did take the opportunity in 1914 to reduce the ECC's capital stock from 2,000 shares at $100 per share face value, to 500 shares.

By World War I, Charles Eckhart had fallen into bad health. Spending his last days in Auburn, Charles complained to Frank of business troubles. Competing wartime requirements made raw materials difficult to come by. Discussions arose again of selling the company. Charles suggested that "California Tops" should be manufactured at the AAC factory to enclose touring models. He also mentioned that the carriage business was about finished. Charles, writing to Frank in a letter dated June 13, 1915: "Our business at the carriage factory is very dull. You will no doubt get your statement by the time you get this letter and it shows at least 500 jobs less than last year." Shipments of carriages dropped from 3,454 in 1914 to 2,669 in

1915. Efforts were made to meld the carriage business into other vehicle ventures. In the November 1915 issue of *Motor Bus*, the ECC took out a full-page advertisement for a new product, a Jitney (bus) body for a Ford chassis. "MAKE MONEY," the ad exclaimed, "Enter 'Jitney' business in the right way. We sell to you the real class in a bus body for Ford chassis . . . Seat seven passengers regularly, nine if necessary . . . The body you must have to make money. Praised by all users. Write for our price before you buy. Eckhart Carriage Company, Auburn, Indiana."

Auburn continued to offer both four- and six-cylinder lines for 1915. "The owner of any one of these new 1915 Auburn cars possesses more than reliable machinery, skillfully put together and graced by a luxurious carriage," the company's catalog boasted. "True, these new 1915 Auburn cars are first of all mechanical things, self-propelled vehicles. But there is a bigger asset in Auburn ownership than this. It is the results you enjoy from their mechanical perfection, and the completeness and comfort of their luxurious bodies." The Auburn Six was now tagged the 6-47, powered by the same 348-cubic-inch Continental straight six. Auburn sixes came with left-hand drive only (earlier models offered either left- or right-hand drive). The 6-47's wheelbase grew to 135 inches, but the 37-inch wheels of the 1914 Auburn Six remained. Price for the six-passenger touring came to $2,000, down $100 from 1914.

The 1915 catalog was a muddled affair. Auburn added another six-cylinder model, the 6-40, but mention is made of it only in captions under illustrations of the cars. The 6-40 rode on a 126-inch wheelbase, using a Continental 288.6-cubic-inch straight six. It was available in touring ($1,550) and roadster form. The 4-40 returned as the 4-43, with few changes but the prices (six-passenger touring, $1,500). A smaller Auburn four also appeared, known as the 4-36 and using a 221-cubic-inch T-head engine on a 114-inch wheelbase. The 36 range included a five-passenger touring ($1,075), a roadster ($1,075), and a formal coupe ($1,350) using the same lines as the 1914 4-40 coupe. Alas, by now the Auburn roadster was but a shadow of its former glory. Gone were those wonderful, vestibuled roadsters with prominent fuel tanks. The roadsters were now streamlined in the back, fashioned with unusual bodywork. From a strictly side profile, the roadster appeared to have a trunk. In fact, from the back one could see a large, horseshoe-shaped indentation formed in the sheet metal, holding the spare tire inside and parallel with the rear deck line. The only access to the trunk was via what would later be known as a "golf-bag door," a small door on the side immediately behind the driver's door. Despite a few flairs, this new roadster design looked cheaper, more like a Ford Model T than an Auburn.

Auburn Acquires a Local Competitor

"I think there will have to be a radical change in our overhead expenses, which are too high at this time," Charles wrote in a letter to Frank. "By taking over this other business, it is necessary to make some radical change." This "other business" refers to the Eckharts' purchase of the Zimmerman Manufacturing Company (see sidebar). John Zimmerman, former president of the Zimmerman Manufacturing Company, and the Eckharts created the Union Automobile Company in 1916, housed in the former Zimmerman factory buildings.

The Union was basically an Auburn with two key differences: It was only available with a four-cylinder engine, and it listed at $895, less than any Auburn model. A five-passenger touring or a two-passenger roadster could be had for that price. Union as a company was never incorporated. It's just as well, as Union survived for only one year. John Zimmerman, however, went on to work for the AAC as a purchasing agent.

Discussions arose again over selling the AAC. Charles mentioned to Frank of "parties from New York" who wished to "take over this business in connection with the Rutenber Motor Company at Marion, with whom we have a contract. . . . Morris wants to know . . . whether you will consent to sell out provided you can get your own money out—something similar to arrangement we made with other parties last winter in New York." So now we know that the Eckharts tried to sell the AAC in 1911, 1914, and 1915. Perhaps even other attempts were made. Selling the company certainly appears to have been an ongoing consideration. One has to wonder how attractive the AAC actually looked to potential buyers. Charles wrote that business "is very good now and if we had the material we could turn out lots of cars, but lack of material is the trouble. It seems that everybody else wants material as badly as we do and the result is we cannot get it very promptly." Yet, look at the low production numbers: "However, we are going to get out about 20 cars this week and possibly double that number next week if we are successful in getting the material we expect." These numbers are in line with what we know of Auburn production for the year. If one can rely on serial numbers (provided no number was skipped), only about 1,475 Auburns rolled out of the factory in 1915.

Unfortunately, Charles never lived to see the AAC sold; he died at his home in Auburn on September 30, 1915.

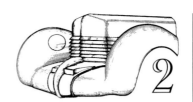

The Chicago Gang
1916-1923

 new Auburn model for 1916, selling for less than $1,000, no doubt went a long way toward helping Auburn's fortunes. The Auburn 4-38 touring and roadster ($985) used the wheelbase of the 1915 4-36, but was powered by a Teetor T-head four that now displaced 235.8 cubic inches. These were the only four-cylinder models offered for the year. Gone was the 348 six. Now the 288.6-cubic-inch six-cylinder of the previous year's 6-40 became the dominant engine model. It was labeled the 6-40A for 1916. The touring model ($1,375) now held seven passengers. The roadster was again available, for the same price as the touring model. Auburn placed a small six, displacing 212 cubic inches and manufactured by Model Gas, into a model labeled the 6-38 Light Six. It rode on a 120-inch wheelbase. Now a prospective

buyer could obtain an Auburn six touring or roadster for just over $1,000 ($1,050, to be exact). All Auburns used cantilevered, semi-elliptical springs on the rear axle, a design that would not last long.

By 1916, Frank spent most of his time in California. His fragile health (it is not recorded what his maladies were) required a more temperate climate. Frank soon became active in his new surroundings. He was president of the Los Angeles-area YMCA for twelve years, a trustee with the Methodist Church, and a vice president and trustee of the University of Southern California (having donated $15,000 toward a hall of philosophy on the USC campus).

Charles Eckhart's death forced the reorganization of the AAC. This was finally accomplished on January 27, 1917. The figures are interesting because they provide a rare glimpse of the company's financial performance under the family's ownership. Capital stock was valued at $3 million, with 10,000 shares of preferred stock accounting for $1 million, the other 20,000 common shares covering the remainder. Until 1919, the company stock remained privately held by the Eckhart family. As for the company's performance, gross sales from July 1, 1916, to October 31, 1917, came to $3 million.

The four-cylinder Auburn disappeared in 1917, only to return briefly in 1926. Until then, Auburn would make its stand mainly on the six-cylinder. At this time, Auburn also shifted its advertising emphasis in brochures from quality to features, a reaction to the realities of a marketplace driven by price. Such market savvy probably accounts for its survival during the World War I period, a time when

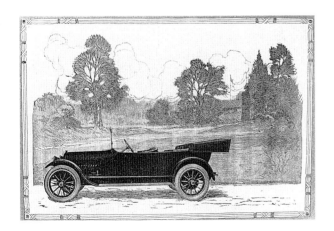

Auburn's 1916 4-38, shown here in an illustration from a sales brochure, was the last four-cylinder model to emerge from the company until 1926.

In its early years, Auburn management insisted every vehicle be road tested before shipment. In the winter, this could be a brutal trial.

numerous other automakers dropped by the way-side. Obtaining raw materials was difficult during the war, and a postwar recession did little to lighten the burden on manufacturers.

For 1917, Auburns were divided between the 6-39 Light Six and the 6-44 lines. The 6-39 used a 120-inch wheelbase and included a five-passenger touring, a 6-39C four-passenger roadster, and a 6-39M two-passenger roadster, all priced equally ($1,145). The 6-44 rode on a 131-inch wheelbase with either a seven-passenger touring or a four-passenger roadster body. Prices remained the same within the 6-44 series ($1,535) as well. No engine from Auburn's 1916 models survived into 1917. The two sixes for the year included a 230-cubic-inch Teetor in the 6-39, and a 303-cubic-inch Continental 9-N in the 6-44. Only the 6-44 retained the cantilevered semi-elliptical rear springs, while the 6-39 used the standard semi-elliptical springs. Auburn started to use Columbia rear axles at least as early as 1917, possibly earlier. This was the beginning of a long relationship between Columbia and the AAC, with Columbia Axle eventually becoming a sister company to Auburn.

A new feature for 1917 was the "detachable sedan top," offered on all Auburn models. It was, to use modern terminology, a removable hardtop. All window glass could be detached while the hardtop remained in place, for those desiring a rush of wind. "Jiffy curtains" remained in storage compartments until inclement weather forced their use. Otherwise, an owner could remove the entire hardtop and use the conventional fold-down soft top. It's obvious the soft top would have to be removed to attach the hardtop, but exactly how many steps that entailed remains obscure. The detachable sedan top added $175 to the cost of a 6-39 and $250 to the 6-44.

For those whose minds are muddled by Auburn's alphabet soup model designations, 1918 comes as a bit of a relief. The 6-39 Light Six and 6-44 lines carried over, and no new model lines were added. To be sure, suffixes were toyed with and new body styles introduced, but for a while a bit of blissful continuity more or less reigned. The 6-39 line included the 6-39-B touring ($1,345), the 6-39 Sport ($1,395), the 6-39-E Chummy roadster ($1,345), and the 6-39-B convertible ($1,595). The convertible was, in fact, a touring body that came with the detachable sedan top offered optionally the prior year. The Chummy roadster held four passengers and sported a roadster-like rear deck. The Sport was a two-door, close-coupled body, using seating akin to a 2+2 arrangement, the rear being vestibuled similar to a touring car. In the 6-44 line, the seven-passenger touring returned ($1,685), and the convertible was also offered ($1,985). Auburn also introduced a formal, seven-passenger "Springfield-Type Sedan" ($2,450) that decidedly moved Auburn upscale again. Each series retained its wheelbase of 1917. Auburn offered wire wheels as an option for the first time, adding $125 to the prices.

Auburn now bought all of its engines from Continental (it would continue to use Continentals, though not exclusively, through 1928), so the 6-44 returned with its 303-cubic-inch six-cylinder, and the 6-39 used a Continental 7-W 224-cubic-inch straight six. Auburn resumed advertising horsepower, with the 303 capable of 55 horsepower at 2100 rpm. The 224 was good for 43 horsepower at 2100 rpm. These six-cylinders were a far cry from the Auburn's 10-horsepower single poppers of yester-year. During this period, however, Auburn avoided making any public references to outsourcing its engines. For example, Auburn's 1918 catalog mentions, "In designing the engine for the 6-39 . . . the engineers of the Auburn Automobile Company . . ." This amounted to a farce as the company never had an engineering staff for engines, nor did Auburn ever manufacture them. Gross sales from November 1, 1917, to September 30, 1918, tallied $1.7 million.

Pearl Watson joined the AAC in 1918, acting as superintendent until 1926, when he was named a vice president at Duesenberg, Inc.

Good-bye, Eckhart Carriage

The Eckharts decided to officially liquidate the ECC in December 1918. One may wonder why it took so long to dissolve the old carriage company. In fact, despite this late date for closing such a company, its gross sales in 1917 amounted to over $208,000 (its highest since 1909's $291,000 in sales). Jobs shipped in 1917 came to 2,228, down from 4,534 in 1907. At the ECC's last shareholders' meeting, those present voted for distributing a $65,000 cash surplus among holders of the company's stock. The old factory complex was sold by 1920. Part of the complex was quickly demolished. The J. K. Moon Carpenter Shop took over one of the buildings with frontage on Seventh Street. Other buildings remained vacated, or were used to store automobiles or hay. The company that Charles Eckhart had struggled to create was now gone; transportation technology had overtaken the carriage. Yet, even Charles, if he had survived to

Auburn's detachable sedan top offered motorists the cold-weather protection of a sedan and the open-air joys of motoring in the summer.

Auburn Seven-Passenger Six, Model 6-44
$1535, f. o. b. Auburn

Interior View of Auburn Seven-Passenger Six, Model 6-44

Auburn 6-44, Seven-Passenger Touring with Auburn detachable Sedan top, including regular summer top, and jiffy curtain. $1785, f. o. b. Auburn

The former Eckhart Carriage Company complex, 1920. Only a scant two years separated the dissolution of the carriage maker from the date this insurance plat was drawn. Already most of the buildings formerly used by the company are gone.

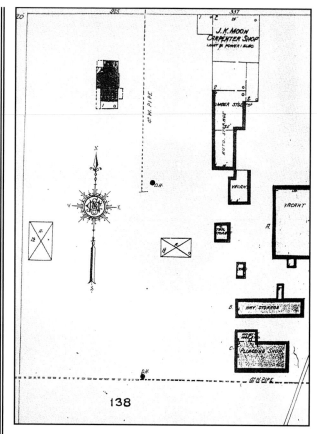

see its demise, would not have shed a tear. He, like many Victorian gentlemen of the time, knew that progress was necessary. There was little money to be made in nostalgia.

After the Eckhart family laid the ECC to rest, the move to sell the AAC continued. After some eight, perhaps more, years of discussions with potential buyers, the availability of the AAC must have been a well-known fact among those in investment circles. This is particularly true in Chicago, a city whose financial institutions were used regularly by the Eckharts for corporate business. Exactly how the Eckharts finally found a group of investors interested in purchasing the AAC has been lost to history. Fortunately, the paper trail surrounding the sale still exists, and its details can be woven together. Frank must have known the sale of Auburn was imminent. In April 1919, he sold 730 shares of Auburn stock for $219,000. Some 83-1/3 shares went to Morris, but Frank sold the remainder to 28 other individuals, the first time a substantial block of AAC shares went outside the family. The AAC sale was finalized by that summer. "The Chicago Gang"—as they were later referred to by a hometown employee of the AAC—filed Articles of Incorporation with the State of Indiana on June 25, 1919, with all assets transferred the following day. (The new owners dropped the "The" from the official title of the company.)

The Chicago Gang revolved around the officers and directors of F. B. Hitchcock and Company, an investment banking firm located in Chicago. Officers and directors from the First National Bank of Chicago were also involved. F. B. Hitchcock was a middle-aged investment banker running his own firm in 1919. His father, H. H. Hitchcock, was a vice president of the firm, a director at the William Wrigley, Jr., Company, and a director and chairman of the board at the First National Bank of Chicago. Another young but upwardly mobile director from the Hitchcock firm who sat on the AAC's board was Ralph Bard, who would later play a key role in the AAC's survival. William K. Wrigley, Jr., being associated with H. H. Hitchcock, was invited to help finance the buyout of the AAC. This is the same Wrigley whose name graces the packages of chewing gum. Wrigley was also a director at the First National Bank of Chicago. A. P. Kemp also hailed from the First National Bank of Chicago, and his contribution was pivotal. Kemp specialized in financing automotive manufacturers, and he knew the automotive business, at least from the banking angle. Kemp filled the position of first vice president and treasurer. James Indus Farley became sec-

It discounts every bill; buys material on the most favorable terms; gives its customers and dealers generous support.

A. P. KEMP
President and Treasurer of the Auburn Automobile Company; formerly second Vice-President of the H. H. Franklin Manufacturing Co. of Syracuse, N. Y. for 19 years with the First National Bank of Chicago where, during the last few years of his association with the bank, he specialized on automobile financing.

J. I. FARLEY
Vice-President of the Auburn Automobile Company and Director of Sales; actively associated with the Company for the last fourteen years during which time he has been closely allied with its success.

WM. WRIGLEY, JR.
Founder and owner of Wrigley's Chewing Gum enterprises; a great merchandiser of national fame. Director of the First National Bank of Chicago; Director of the Consumers Company, Chicago; Director of the Erie Railroad Company and Director of Wm. Wrigley, Jr. Company; Director Pacific American Fisheries Co.; Director National Safe Deposit Co.

H. H. HITCHCOCK
Formerly Vice-President, now Chairman of the Board and a Director of the First National Bank of Chicago; Vice-President of F. B. Hitchcock & Co.; Director of First Trust & Savings Bank; Director of Wm. Wrigley, Jr. Company; Director Pacific American Fisheries Co.; Director National Safe Deposit Co.

I N financial strength, and ability to exercise the magic force of ready money, the Auburn Automobile Company is one of the strongest in the industry.

Every bill is discounted. There are always ample funds available to take advantage of favorable purchases for a long time ahead. No activity of the company is in any way cramped for lack of funds.

This condition has always been true of the Auburn Company even during the recent depression which left so many automobile companies in a precarious condition.

It is a fact of big moment to the owner of an Auburn car for it means that Auburn is

in the business to stay — as it has stayed with steadily increasing success since 1900. It means that every Auburn owner can buy an Auburn car with perfect assurance that the service and the backing of the factory will continue for years to come.

It means, too, that Auburn is able to support its dealers with everything necessary

The Auburn Magazine—Page 2

ond vice president for the AAC. Farley had sold Studebakers before joining Auburn in 1908 as a sales manager. (Farley assumed the post of president for the AAC in 1923, eventually turning this office over to E. L. Cord in 1926. Farley later became a U.S. representative from Auburn's district.) Another holdover from the old AAC was E. A. Johnson, who was named assistant treasurer. Johnson wrote to George Eckhart in 1951, briefly outlining his tenure with the AAC: "I [joined] the carriage company on September 7, 1899; was with them until we decided to close it out, and went over to the automobile company in September 1918 to take on the work of Mr. [F. B.] Sears, who was away on an extended leave due to a [nervous] breakdown. I stayed with the [AAC] until they were about out of the picture, leaving . . . about April 1, 1936." Johnson was a purchasing agent and general manager at the ECC, and an assistant service manager and later a director of service at Auburn. Finally, there was James H. Rose, lawyer to the Eckharts for some years. Rose's contribution to the family was great, as he tried to keep the family abreast of corporate and legal matters. Last-minute legalities kept the paperwork of the AAC sale tied

The Home of the "Auburn," Auburn, Ind.

for aggressive and successful conduct of their business — and that is the reason that so much value is attached to the Auburn franchise by aggressive and successful selling companies in all parts of the country.

Likewise, Auburn is able to get the best service from manufacturers of material of all kinds, and is able to hold its costs as low

F. B. HITCHCOCK
President and Director of F. B. Hitchcock & Co.; Director Chicago Mill & Lumber Co.; Director of Vesta Battery Corporation.

RALPH A. BARD
Vice-President and Director F. B. Hitchcock & Co.; Director H. W. Gossard Co., Inc.; Director Barco Manufacturing Co.

HON. J. H. ROSE
Former Judge of the Circuit Court of Indiana for DeKalb County, and a well-known counsellor and attorney.

E. A. JOHNSON
Secretary of the Auburn Automobile Co. and Director of Service. Has been connected with the Company since its inception.

ests in many kinds of business and all of whom have been successful.

The present enviable position of the Auburn car is the result of steady growth since the company began the manufacture of automobiles in 1900.

During all that time the company has been able to maintain a volume of production that won for it large operating and marketing advantages — and each year those advantages have become more pronounced.

They are all expressed in the remarkable value that the Auburn is able to give its customers — a value not surpassed by any other maker of fine motor cars.

as they can be held for a car of the high Auburn quality.

The great business strength of the Auburn is indicated by the personnel of the board of directors—men who have wide-spread inter-

The Auburn Magazine—Page 3

up, due in part to the Eckhart's neglect in keeping accurate records.

Wilson H. Denison filled in as secretary for the new corporation. Directors for the new AAC included Eckhart, Farley, Denison, Johnson, Rose, A. M. Graffis, and Virgil B. Walling. Morris Eckhart stayed on as president through 1921, helping the new management team with the transition. Morris was supposed to remain for three years, but he managed to bow out of the picture sooner. When Morris left Auburn, the Eckharts faded from the little town of Auburn for good. The name remained on a library and a park only.

The Chicago Gang organized the AAC with a capital stock consisting of 10,000 shares of preferred stock holding a 7 percent dividend rate and valued at $100 per share ($1 million total value) and 30,000 shares of common stock valued at $25 per share ($750,000 total value). The former stockholders received more than $119,000 in cash and 10,000 shares of common stock ($250,000 face value on June 26, 1919), distributed according to the proportions in which they held the old company's stock. Acting on his behalf and as trustee for the former stockholders in his family, Morris received 20,000 shares of common stock ($500,000) and 7,500 shares of preferred stock ($750,000). Although this tallies to $1.25 million, Eckhart, et. al., sold the stocks back to F. B. Hitchcock and Company, for $750,000. Morris received $87,280 in cash up front, along with $28,910 per year payable to his person for the next three years. Frank's portion of the sale amounted to more than $150,000 in cash and stocks. This, along with Frank's previous stock sale of $219,000, gave him a nest egg of $369,000, which does not include his proceeds from the sale of

An exterior view of Auburn's original administration building. It served the company until 1930 when a larger building was erected to the south. This building remains extant, albeit only one story.

The Chicago bankers and financiers who bought the AAC from the Eckharts in 1919, later referred to as "the Chicago Gang."

the ECC. The remaining 2,500 shares of preferred stock were sold by F. B. Hitchcock and Company for $237,500, the cash being deposited into the AAC's treasury for new capital. The preferred stocks were to be retired annually at a rate of $100,000 per year, with the final payoff by January 1, 1930.

The Chicago Gang did well with this arrangement. By June 30, 1925—shortly before all remaining preferred shares were retired—they collected over $262,000 in interest. A "sinking fund" was established to cover any lean years. The Chicago Gang also picked up all payable taxes for the fiscal year starting October 1, 1918, and paid all contractual obligations of the former owners, not to exceed $15,000. At the time of the sale, total assets amounted to $2.4 million, total liabilities some $668,000, making the net worth of the company $1.7 million.

During the transition year of 1919, A. H. McInnis arrived at AAC, joining its service department and eventually becoming director of service. From October 1, 1918, the start of the fiscal year, to June 26, 1919, the day AAC ownership was transferred, gross sales for the company amounted to $2.5 million. It was an astounding performance, and

the Eckharts sold the company on an upswing. No little help was coming from Auburn's new model, dubbed the Beauty Six. It is commonly thought that the Chicago Gang introduced the Beauty Six, but the paper trail does not substantiate this. If the Chicago Gang did indeed introduce the Beauty Six, the earliest this could have been accomplished was for the 1920 model year. All Auburn literature from 1919 has the Beauty Six model listed, the early catalogs and brochures being printed in late 1918. Also, the AAC displayed the Beauty Six at all the auto shows in January 1919, six months before the Chicago Gang moved into town. Therefore, credit must be given to Morris Eckhart and company for the creation and introduction of the Beauty Six. With the company's phenomenal results for the first six months of the year, the Beauty Six proved to be a sales winner for the small company. It also shows there were those within the AAC who had the moxie to market and sell the Beauty Six properly.

The Beauty Six carried the underpinnings of the

previous 6-39 models, but with a new body style. It sported a higher beltline, running from the radiator to the cowl on most models, and from the radiator to the vestibule at the rear of the touring model. This was done simply by squaring the body lines, eschewing the softer corners of previous models. A new radiator shell blended with the updated style. Auburn continued to use the 224-cubic-inch Continental six in the Beauty Six. The company relied on Rayfield carburetors (the Model S for 1919) for the remainder of the Beauty Six's life cycle (fewer and fewer automakers used Rayfield carburetors until the name disappeared completely after 1927). The Continental six pulled the same 120-inch wheelbase chassis of the 6-39, riding on 33-inch artillery type wheels. The rims were shod with Goodrich straight-side tires, the nonskid variety on the rear.

Auburn offered five models for 1919, still using the 6-39 nomenclature, but the AAC most promoted the Beauty Six. The 6-39-H designated the touring model ($1,595). Auburn dubbed the 6-39-K as the "Smart Tourster" ($1,595). For its roadster, Auburn used the 6-39-R designation ($1,595). For whatever reason, Auburn avoided letters when referring to its remaining two models, simply labeled the 6-39 sedan and the 6-39 coupe. The price of the sedan and coupe, however, rose precipitously over the lettered models. Each of these latter models retailed for $2,375. Any of these models could be finished in Royal Blue, Purple Lake, or Auburn Gray.

The Auburn continued to be an assembled car, relying heavily on outside suppliers. In addition to Continental engines, Auburn also installed parts from the following companies: Borg and Beck (clutch), Grant and Lees (three-speed transmission), Jacox (steering gear), Jamestown (radiator), and Remy (electrical). Auburn even outsourced its frames, obtaining them from the Parish Bingham firm. Since the Beauty Six can be attributed to the former owners, one might wonder what the Chicago Gang brought to the table. Not much, save for a reason in the future to bring an upwardly mobile Moon salesman on board to salvage the company (see chapter three).

For the short term, Auburn's investors could stay optimistic about the company's prospects. The success of the Beauty Six had an effect on those common stocks recently changing hands. From September 1, 1919, to January 13, 1920, Auburn common shares rose from $38 per share to $80 per share. Riding on the wave of momentum created by the Beauty Six, net profits from June 26, 1919, to December 31, 1919, amounted to almost $1 million. All profit figures from 1919 to 1924—quoted after federal taxes were paid—came from financial statements filed by the AAC with the State of Illinois in 1925.

By 1920, these profits would dip only slightly, to some $802,000 for a 12-month period (*Moody's* reported just over $622,000 in profits, from $1.1 mil-

A 1919 Auburn 6-39H five-passenger touring Beauty Six.

lion in revenues). To make matters better, the Chicago Gang didn't have to change Auburn's model line for the year. The Beauty Six remained intact, although management took advantage of the Beauty Six sales and raised prices $100 per model. Blaine O. Snepp joined Auburn in 1920, after having put in a stint with the Eckhart Carriage Company. He served as the head of cost and accounting and served as the AAC's assistant secretary starting in September 1923, assistant treasurer in May 1924, and treasurer in 1926.

The year 1921 presented another story. Suddenly, the Chicago Gang received a wake-up call, realizing the hard way that this automotive manufacturing business wasn't always so friendly. Profits and losses could change overnight. The public, after rushing to buy the latest and greatest model, soon tired of it. Most of all, economic crunches, such as the one suffered in the United States during this period, could have a devastating effect on margins. If management didn't prepare for the worst during good times, the bad times were harder to bear. Although late in the model year the AAC rolled out a slightly larger model with increased horsepower, the more bang for the buck theory didn't work with the buying public. Net profits dropped to just under $307,000 for 1921, and *Moody's* reported just over

$632,000 in revenues. Though it may have been necessary, the Chicago Gang's capital investment in the company by expanding facilities and upgrading its tooling didn't help matters. There's nothing wrong with capital investments, as long as the boom holds out long enough to cover the outlays. This, alas, didn't happen, as the Chicago Gang's expenditures collided headlong with an ongoing postwar depression. This made financial matters that much harder for the AAC to manage when the crunch caught up with the company. Early in the 1921 model year, the 6-39 returned to the line-up, now with disc wheels, all the rage, as an option. The Chicago Gang didn't help the AAC's sales by raising prices of the 6-39-H, -K, and -R models to $1,895 per copy. The sedan and coupe rose to a dizzying $2,995 per model.

Late in the year, the AAC introduced the 6-51, replacing the 6-39 but still calling this model the Beauty Six. The 6-51 rolled on a 121-inch wheelbase with 32-inch artillery wheels installed. Continental's new 7-R engine—introduced in 1920—provided power. Displacement (and bore and stroke) remained the same as the 7-W at 224 cubic inches, but the number of main bearings increased to four. The 7-R featured an aluminum cylinder head and a cast-iron crankcase. More important, horsepower climbed to 55 at 2600 rpm. The 6-51

The 1921 Auburn Beauty Six shows essentially the same body style as when the Beauty Six line was introduced two years earlier.

An Auburn ad for its Beauty Six line. The *Saturday Evening Post* was one of the AAC's main advertising outlets for years, a tradition begun when the Eckhart family still owned the company.

model line included a five-passenger touring ($1,695), a seven-passenger touring ($1,760), a two-passenger roadster ($1,670), and those expensive sedans and coupes (albeit some cheaper at $2,475 each). With the switch to the 6-51 model, the roadster gained a legitimate trunk, with the spare now mounted on the rear bumper. New paint selections included Brilliant Blue and maroon, with Auburn Gray returning and Rolls Royce Blue still available on the roadster.

Although one could easily assume the 6-51 carried into 1922 without a change, such was not the case. Auburn switched to Continental's 8-R engine, which used the same stroke as the 7-R but a 0.125-inch bigger bore. Total displacement equaled 241.5 cubic inches, and horsepower rose to 58 at 2300 rpm. Some sources cite 60 horsepower at 2650 rpm. Auburn continued to ship a few 6-51s with 7-R engines early in the year to use up remaining stock. The five-passenger touring and roadster (both $1,575), seven-passenger touring ($1,615), sedan ($2,395), and coupe ($2,275) all returned. The latter two still demanded premium money, although prices had dropped to 1919 levels. Auburn equipped its

models with aluminum body molding, and the touring models had a walnut storage cabinet behind the front seat for the side curtains. A new, and by far the most exciting, model to come along since the vestibuled roadsters was simply dubbed the "Sport." Unlike the Sport of 1918, this model was unique. The Sport bore stylish disc wheels ("disteel wheels"), step plates instead of running boards, motorcycle fenders, side-mount trunks (holding a set of custom-fit luggage), a raked windshield with side wings, and a rear-mounted spare tire. Yet, with all these features, it sold for less than the coupe and sedan ($2,195). More important to our story is the Sport's wonderful color scheme—a Napier Green livery with door panels and disc wheels in Sage Brush Green, topped with gold pinstriping. Nickel-plated hardware adorned the Sport, including the radiator shell, lamps, and bumper. Many have cited E. L. Cord with painting a back lot of Auburns in two-tone schemes and throwing on a bit of nickel plating in an attempt to sell them quickly. Perhaps Cord did do this, but he certainly was not the first to dress Auburns in such decor. Disc wheels were standard and wire wheels optional. Wheel and tire sizes were a jumble, with the

The smart 1922 Auburn 6-51 Sport, with luggage boxes, step plates, and disc wheels. Auburn painted Sport models in a three-tone scheme and lavished the model with nickel-plated trim.

Roy Faulkner joined Auburn in 1923 as a sales manager. Faulkner faced a grim financial situation when he arrived at Auburn but made the most of the situation.

touring and roadster models using 32x4-inch tires, the Sport holding 32x4.5-inch tires, and all closed-body models 33x4.5 inch. In addition to the Sport's color scheme, the AAC continued to offer Brilliant Blue, maroon, and Auburn Gray for its other models. A buyer of the Sport could choose these colors as an option, too. Late in the year, Auburn offered Belgian Blue as the color of choice for the roadster. Unfortunately, though dashing, the Sport did little to raise Auburn's fortunes.

Net profits now dropped to under $139,000, while *Moody's* reported revenues of over $541,000. Morris Eckhart left the AAC's president position by 1922, and A. P. Kemp took over this office and that of treasurer. J. I. Farley moved from treasurer to vice president, and E. A. Johnson remained as secretary. James Crawford joined the AAC in 1922, the company's first chief engineer. He remained with the company in that position until 1927, overseeing the transition of models that came with E. L. Cord's new leadership.

The Chicago Gang started to take steps to turn its flagging fortunes around. They hired Roy Faulkner in late 1922, who became a key figure in the company's history. Faulkner hailed from Pittsburgh, born there in 1877. Little is known of Faulkner before he served as county recorder at the Allegheny Court House in Pittsburgh. He then worked for a short time as a lumber salesman before selling Oaklands at that company's dealership in Pittsburgh. Faulkner subsequently became a sales

manager for the Reo and Stutz dealer in the same city, and served in the same capacity at the Frank Santry Motor Company, the Nash distributors in Cincinnati. His reputation as a salesman flourished throughout the Midwest during his tenure in Cincinnati. At 45 years of age, Faulkner filled Auburn's sales manager position. The company was severely bleeding red ink, and desperate measures were needed. Faulkner did not join the company with the same mandate that E. L. Cord would later enjoy. Faulkner did not have the power to dictate model lines, equipment offered on those models, or sources for parts. Hence, turning Auburn around was a difficult task for Faulkner.

While the AAC's net profits for 1923 dipped to a low $8,342 after taxes, a definite upswing in the company's fortunes can be traced even in this gloomy picture. If one pulls out the net profits made by the AAC in the last half of 1923, it shows a figure of some $62,000. Considering the financial free fall AAC must have been in by the time Faulkner arrived, a six-month lag in his efforts to raise sales is not unreasonable to expect. *Moody's* listed revenues at $4.4 million for 1923. This is no doubt a change in accounting methods rather than any huge upswing in sales. Otherwise, what is known of production figures does not warrant such an increase for 1923 when compared to better sales years such as 1919 and 1920.

In 1923, J. I. Farley rose to Auburn's presidency, remaining there until 1926. It is unknown who served as vice president during this period, but W. C. MacFarlane filled in as treasurer, while Judge Rose served as secretary. Auburn's 1923 model line-up is one of the most difficult to follow. Three different lines were offered, all using the same body style names. This situation is made even more confusing because Auburn noted few, if any, reference points—wheelbase, engine, or series number—in many pieces of sales literature. As an example, in a Sport brochure, one is left wondering whether it refers to the 6-43 Sport, the 6-51 Sport, or the 6-63 Sport. Perhaps this was a ploy to save printing costs. If so, it wasn't working; Auburn produced approximately 12 different pieces of literature for the 1923 model year, the highest total ever.

In the sales literature, Auburn no longer referred to the 6-51 as the Beauty Six, but simply the "6-51." As the company had rarely made reference to the Beauty Six's model numbers in previous years, this made the 6-51 appear to be a new model. Regardless, Auburn had to sell the 6-51 inventory before offering the 6-63. This led to an unusual situation in which Auburn slowly released various 6-63 models (called "The Six Supreme") over the course of the year. In fact, *MoTor* magazine doesn't even list the 6-63 in its 1923 roundup. On the other hand, the 6-43, another of Auburn's many attempts to drop into a lower-priced market, was offered

An early view of the Auburn assembly line, as found before Cord's takeover of the company. The term "assembly line" is used loosely; note the use of sawhorses to assemble a chassis until the wheels were ready for attachment.

immediately. The 6-43 rode on a 114-inch wheelbase and was powered by a 195.6-cubic-inch Continental 6-Y straight six. This unit was good for 50 horsepower at 2600 rpm. Early in the model year, Auburn offered the 6-43 as a five-passenger touring ($1,095) and a touring sedan ($1,465). Later in the year, while the five-passenger touring remained, the touring sedan was dropped. Other 6-43 models included the Sport ($1,325), touring coupe ($1,495), and the five-passenger sedan ($1,595). Within the 6-51 series, the five-passenger touring ($1,275), seven-passenger touring ($1,345), Sport ($1,895), and five-passenger sedan ($2,245) all returned. Auburn briefly produced a 6-51 brougham ($1,965).

The product planners must have gone mad. Here was a company in dire financial straits, yet in one year it introduces a new model (the 6-51 brougham), only later to drop it along with the entire 6-51 line. The same thing occurred with the 6-43 touring sedan. Although the 6-43 line remained, within months the touring sedan was replaced with the touring coupe. To top it off, Auburn decided to launch the 6-63 Six Supreme, using an expensive Weidely engine. At the beginning of the year, Auburn only introduced the $1,650 Six Supreme five-passenger touring (the company eventually dropped the 6-63 touring's price by $55). Later, the Six Supreme Sport ($1,850), brougham ($2,145), and five/seven-passenger sedan ($2,345) appeared. These models sold for approximately the same price as their counterparts in the 6-51 series, but featured the more expensive Weidely.

The Six Supreme used a Weidely straight-six, an expensive but technically wonderful engine.

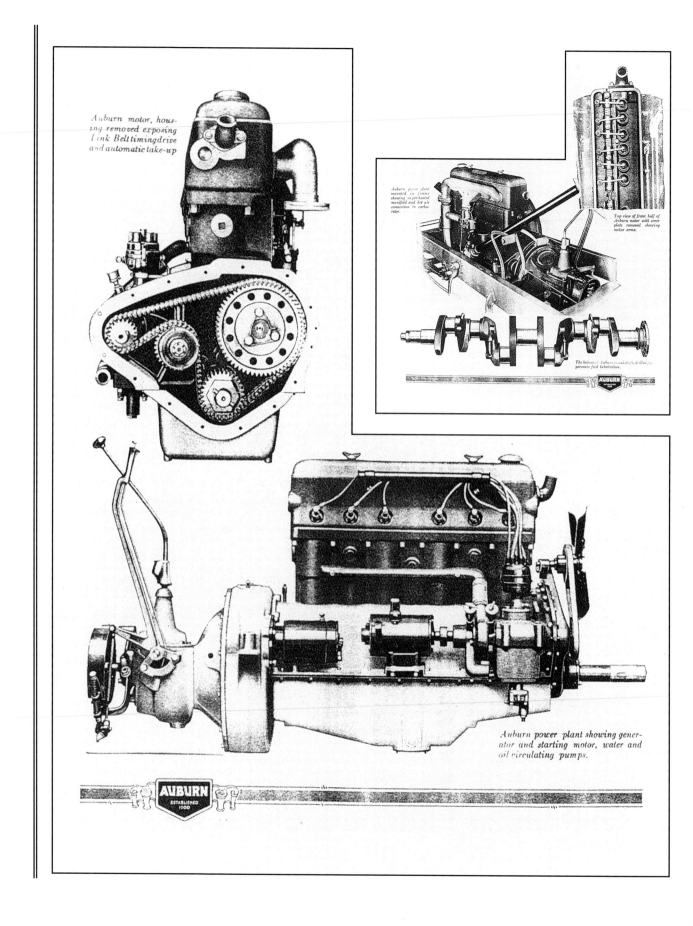

Auburn motor, housing removed exposing Link Belt timing drive and automatic take-up

Auburn power plant mounted in frame showing super-heated manifold and hot air connection to carburetor.

Top view of front half of Auburn motor with cover plate removed showing rocker arms.

The balanced Auburn crankshaft, drilled for pressure feed lubrication.

Auburn power plant showing generator and starting motor, water and oil circulating pumps.

There's no doubt the Weidely-powered Six Supreme packed the most punch enjoyed by an Auburn to that date. Perhaps unnecessary in light of the company's woeful finances, the Weidely in any other situation would have been a nice touch. This 248.9-cubic-inch six produced a respectable 63 horsepower at 3000 rpm, better than many other six-cylinders of the day. Very few engine makers could claim such a high redline. No question, the Weidely was built to run. It ran overhead valves operated by hollow pushrods in a day when most engines had side valves. The water jacket surrounded the spark plugs. Auburn claimed the engine as its own, and though it may have had some features uniquely designed for Auburn, it was a Weidely through and through. Auburn claimed the Six Supreme's top speed was 70 miles per hour and that 5 to 50 miles per hour came in 11 seconds. The Six Supreme sported a wheelbase of 122 inches, again incrementally increasing the size of Auburns. Engineers at the AAC moved the emergency brakes from the rear wheels to the transmission to reduce unsprung weight. Advanced for its day, the Six Supreme used a variable-ratio steering gear. Five-ply laminated wood was used for the body framework, eliminating splitting and breaking of dimensionally unstable hardwoods. Auburn used cork on its body mount pads to eliminate squeaks.

The 1923 Sport models enjoyed the same accouterments as in 1922. Auburn described the 1923 Sport as having hand-buffed Spanish brown leather upholstery, with a beige-brown body color, black fenders, a lighter shade of "greenish brown" in the door panels and the disc wheels, and pinstriping of scarlet, black, and gold setting off the two-tone livery. Auburn delivered the Sport with an olive drab mohair top. What were described as "unusually large tires"—32x4.5 inches—were actually standard fare in the rest of the Auburn line. With the Weidely engine, the 6-63 Sport lived up to its name. Auburn sales literature described it as "pre-eminently the car of youth and style. Like a well-cut suit or a carefully chosen cravat, it adds a touch of dash and sparkle to the personal equipment of its owner. Everywhere, the sport car by its vividness and grace attracts admiring attention. It is pert and voguish, but never so extreme as to pass the bounds of good taste." The copywriters signed off the brochure, as with all Auburn sales literature for 1923, "Once an Owner— Always a Friend."

The 6-63 sedan's body was built under contract by McFarlan Motor Car Company of Connersville, Indiana. This provided the first key link to that east central Indiana town, a town that would play an ever greater role in Auburn's fortunes starting in 1924. McFarlan used aluminum panels for the sedan, a material usually reserved for custom coachwork bodies. All 6-63 closed-body models came equipped with door locks. The 6-63 touring's top was permanent, although customers could order a folding top. Available colors included Maroon Lake, Auburn Gray, or Brilliant Blue. At times, brochures listed a DeKalb Blue, which one suspects was the same color as Brilliant Blue but represented a noble gesture toward the home county.

Auburn literature listed the 6-43 open and closed models arriving in Brewster Green. The 6-43 Chesterfield touring ($1,395) was a step up in the small Auburn line, coming equipped with a Blue Jay Blue livery over a two-tone brown Spanish leather. Standard equipment included a nickel-plated radiator shell, front bumper, cowl lights, Boyce Motometer, windshield wiper, transmission lock, step pads, spare tire, and walnut dash.

Despite the company's product weaknesses, Auburn was on the leading edge of marketing. Recognizing early the power and independence women were gaining in society, Auburn's literature depicted photos of women at the wheel of its automobiles.

Regardless of who the company was trying to reach, it wasn't working. The Chicago Gang, looking at a troubled profit line for the year, was in grave condition.

Little did anyone suspect that Ralph Bard would soon stumble into Auburn's salvation.

Auburn's Six Supreme chassis was rather standard engineering fare for the day. It was a stout unit, but not excessively so.

The Cord that Binds

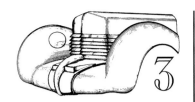

1924-1926

3

hile there was a marked increase in the AAC's activities in the latter half of 1923, the turnaround wasn't sufficient to place Auburn on the high road. Something else was needed. In a brief history written for the Indiana Historical Society's quarterly publication, *Traces of Indiana and Midwestern History* (spring 1994), it was noted, "The . . . three marques . . . Auburn, Cord, and Duesenberg emerged from under one corporate umbrella. Yet the company never once produced more than 50,000 automobiles in any given 12-month period, only enjoyed a few years of relative financial security, mostly labored under a tenuous management arrangement, and dissolved into bankruptcy by the end of the 1930s, like so many lesser automakers before. So why have the names of Auburn, Cord, and Duesenberg come to the forefront of our attention today? Why do they serve as the epitome of the Classic Car? History reveals the answers in a fortuitous set of circumstances that merged within a limited time frame to produce a unique result." That fortuitous set of circumstances arrived at Auburn in the person of Errett Lobban Cord, a man who first made his mark as a highly successful automotive salesman in Chicago(see sidebar).

Cord, his appetite whetted for the automotive business, had decided by 1924 that he wanted to manufacture cars. Understanding the success an assembled car could obtain, he started to look for an available company. No doubt Cord preferred a manufacturer on the skids—a company came cheaper that way. Helping Cord shop for a prospective company was Lucius Bass Manning, a security salesman in Chicago.

Manning was born in 1894 in Tacoma, Washington. His parents, good Victorians that they were, believed in an eastern education. They sent Manning to a boarding school and eventually to Yale's Sheffield Scientific School, but he did not complete his studies there. According to *Who's Who in America 1938-1939*, Manning worked as an automobile salesman from 1915 to 1917. After a stint as an aviator

director from the AAC buying a Moon? Perhaps it was nothing more than a means by which Bard could meet Cord. That he had to buy a Moon to do so says volumes about Cord.

Cord's success as an automotive entrepreneur was well known in Windy City business circles. As Bard later explained, "We had heard that Cord was cocky, footloose, and feared nor respected nothing in the automobile game." It was this kind of savvy the AAC desperately needed. Bard listened to Cord's plans and invited him to speak to the other AAC directors. Cord was ready; he already knew in his head what he wanted out of the deal. Bard was painfully aware his money was stuck in the AAC. The remainder of the Chicago Gang was less than thrilled. The prospect of this 29-year-old hustler from Los Angeles taking charge of Auburn was less than palatable. Bard, however, told fellow board members in no uncertain terms that they had managed only to drive Auburn into the ground. If they ever hoped to see a return on their investments—not to mention the original investment itself—then they had better consider the deal Cord was offering.

Cord, of course, wanted more than to just play the white knight riding into town to save Auburn from oblivion. He wanted to own the company, and part of his plan allowed for him to do just that. Lacking other ideas, the Chicago Gang must have

L. B. Manning served in the Army Air Forces during World War II.

Ralph Austin Bard played a key role in bringing Cord to Auburn as a means of salvaging the company from obscurity.

for the U.S. Signal Corps during World War I, he traveled to Chicago finding employment at a brokerage house. He was still working there when he was introduced to Cord. Cord and Manning soon became close business partners. Manning directed Cord's search for an automaker toward the Haynes Automobile Company, in Kokomo, Indiana. But before anyone could put ink to the Haynes deal, however, Auburn's Ralph Bard intervened. According to Ames, Bard purchased a Moon from Cord, which is how the two met. This alone is strange; why was a

grudgingly given in to Bard's admonishments. Cord was on his way to making a big name for himself in automotive circles.

Cord took his first view of the AAC in June 1924 and summed up the situation in his head. Sprawled over 18-1/2 acres were a number of long factory buildings offering 527,000 square feet of floor space. Cord, in a 1925 prospectus, noted, "The capacity of the plant can be brought to 100 cars per day with slight additional capital expenditure." True, perhaps,

but the need was hardly there. More than 700 Auburns collected dust in the back lots of the factory complex, and there were enough parts in the factory for the assembly of that many more. Cord knew exactly what would be required to move these cars. He had, while still working at Quinlan Motors in Chicago, designed his own dream automobile. "Designed" in the sense of sourcing the parts he would rely on to build the car's skeleton, then contacting the appropriate parts suppliers to obtain

An aerial view of the Auburn complex at its peak in 1931. The newest building in the photo is the J-shaped administration building (foreground), built the previous year. The Quonset-style and rectangular buildings immediately behind it still remain, as does the power plant, sans smokestack, seen in the upper left of the photo.

continued on page 44

Errett Lobban Cord

The stories of Charles Eckhart and Errett Lobban Cord are studies in contrasts and similarities. Both were self-made men. Both passed through a number of jobs and positions before they finally reached the circumstances that would bring them wealth. Both were teetotalers, although Cord was not adamantly opposed to others drinking. And neither man enjoyed an extensive education. Here the similarities end. Eckhart immersed himself in matters of the church and community. Cord remained reclusive, attending only to his business affairs. Eckhart held to a Victorian-era code of business, conservative and deliberate in his management. Cord's management style was very much a part of the Roaring Twenties, quick to move from one opportunity to another and always trying to stay one step ahead of the competition. Eckhart would have passed into obscurity were it not for Cord's impact on the AAC. Cord's story is compelling enough that a massive compilation of his life's work was written by automotive historian Griffith Borgeson (*Errett Lobban Cord: His Empire, His Motorcars: Auburn, Cord, Duesenberg*).

In October 1882, the Reverend Isaac Errett joined Charles William Cord and Ida Lewis Lobban in matrimony. It's easy to deduce how Charles and Ida Cord named their first son, born July 20, 1894, in Warrensburg, Missouri. Charles Cord was the proprietor of a general store in Warrensburg, which placed his family in a comfortable middle-class setting. During an economic downturn, Charles moved his family to Joliet, Illinois, for a time, working at his brother-in-law's jewelry store. From there, the family eventually moved to Los Angeles, where Errett attended the Los Angeles Polytechnic High School. In Cord's biography, Borgeson made note of an essay Cord wrote in high school.

Errett Lobban Cord, as he appeared early in his tenure with the Auburn Automobile Company.

Helen Cord, photographed during a recreational swim.

Most significantly, a sentence in the essay showed that Cord was already concocting his later-famous insights: "Genius is born to a man. Talent is obtained by a man."

In 1911, while Cord was in high school, his father died. After high school, Cord took a job selling used automobiles on a lot owned by Earle C. Anthony of L. A. Packard dealer fame. The entrepreneur-in-the-making was already fascinated by cars. At night, Cord took evening classes in business at the local YMCA. Like Charles Eckhart, Cord retained a lifelong fondness for that organization. Coincidentally, the YMCA that Cord attended—being a part of the Los Angeles area—would soon be presided over by Frank Eckhart. Cord's brush with his destiny was amazingly close.

In 1913, after a stint with a Buick dealer and a crew installing a pipeline for the Los Angeles Department of Water and Power, Cord found a better way to make money. He purchased a used Ford Model T for $75, turned it into a speedster—with one of any number of kits available for this purpose—and sold it to a Chandler dealer for $675. Cord then bought a new Model T with the profits, again converting it into a speedster, and this time selling it for $1,200. By the end of 1914, Cord had converted approximately 20 Model T speedsters, netting an average $500 a pop for the cars. It doesn't take much math to figure he had accumulated for himself $10,000 from the effort. Cord eventually took a job at the J and B Auto Company, in Los Angeles. The company's name was more impressive than its environs. It was basically a service station, and Cord used the bays after hours to continue his Model T conversion work. The budding entrepreneur also tried to start a car wash, known as the Cord Auto Washing Company. Apparently, this business was nothing more than a bucket and chamois at J and B.

Fate called again when Cord's mother obtained a lease on a 20-unit apartment building, aptly dubbed the Lobban Apartments. In 1913, one Emma Frische rented an apartment to share with her 21-year-old niece, Helen Marie Frische. It wasn't long before fondness welled up in the eyes of Cord and the young Frische. In September 1914, the two eloped in one of Cord's Model T speedsters.

With responsibilities building on his shoulders, Cord took a steady job hauling ore in Arizona with his cousin John Cord. E. L. and Helen's first child, Charles Errett, arrived soon after, born December 31, 1915. Cord, deciding to remain in Arizona, started selling Paige automobiles in Phoenix. His budding family followed, but Helen returned to Los Angeles while she was pregnant with their second son, Billy James, who was born September 19, 1917. At the end of 1918, Cord returned to L.A. as well.

How Cord decided to venture to Chicago was explained by Harold Ames in a 1976 interview conducted by the Auburn-Cord-Duesenberg Museum. "I was a pilot in World War I," Ames said. "Cord decided about that time to come to Chicago and get a job selling automobiles. He had a friend in Los Angeles that . . . was in my squadron during the war. Prior to my joining the [Signal] Corps, I had sold Chandler automobiles in Chicago. This gentleman knew about it and he told Cord, 'If you're going to Chicago to get a job, why not go in to see my friend Harold Ames at Thomas Hay?' [Hay was the] Chandler distributor . . . at 25th and Michigan Avenue." Ames returned to selling Chandlers for the Thomas J. Hay Company in January 1919. Cord arrived in Chicago later that month, just after Ames had returned to work. After the customary introductions, Ames arranged an interview for Cord with Hay. Ames, unfortunately, neglected to forewarn Cord about Hay's distaste for smokers. When Cord lit up during the interview, Hay showed him the door. Soon afterward, Hay left for his customary February vacation in Florida. Ames convinced Jack Quinlan, the agency's sales manager, to hire Cord. When Hay returned from his vacation, he found Cord in place and doing quite well selling cars. Hay let him stay, but Cord didn't remain long. He moved to other automotive agencies in a short time span. Eventually, Quinlan moved out of the Hay agency after obtaining a Moon dealership. Cord returned to work for his

Harold Ames became well-acquainted with Cord before the entrepreneur took over the Auburn Automobile Company. In 1926, Ames joined the company, becoming Cord's right-hand man for years to come.

former sales manager. It was around this period that Cord's family finally joined him in Chicago, moving there in the summer of 1919. But Cord was always itching for some bigger action, and the Cords returned to L.A. in 1920 when Cord obtained an exclusive California distributorship for a gas heater. The new enterprise was soon foiled, however, when legislation passed in California governing the acceptable designs of gas heaters that could be sold in the state. Alas, the gas heater Cord tried to distribute failed to meet these new standards. Cord was broke once again. He dabbled in real estate for a while, but soon returned to Chicago. Quinlan, his agency doing very well with the Moon, induced the Moon Motor Car Company of St. Louis to award him a distributorship for the region. Ames states that Cord returned, and got "25 percent of [Quinlan's] business that he [purchased] out of his commissions."

Moon automobiles enjoyed a good reputation. Although assembled from parts sourced elsewhere, Moons were well built, solid, and wrapped in an attractive body. This would later influence Cord's approach to Auburn. In 1921, Moon offered two models, a 6-48 and a 6-68. The 6-48 used the Continental 7-R six, and the 6-68 sported the Continental 9-N. Auburn had also used both engines. Prices ranged from $1,885 to $2,995, placing it in the same price arena as Auburn. Auburn, however, wasn't benefiting from the sales savvy of Cord in 1921. Quinlan and Cord were selling up to 60 percent of that factory's output. Little wonder the two became the darlings of the Missouri company. Moon offered additional territory, and Cord took on the company's distributorships in Iowa, Minnesota, and Wisconsin. Cord moved to Milwaukee for a while, where he based his newfound operations. He built up a good business, was offered $10,000 for the distributorship, took the money, and returned to Chicago. During this time, Cord learned well the automotive business, including marketing, distribution, and financing. By 1922, Cord bought back his partnership in Quinlan Motors and proceeded to oversee the selling of 5,000 cars in six months. The commissions were piling up in the bank. Ames, still selling Chandlers at Hay, recalled a discussion Cord and he had a few years earlier. "We . . . had an understanding, the two of us, that when we got $50,000 saved up, we'd quit and go do something else." This Cord did, by 1923.

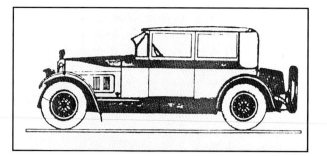

E. L. Cord's dream car, as rendered previous to his ownership of the AAC and published in *Sales Management*.

Cord no doubt drew inspiration for his dream car from this Millspaugh and Irish brougham (albeit with four doors instead of two) pictured on the front cover of the 1922 Duesenberg catalog. At the time, Cord probably didn't realize he would soon own that company as well.

continued from page 41

quantity pricing. "He got an [engine] price out of Lycoming, and it was better than Continental's," noted Ames.

Cord hired a graphic designer to draw the car's exterior, guiding the designer's every pen stroke to match his desires. It was a smart design for the time, the intention being to place the car in production, not to create a one-off custom with pricey embellishments. Cord's dream car shows his attraction to Duesenberg even at this early date. The car appears to be roughly based on a Duesenberg Model A four-door brougham by Millspaugh and Irish, as published on the front cover of a 1922 Duesenberg Automobile and Motors Company catalog. The rounded radiator shell and plummeting beltline certainly found their inspiration in the Model A. Unlike the Model A, Cord's dream car sported balloon tires and more flowing lines, especially in the roof area. The rear roofline dropped below the beltline, halting its advance at the rear quarter panel. A Brewster windshield was also

shown. By the end of the project, Cord knew the car's complete bill of materials, and the costs per part per number of thousands. (*Sales Management*, in its May 1, 1926, issue, printed a reproduction of Cord's dream car concept in a discussion of the managerial approach used at the AAC.)

When Cord made his pitch to the Chicago Gang, he had all this information in his head and did not ignorantly promise the stars without knowing what was involved. He certainly must have felt confident, the pieces were all out there waiting to be gathered and made into a complete automobile. In return for his efforts, Cord looked after himself. Over the years, much conjecture has been offered as to exactly what kind of a deal Cord worked out with the Chicago Gang that enabled him to eventually take over the company. Much of it has been wrong. It wasn't until this author uncovered some old forgotten photocopies at the Auburn-Cord-Duesenberg Museum that the inside story can now be sorted out.

The details of this breakthrough are fairly simple. It was discovered in the past 20 years that the State of Illinois still retained a number of legal documents regarding the AAC. In the summer of 1925, a Chicago stock brokerage wanted to sell a portion of a new securities offering made by the AAC. Hence, the appropriate paperwork had to be filed with the Illinois Secretary of State's office, where it remained for some 50 years before being uncovered. A plethora of legal papers emerged from the AAC in 1925. No doubt the instigator behind this flurry of AAC security activity was Cord himself. Within the filings one can find the arrangements Cord had worked out between himself and the Chicago Gang. The paperwork was generated over the AAC's "Application for Preliminary Approval of Class 'C' Securities, Under Provisions of Par. (b) Sec. 7 of the Illinois Securities Law." The filing took place August 7, 1925. The request was for issuance of 60,000 shares of capital stock, with a par value of $25 per share. The shares were offered at $31.50 each. The Chicago Gang's law firm of Loucks, Eckert and Peterson, Chicago, filed the papers with the Illinois Secretary of State's office. Wm. H. Colvin and Company, the interested Chicago stock brokerage, offered 17,050 AAC shares on the Chicago Stock Exchange. Authorization to increase the AAC's common shares to 60,000 officially took place August 14, 1925. An authorization to increase the limit to 120,000 shares occurred on November 19, 1925. What would become the final increase in shares authorizations of 500,000 passed on July 1, 1927. At the AAC common stock high point in 1933 some 224,730 shares were outstanding, just less than half of the authorized limit. Digression aside, the 1925 disclosure statements from the company's officers and directors were required for the share offering. At interest is Cord's form, which discloses his salary arrangement with the Chicago gang. Cord reported an "Employment contract as general manager, expiring December 31, 1927, for $1,000 per month or 20 percent of net profits, whichever is greater." Knowing that AAC net profits tallied to $359,592 (after federal taxes) for the first half of 1925, Cord had already accumulated some $70,000 in six months. Returning to Cord's disclosure form for the moment, another question asked, "How much time do you devote to the business of the company?" to which Cord tellingly replied, "24 hours a day." Ames readily verified this: "(Cord) was the hardest working man I've ever known in my life. . . . He was shy, very modest, a very analytical mind, a very inquisitive mind. As far as [the people of] Auburn [were] concerned, he was unsociable because he never did anything [but work]." In reference to the disclosure form's inquiry into Cord's previous employment, he wrote, "May, 1919 to June 30, 1924, General Manager, Quinlan Motors Co., Chicago. Since July, 1924, General Manager, Auburn Automobile Company." For all his positions held with AAC, Cord listed "Vice President-General Manager-Director-Treasurer."

Cord's appointment to these positions was announced in the September 27, 1924, issue of *Automobile Topics.* At this point, Cord owned "Eighteen thousand shares common" purchased in a range "from $7.50 to $32.00 per share." The $7.50 per share seems to have been a low point for AAC shares, as that figure was also used by other company officials on their disclosure forms. It is also obvious that Cord controlled the lion's share of the company's stock. Noteworthy is another statement, in which Cord divulges he was in debt "approximately $250,000 to bankers." The form was signed by Cord on August 29, 1925. Other officers filing included J. I. Farley, president, 2,020 shares; James H. Rose, secretary, 400 shares; Ralph Austin Bard, director, 600 shares; L. B. Manning, director, 300 shares.

It wasn't long before Manning established Manning and Company, with the new company's main purpose being to serve as a financial banker and personal holding company for Cord. Wm. H. Colvin and Company, informing the Illinois Secretary of State's office of the firm's intention to offer the AAC stock, made note of the AAC's historical share performance:

> "The undersigned is submitting herewith a certified copy of the balance sheet of the Auburn Automobile Company as of June 30, 1925, certified to by Arthur Young and Co., and a condensed profit and income account made by them for a period of six years, showing a net average earning over a period of two years ending June 30, 1925 (after paying preferred dividend) in excess of $1.40 per share per annum which is 4.19% on selling price and showing a net average earning of more than $6.00 per share, per annum over said six-year period. *Attention is also directed to the fact that all of preferred stock is now retired or deposit made for retiring of same* [emphasis added]."

This statement was signed February 12, 1926. Cord retired the remaining preferred stocks by issuing $600,000 of $1,000 debenture 6 percent gold notes. The issue's initiation was dated November 1, 1925. The first notes came due November 1, 1926, with $100,000 payable. Each successive year called for payments of $125,000, the final set of notes to be retired by November 1, 1930. Each note was convertible to 16-2/3 shares of AAC common stock. These notes were used to pay off the Chicago Gang to gain control of the AAC.

How it all played out was closer to this: By 1929, the AAC's annual report listed $675,000 in outstanding payable notes. In 1930, this figure increased to $1.6 million, as Cord went into more debt. Yet, by the company's 1931 annual report, all traces of payable notes vanished. According to the AAC's balance sheet for September 30, 1926, an additional $45,000 in gold notes came due on October 26, 1926. The reason for this issue is unclear. In addition to retiring Auburn's preferred shares, Cord was also required to take out a life insurance policy for $250,000.

Before Cord could take over the AAC, plenty of work lay before him. Cord worked hard at recreating a vibrant dealer network. The bigger dealerships were convinced to stick around; better days were on their way. Plenty of them had been straddled with Auburns shipped on consignment. Some dealers were deeply in debt, others had borrowed from the company just to have the ability to buy Auburns. A

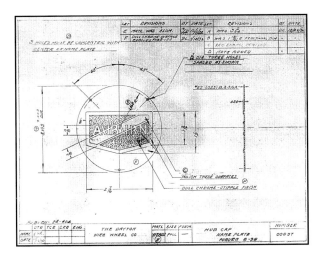

This engineered drawing of the Auburn Automobile Company's logo was used by the Dayton Wire Wheel Company to manufacture hubcaps for Auburn. The "home plate" Auburn logo has been credited to Bruce Guilford, a body striper at the company.

A rather cheeky Auburn ad, circa 1923, depicting a Sport model. The ad purports that Auburns are blue bloods within the automotive family.

AUBURN

BLOOD WILL TELL!

What car attracted the crowd at the first automobile shows in 1903? The Auburn! What name has been on everybody's lips at the 1923 shows? Auburn! ❡ What is it that has enabled Auburn not merely to survive but to stay in the very forefront of the dozen cars that date back to the beginning of the industry? If there is one word that describes it, that word is "distinction." Auburn always has had that "something" about it which makes experienced motorists pick it out intuitively. ❡ Today that originality, skill, diligence, ambition—call it what you will—refined, developed and inspired by a twenty-three-year record of continuous success, is producing by far the most distinguished cars in Auburn's history.

Sport (illustrated) fully equipped $1895. Other Auburn Models — 6-43 Touring $1095, Touring-Sedan $1465, 6-51 Touring $1275, 7-passenger Touring $1345, Brougham $1965, Sedan $2245, 6-63 Touring $1650. *(Freight and war tax extra.)*

Dealers: It is a piece of genuine good fortune to have the complete Auburn line in 1923. Your territory may be open—wire.

Auburn Automobile Company, Auburn, Indiana

"ONCE AN OWNER ALWAYS A FRIEND"

few dealers hadn't sold an Auburn in two years. The not-so-productive franchises were eliminated; some were nothing more than a service station with one demo model and a proprietor willing to sell it or send in an order.

Cord wasted no time in moving the dusty Auburns, either piecemeal or in wholesale lots. This generated enough capital to allow Cord to pursue the dream car he had envisioned in his not-too-distant days at Quinlan Motors. Cord's method of market analysis was simple. He traveled the country, talking directly with the dealers and customers. He learned of their dislikes and preferences. It was during this time that Cord issued any number of axioms. A few examples include:

- "Be different if you can't be biggest."
- "There will always be a market for the product that is distinctive . . . that appeals to the man who wants something that isn't exactly like the products owned by all his neighbors."
- "Brains are the most important ingredient in a motor."

As the last remnants of the Beauty Sixes finally faded (the 6-51), the AAC entered the 1924 automotive market with only the 6-43 and the Weidely-powered 6-63. The 6-43 and 6-63 carried over intact—feature and price-wise—with only minor embellishments added. Most models now came equipped with disc wheels, the sole exception being the standard touring. Auburn supplied this model with wood wheels (all models could be ordered with wood wheels as an option, except the Sport). The 6-43, previously referred to as the Chesterfield touring, was now known as the special touring model. Although 1924 specifications mentioned a permanent top for this model, sales literature in 1923 did not list this feature. The special touring, the touring coupe, and sedan came with DeKalb Blue or Maroon Lake livery. The standard touring was available only in DeKalb Blue. The Sport, instead of wearing a two-tone color scheme, arrived in dashing Cherry Red. As Auburn's literature promoted, "These cars are built by a home-owning group of workmen in Auburn, Indiana, whose big purpose in life is the Auburn car. They build it with that exacting care that makes a good car a better one." For Cord, however, the Sport could no longer be justified; it faded, along with a number of other models, by year's end. The 6-43 dwindled to the special touring, sedan, and the English coach ($1,945).

When Auburn introduced the straight-eight, the company heavily promoted the new engine.

Cord wasted no time in promoting the English Coach, a model by which he hoped to attract customers to ailing Auburn dealerships.

This latter model was one of the first Auburn products to be impacted by Cord. It was a transition model with some of the details from Cord's dream car, but falling short of using all of his prototype's themes. For instance, the English Coach used a rounded top, like the Cord dream car, but wore a high waistline. The front overhang of the roof acted not only as a visor, but also as a ventilator. It was not, however, of the Brewster variety. Auburn supplied the English Coach only in Sage Brush Green. Balloon tires (another feature from Cord's dream car) and four-wheel brakes became standard features on all models, the first year for both. For now, the 6-43 continued to use the 195.6-cubic-inch Continental straight six. Now using the Continental 7-U, power ratings edged up nominally to 52 horsepower at 2600 rpm.

Cord also phased out the Weidely-engined 6-63. It wasn't that Cord found the Weidely too expensive, but the same money could be channeled toward an engine with more marketing impact. Basically, he threw the Weidely contract overboard. No doubt the AAC's legal team used more tactful terms, but the net effect still cut off Weidely, now in financial trouble due in part to the Auburn contract. A securities document filed with the State of Illinois, refers to what became of the AAC's association with Weidely: ". . . an action [was] brought against [the AAC] by the Receiver of Weidely Motor Company to recover damages alleged to have

OPPOSITE
In 1923, Sport models wore a two-tone brown livery. This model, parked in front of the Auburn Country Club, wears that paint scheme, though it's difficult to detect in this black-and-white photo. In the following year, Sport models came with a single-tone, dashing, Cherry Red paint scheme.

Lycoming's straight-eight engine became an Auburn hallmark from 1924 until the marque's demise in 1936.

been sustained by an alleged refusal to accept motors," the document reported. "Said action is pending in the DeKalb Circuit Court, undetermined."

Cord didn't want to deal with anything that dictated how he could use Auburn's dwindling resources. As Ames verified, Cord, working up the specs for his dream car, had found that Lycoming could deliver an engine at a better price. Never putting the company out of his mind, Cord wasted no time calling on the engine maker to deliver what would be one of the biggest marketing boosts the AAC ever enjoyed.

Founded in 1908 as the Lycoming Foundry and Machine Company, Lycoming started to produce automotive engines in 1912. By 1918, only four U.S. marques out of the some 119 that existed used Lycoming engines in their products. In 1920, the company was reorganized as the Lycoming Motor Corporation. According to *MoTor*'s annual listing of car specifications for 1924, Lycoming produced two engines, each a four, for the market. These were used by Elcar and Gardner. In May 1924, Lycoming announced the availability of a straight eight. By 1925, the Pennsylvania-based company provided straight eights (known as the 2-H) to Auburn, Elcar, Gardner, and a variation to Kissel (the 287-cubic-inch 3-H). As a result of the straight eight, Lycoming saw its sales grow 16 percent from 1925 to 1926, and some 25 percent in 1927, topping over $8 million.

Auburn's entry into the straight-eight market was one of the main reasons the company survived past 1924.

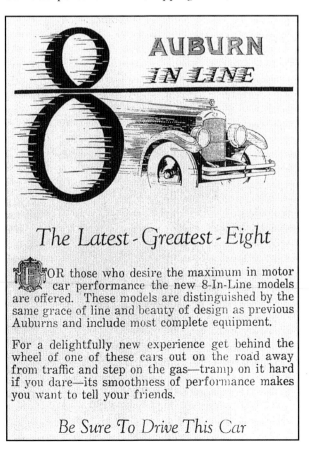

The Latest - Greatest - Eight

FOR those who desire the maximum in motor car performance the new 8-In-Line models are offered. These models are distinguished by the same grace of line and beauty of design as previous Auburns and include most complete equipment.

For a delightfully new experience get behind the wheel of one of these cars out on the road away from traffic and step on the gas—tramp on it hard if you dare—its smoothness of performance makes you want to tell your friends.

Be Sure To Drive This Car

By the fall of 1924, Auburn would tackle the market with the Lycoming-powered "Eight-In-Line." Dubbed the "Latest Greatest Eight," Auburn offered the 8-63 in the former 6-63 body styles of the aluminum-bodied sedan made by McFarlan ($2,550), the special touring ($1,895 and also with a permanent top), and four-door brougham ($2,395). The AAC also positioned the English Coach ($2,650) in the 8-63 line. Cord used the English Coach, in particular, as a salesroom draw. Here was an Auburn with the latest in production-car styling, yet the dealer could also offer older Auburn models at deeply discounted prices. This was key to Cord clearing out those back lots. The showcase of the 8-63, of course, was the Lycoming 260.8-cubic-inch straight eight. With a bore and stroke identical to the Continental 7-U, it produced 58 horsepower at 2850 rpm. Although the eight had almost the same power as the six-cylinder Weidely engine, this misses the point. The straight eight *sounded* bigger. Lycoming bedecked the engine with a "swan [intake] manifold," five main bearings, vibration dampeners, and a side-valve configuration. The 8-63 rode on a 124-inch wheelbase and came equipped with balloon tires and four-wheel brakes. The brake system used a proportioning system, but only the front brakes had internal shoes. The rear brakes used a rather antique external contracting band arrangement. More advanced was the steering system's variable-ratio gear box.

All the various components of the 8-63 were the purchasing responsibility of Harry L. Dunn. In charge of purchasing as of 1924, he eventually became vice president of the department. For 1924, some 2,400 cars rolled off the assembly line. Revenues amounted to $3.4 million. Net profits tallied over $60,000, and the cash surplus rose to just under $985,000. To be sure, Cord was using every bucket he had at his disposal to bail the company out. Yet, these numbers conflict with those listed in *Moody's Manual of Investments*. While gross sales figures remain the same, *Moody's* reported a loss of $37,951 and a deficit of $69,830. Since the AAC likely supplied both sets of numbers, one must question its bookkeeping practices.

Simultaneously with the small miracle Cord was working in the latter half of 1924, he also had to tackle the Herculean task of bringing out a new Auburn by 1925. At the very least, prototypes had to make the all-important New York show or momentum would be lost. What little capital Cord was able to muster had to be stretched. He pitched his ideas to suppliers, bolstered the company's image, and asked for and received sub-wholesale prices. Of particular importance—both for the task at hand and for the AAC's future—was Cord persuading the Central Manufacturing Company to run 100 of the upcoming Auburn bodies on credit and at a bargain price. Cord needed more bodies than Auburn could

produce, and he approached Central in March 1925 to inquire of its willingness. At that time, 27-year-old Central was dying. The Connersville company had incorporated in 1898 for the purpose of manufacturing carriage body woodwork. In 1903, Central made its first automotive bodies, shipping them to Cadillac. The company went on to provide bodies for Stutz, Overland, Paige, Haynes, Apperson, Gardner, Cole, and Moon, among others. Cord probably became aware of the operation while selling Moons. At any rate, Central wasn't the only company in Connersville gasping for breath. The town's once massive automotive empire was now in a shambles, and any chance of salvation probably looked good. Central accepted the deal Cord offered.

Cord's salvation didn't stop with a 100-body order, however, as he sent ever more business to the east-central Indiana town. Eventually, an 18-month

contract worth $1.5 million was signed, and Central henceforth played a key role in the AAC's affairs.

Two prototypes for 1925 made the New York show and promptly received an enthusiastic response from the dealers, the very crowd Cord most had to please. Auburn's new models, the 8-88 and 6-66, created quite a stir. They brought to fruition Cord's efforts to transform Auburn's product line into a cohesive entity. The new line offered a wide array of body styles for differing tastes. Particularly interesting was the brougham. Here was Cord's dream car, designed just a few years earlier, incarnate. The beltline started on top of the hood, just behind the radiator shell, then swept down and followed the lower side of the greenhouse in more traditional form. The Brewster windshield was there. All Auburns used a rounded radiator shell treatment just as Cord envisioned it from the Duesenberg Model A. The early 8-88 prototype had a chrome strip running diagonally from the upper left corner of the radiator shell to the lower right corner. This feature can be seen on an Auburn depicted on the cover of the earliest 8-88 brochure, *Worth vs. Words*. Auburn never used this radiator trimming on production models. The hood held four groups of four louvers each, all leaning forward. Auburn offered disc wheels or six-spoke pressed steel wheels. Parts were kept as interchangeable as possible. Relying on one supplier for a component also helped control costs. For instance, the AAC now purchased all of its engines from Lycoming.

The Roadster

The 8-88 and 6-66 represented styling far in advance of anything Auburn had previously manufactured. Although the prototypes made the New York show in January, the new Auburn models didn't roll off the production lines until later in the year. The new models cost the company an average of $1,000 each to produce. The buying public had a choice of a sedan (6-66:$1,695, 8-88: $1,995), coupe ($1,445/$1,745), brougham ($1,495/$1,795), touring ($1,395/-$1,695), roadster (a style not available since 1922 and listing for $1,395/$1,695), or a Wanderer sedan ($1,745/$2,045). The latter was simply a sedan, but the back of the front seat folded down to meet the bottom cushion of the rear seat. In effect, this created a large mattress for the ultimate in car camping. The roadster had an unusual feature as well: a small side door and a flip-up panel, which prevented rear passengers from having to climb over the side of the body to access the rumble seat. Windshield wings returned to open-body (the roadster and touring) Auburns after disappearing on the 1923 Sport. Instead of a Brewster windshield arrangement, the roadster and touring used a two-piece ventilating type. The coupe used a body built up from a process similar to the Weymann technique, whereby a padded fabric—known as Meritas—was stretched over wire mesh. The fabric itself was dyed, not painted. This made for a very light body shell in its day. Upholstery choices for the year included a silk-finish wool mohair in the sedan, high-quality velour in the coupe, and Spanish leather in the open-body models. The 6-66 used a Lycoming 207.1-cubic-inch six-cylinder, good for 48 horsepower at 2600 rpm. A slightly bigger six, bored out to displace 224 cubic inches, replaced this earlier version by the beginning of 1926. This engine was mounted in a 120-inch wheelbase chassis rolling on 30-inch tires. The 8-88 used Lycoming's 2-H straight-eight again (previously found in the 8-63), but now displacing 276.1 cubic inches. The updated 2-H used the same bore as the previous eight, but with a slightly longer stroke. It produced 60 horsepower at 2850 rpm and would propel an Auburn to 68 miles per hour. The 8-88 enjoyed four-wheel mechanical brakes with a proportioning system on a 129-inch wheelbase chassis. Like the 6-66, Auburn used 30-inch balloon tires, albeit wider. The 8-88's long semi-elliptic springs were *de rigueur* in 1926 for providing a soft ride.

The year 1925 started as a seller's market for the auto industry; so was the new Auburn a hit or just riding a sales wave? By summer, discounting erupted, turning the market toward buyers, but Cord stuck by his original prices. Auburn sales kept pace: the AAC averaged sales of 419 cars per month during the first half of 1925, jumping to an average of 496 cars per

ABOVE
The Wanderer sedan, as shown in this ad, was essentially a standard Auburn sedan on the exterior, but with a fold-down front seat inside.

RIGHT
Workers are shown assembling 1925 Auburn coupes, using the Weymann method of covering bodies with mesh, padding, and a leatherette material.

OPPOSITE
Wade Morton, Neil McDarby, Cliff Henderson, Roy Faulkner, and E. L. Cord pose beside a Cord L-29 phaeton-sedan. In the background is the Eckhart Library of Auburn, Indiana.

Soon after Cord's takeover of Auburn, the company's ads and sales literature started to reflect its latest logo: "If it does not sell itself, you will not be asked to buy." The slogan reflects a hardy belief in the company's products, and their superiority over the competition.

month in the second half. Cord now knew he had a hit on his hands. With 5,493 Auburns sold, sales for 1925 climbed to $7.9 million, with profits exceeding $750,000. Cash surplus for the year tallied some $655,000. According to the company's annual report, working capital climbed to over $3.8 million. Some 60,000 AAC shares were outstanding at the end of the year, trading in a high/low range from 56-1/2 to 31-3/4, the latter figure representing face value upon issue earlier in the year.

On February 13, 1925, the AAC filed a corporate resolution reducing the number of directors from seven to five. The AAC hired Neil McDarby as a general sales manager in 1925. In July 1925, Cord started to establish distributorships, the first located in New York, Boston, and Chicago. An export department was also formed, managed by Robert S. Wiley. In Griffith Borgeson's book on Cord, the author noted, "Also new to [Cord] was running a good-sized manufacturing and sales organization. What had been esteemed as good business practice under the administration of the bankers seemed ridiculous to him. He tore out lint-picking, time-wasting systems which had satisfied the criteria of efficiency experts, got rid of tons of paperwork, and set up a new order of common sense." The point is, Cord didn't come to the AAC burdened with ingrained management paths upon which to move. If one didn't know better, his revamping of the company sounds like an example of re-engineering in the 1990s. By November 1, 1925, the AAC was out of debt, the banker's preferred stock liquidated, and Cord's takeover complete.

Duesenberg Enters the Picture

Auburn offered a four-cylinder in 1926, the first Auburn four since 1916. Its return would be brief. The company offered the 4-44 in a sedan ($1,195), coupe ($1,175), touring ($1,145), or roadster ($1,145). Auburn 4-44 customers received a Lycoming CF 206.4-cubic-inch four-cylinder, producing 42 horse-

power at 2200 rpm. Unlike the 6-66 and 8-88 models, the 4-44's windshield was a one-piece affair. While the 4-44 gave Auburn a budget-priced model, it never caught on. Its larger brethren outsold the small Auburn three to four times in volume.

The 6-66 and 8-88 models returned, with only minor updates to their drivetrains. The 6-66 now used a larger Lycoming straight six, the SM model displacing 224 cubic inches and delivering 55 horsepower at 3000 rpm. The Lycoming straight eight (now labeled the HM) also took a jump in cubic inches, to 298.6. With an increase in the bore, this engine produced 68 horsepower at 3000 rpm. Although never advertised in 1926, an Auburn retail price sheet showed a 147-inch wheelbase 8-88 seven-passenger sedan as being available ($2,495). For large families in 1926, the seven-passenger sedan was akin to today's minivan.

Not among the updates was Auburn's brake system. It's interesting to note the company's reasoning for using mechanical brakes. In its sales literature, the company stated: ". . . we tried out the two types of brakes that are now being used on standard motor cars—the Hydraulic and the Mechanical. After these tests we came to the conclusion that the mechanical brake would be most satisfactory in the hands of our owners." Interestingly, this didn't stop the AAC from using hydraulic brakes on the 4-44.

AAC sales in 1926 climbed to $10.8 million, while profits rose to over $942,000. The company's balance sheet, dated September 1926, showed a surplus of $1.7 million. Outstanding shares on November 30, 1926, came to 84,888. The company's high/low trading range covered 72-7/8 to 40-1/2 for the year.

The AAC also took on a new legal firm in 1926, Miller, Gorham, Wales, and Noxon. In particular, it retained one Raymond S. Pruitt as general counsel. When the Chicago Gang finally left town, Pruitt replaced Rose as the AAC's counsel. He would soon become inseparable from the business activities of Cord. Ames also joined Cord at the AAC around this time. "I got married in '25. In 1926, we went on our honeymoon. . . . When I came back, Cleveland [autos] had gone broke! Cord has been trying to get me to come to Auburn. . . . I started, I think it was, September. . . ." Well, Cleveland did disappear, but only because Chandler had absorbed the company. In any case, the situation apparently provided Ames with an excuse to leave Chicago.

In its February 26, 1926, issue, *Automobile Topics* reported, "Cord has acquired a substantial interest in the company, and is now in complete control of its affairs." The transition of power occurred on February 2 at the AAC's annual meeting. Cord, 32 years of age, was elected president. Faulkner ascended to the vice president position, Manning became treasurer, and Pruitt was named secretary.

Cord continued to build his automotive empire. On August 26, 1926, Cord purchased the Ansted Engineering facility in Connersville. Purchase price for the 85,000-square-foot building was $40,000. Three months later, on November 26, Cord was back in Connersville, this time a recipient of a gift from the Bigger and Better Connersville Committee. The committee turned over to Cord a 135,000-square-foot facility formerly belonging to the Lexington Motor Car Company. Due to the rapid decline of several automotive companies in Connersville, the town fathers came to the conclusion that they needed Cord and basically gave him a blank check to the area.

While expanding his presence in Connersville, Cord also purchased Duesenberg out of bankruptcy court for $500,000. Incorporated in Delaware on November 3, 1926, the company complex covered 16.5 acres at 1511 W. Washington Street in Indianapolis. Capitalized at over $1 million, its name changed from Duesenberg Motors Corporation to Duesenberg, Inc. Cord appointed himself as president and Fred Duesenberg as vice president of engineering. Pearl Watson left his post as superintendent of the AAC factory and became vice president of manufacturing. Ames was initially named vice president of sales and was promoted to president in 1930. (The AAC always maintained a majority control of Duesenberg shares.) Though Duesenberg would go on to become the "premier" company of the Auburn-Cord-Duesenberg triumvirate, it would always do so on the back of the Auburn Automobile Company.

An exterior view of the main office building for Auburn's Connersville, Indiana, operations. It bears a likeness to the company's first administration building in Auburn, Indiana.

TB-A I

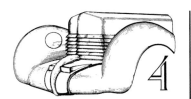

Explosive Growth
1927-1931

4

By 1927, the AAC's fortunes were on the rise, and Cord had come a long way from his days of scratching out a living. Auburn sales had grown the past two years since Cord had taken the helm, and 1927 only continued the upward push. Auburn's growing confidence was reflected in the sales slogan for the period: "Drive an Auburn Straight Eight and if it does not sell itself, you will not be asked to buy."

The 1926 models carried over intact early in the year, followed by a little model shuffling later in the season. With 4-44 sales flat, the company yanked this model. Although Auburn would never again offer a four-cylinder model, prices of the 6-66 dropped sufficiently for it to take up the 4-44's market position. A 6-66 roadster listed for $1,095, ditto for the touring. The sports sedan (previously known as the

brougham) sold for $1,195, and the sedan for $1,295. Early 6-66 models used the 55 horsepower (at 3000 rpm), Lycoming 4SM, 224-cubic-inch straight six, a carryover from 1926. The straight six in the later 6-66 models, however, used a different engine. Apparently, Continental cut a price for its 28L engine that Lycoming couldn't match, and Auburn used Continental engines for what would be the last time. This 185-cubic-inch straight six puffed out 43 horsepower at 2600 rpm. To fill the gap left by the 6-66's move downward, Auburn introduced the 8-77, an economy-priced straight eight with a 125-inch wheelbase. This model used Lycoming's GT eight, a 225.7-cubic-inch engine developing 65 horsepower at 3200 rpm. Again, pricing was the draw: the 8-77 roadster and touring sold for $1,395, the sports sedan for $1,495, and the sedan listed at $1,695. Brakes for the 8-77 consisted of four 12-inch drums.

The 8-88 line remained essentially unchanged, although Auburn increased its wheelbase to 130 inches. Out back, the 8-88 had external contracting brakes working on 15-inch drums, with internal expanding brakes inside 14-inch drums up front. The 298.6-cubic-inch Lycoming now used the model nomenclature of 4HM. This engine spun its Nelson Bohnalite pistons and Duraluminum rods with a five-bearing crankshaft. The Wanderer sedan was still available, and Auburn released a seven-passenger touring, riding on the same 147-inch wheelbase as the seven-passenger 8-88 sedan. In its sales literature, Auburn gloated over the "Marshall-type, double-deck upholstery springs in the 8-77 sedan and 8-88 closed models." Essentially, these

This 6-66 sedan was photographed in front of E. L. Cord's home in Auburn, Indiana.

seat springs had progressive rates that were individually sacked. Shades of Posturpedic.

During the summer, the AAC released the cabriolet, available in all its lines. Auburn was one of the first automakers to build a production cabriolet (a two-door drop top with roll-up windows, as opposed to the side curtains fitted to roadsters).

It was around this time that Cord hired the advertising talents of Peter Paul Willis, more popularly known as P. P. Willis, who operated an advertising agency in Chicago. Auburn's advertising aesthetics took a quantum leap. It was Willis who devised advertising schemes such as white type over a black background. H. Gordon Hersh handled Auburn's advertising campaigns internally. Sales for 1927 tallied 14,517 units, pulling in $17 million, an increase of 57 percent over 1926. Net profits edged up to $1.2 million and, according to the company's annual report, the AAC's cash surplus almost surpassed $1 million. Outstanding shares climbed from 84,888 to 127,600, and the AAC's par value dropped accordingly. For 1927, AAC stock traded in a range from 69 to 123-1/2.

On the heels of this success, Auburn distributors were popping up all over Europe, including Amsterdam, Athens, Berlin, Brussels, Bucharest, Copenhagen, Hamburg, Lisbon, London, Oslo, Paris, Prague, Riga, San Sebastian, Vienna, and Zurich.

Further boosting Auburn's image in 1927 were a set of speed record attempts and races staged throughout the year. These events, however, were not planned by anyone at the AAC. At various times over the years, privateers had raced Auburns, though the marque was not one of the first thought or spoken of when enthusiasts discussed racing. This deficiency in equating Auburn with performance events, however, was about to change.

Auburn Goes Racing

A West Coast Auburn dealer made an ill-fated attempt to break the one-mile stock car record with an unprepared Auburn 8-88 in 1927. Wade Morton, noted race car driver and a former principal of Meteor Motors, Inc., caught wind of the attempt and decided to attempt breaking the existing speed records with a run in his own 8-88. Morton went after the record a little more diligently, however, having his Auburn prepared by Eddie Miller, whose Hollywood garage was the official repair station for Duesenbergs in the mid-1920s and a favorite haunt for racing types. Miller, a former mechanic for the Duesenberg brothers, went through the 8-88's engine carefully, tuning the Lycoming for maximum efficiency. Morton and Miller's extra effort paid off. On March 18, 1927, Morton took the Auburn to the Culver City, California, board track and promptly set a new 1,000-mile record for American stock cars in the 300-cubic-inch class. Setting an average speed of 68.37 miles per hour over

the 1,000 miles, the 8-88's speed average peaked at 82.128 miles per hour over a 25-mile distance.

The news took the country by storm, particularly Auburn dealers and management at the AAC, who had no prior knowledge of the attempt. The competition wasn't about to rest, however. Ever since Marmon had faded from competitive events, Stutz had been the lone wolf in the stock car racing field. Not wanting to be left behind, Stutz one-upped Auburn on April 4 by averaging 68.4 miles per hour for the same record at Indianapolis. The new speed record did not exactly leave Auburn eating dust, something an owner of the much more costly Stutz had the right to expect. This tit-for-tat encouraged a head-to-head match, and that's exactly what occurred next. The high-noon showdown transpired at the Atlantic City, New Jersey, board track on May 7, 1927. It was Stutz versus Auburn in a 75-mile event. But this time Morton and Miller had factory backing. Morton raced an Auburn 8-88 roadster; Tom Rooney piloted a Stutz roadster. The Stutz won, but only by a nose, clocking 86.247 miles per hour at the finishing line, the Auburn a hair behind at 86.240 miles per hour. Once again Auburn had the upper hand in the ensuing

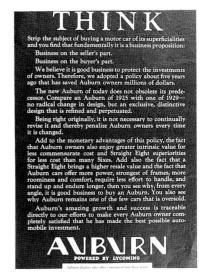

After P. P. Willis started to design Auburn's advertising campaigns, Auburn ads achieved a contemporary look. White letters on black backgrounds and the lack of any illustration of Auburn models are just two examples of Willis' creative thinking.

publicity, giving the Stutz a run for the money at half the cost (or less) in the showroom.

Later that summer, the Auburn gang returned to Atlantic City for a series of speed-record attempts. Four Auburns made the trip: two 8-88 roadsters, one cabriolet, and one sports sedan. Some 45 assistants helped nine drivers—including Morton, Ralph Hepburn, Fred Winnai, and Ab Jenkins—run in relay fashion. The runs took place from July 28 to August 8, 1927. AAC literature painted a picture of the scene: "Officials huddled in a little coop of a judge's stand,

A shop owner in Portland, Oregon, used a First Series 1928 Auburn sedan to decorate his window display in February 1928.

OPPOSITE
For 1927, Auburn offered two models on a stretched 147-inch wheelbase: a seven-passenger sedan and the seven-passenger touring shown here.

An entourage from the Auburn Automobile Company traveled to Atlantic City, New Jersey, during the summer of 1927 to tackle a number of endurance records. A crew is shown here making hasty late-night repairs to one of the 8-88 roadsters participating in the runs.

An Auburn 8-88 roadster churns away the miles over the Atlantic City board track.

A triumphant Wade Morton, part of the team of drivers that ran the Atlantic City track, is seen at the end of the record attempts.

The 8-88 sedan that participated in the speed run at Atlantic City was wrecked during the effort, but that didn't prevent the pit crews from patching it and pushing it back on the track. A board lists the names of the crew assigned to the sedan.

With this latest round of Auburn speed successes, an enthusiastic public could no longer contain itself. Auburn was the talk of the moment in automotive circles. Dealer applications were on the rise, and Auburn staked out a solid place for itself in the automotive market. The company's sales literature now boasted that the 8-88 was capable of an 80-plus miles per hour top speed. Who could have argued? The speed records proved this (if one overlooks the tuning the racers received), and street tires of the day did not allow anyone to test Auburn's claims.

The Premier Auburn: The Speedster

In September 1927, Cord stretched his acquisition binge by buying Lycoming. Lycoming continued to supply other auto manufacturers as well as serve as the exclusive engine for Auburn. Lycoming's sales continued to grow, 15 percent in 1928 and 11 percent in 1929. Cord made his first acquisition in Connersville—the Ansted Engineering facility—as already noted, in

closed in with netting to protect them from mosquitoes, with electric fans to cool them in the Sahara-like heat of the mid-day sun reflected from Jersey sand, and with greatcoats to keep them warm at night." It rained almost every night, with fog setting in by morning. The sedan, purchased back from a physician, was wrecked during the run. The two roadsters, however, went on to grab new AAA stock-car records from the 5- to 15,000-mile marks. Notable benchmarks included the speeds at 1,000 miles, with Auburn obtaining 72.512 miles per hour and 61.377 miles per hour at 15,000 miles. For 24 hours, the average speed was clocked at 72.192 miles per hour. The Atlantic City speed attempts marked the first official relationship between Ab Jenkins and the AAC. (Eight years later, Jenkins would be racing for Auburn on the salt flats of Bonneville.)

Auburn line workers assemble a speedster at Connersville, circa 1928.

Arthur Landis, shown in the latter days of the AAC next to a Cord 810, served as Auburn's vice president in charge of Connersville operations.

1926. By 1928, Cord had purchased Central and the surrounding 83 acres known as "McFarlan's Corn Patch." He ordered two additions to the Central facility, which cost $2 million total and added 1.5 million square feet. Arthur Landis was named vice president in charge of Connersville, and C. E. Hilkey served as the new facility's superintendent.

Continuing Auburn's tradition of introducing models at any time during the year, the company carried over its 1927 models for a short time in 1928. However, the second series of Auburns for 1928 would temporarily suspend the company's use of hyphenated model numbers. When Auburn finally rolled out the new 115, it became Auburn's *pièce de résistance*. In hindsight, many still feel it is one of Auburn's finest. Borgeson quotes Eddie Miller as saying that the 115 was "the first real Auburn." Hydraulic four-wheel brakes stopped the 115, and the famous Bijur automatic lubrication system greased key points of the 130-inch chassis on demand. Wheel size on the 115 dropped to 18 inches, continuing the trend of ever-smaller tires. While styling didn't depart markedly from the

previous Auburn series, hood louvers now leaned rearward instead of forward. Lycoming created a real work of art for under the hood. Called the 4MD, the 298.6-cubic-inch straight eight developed 115 horsepower at 3300 rpm. The engine had, among other tweaks, a dual-carburetor manifold and a better breathing, new combustion chamber design. The 4MD matched Stutz's horsepower jump from 95 horsepower in 1927 to 115 horsepower in 1928. Although Auburn dealer literature claimed a horsepower gain in the 298.6 from 90 to 115, no public source of information ever claimed 90 horsepower from the 298.6-cubic-inch Lycoming (4HM) straight eight as used in the 8-88. In fact, typical listings for the older 4HM quoted 68 horsepower at 3000 rpm, or 72 horsepower at 3000 rpm (*MoToR*). If the latter figures are reliable, this represents a 60 to 69 percent power increase over the 8-88's engine. Even assuming the 90 horsepower figure, the horsepower gain is still a respectable 28 percent. Ultimately, the horsepower discrepancies are unexplainable. What is clear is that Auburn learned a few tricks from its speed-record attempts.

Auburn offered the 115 in a sedan, sport sedan, roadster, cabriolet, and phaeton sedan. This last model represented a more civilized means to enjoy top-down motoring with a four-door model. Unlike a touring model, a phaeton owner enjoyed roll-up windows. Auburn was the first automaker to offer the phaeton body style on a production car. In early dealer literature, the AAC also mentions a touring model. However, the company decided to drop this increasingly unpopular model by the time sales literature was printed for public consumption.

In 1928, Auburn introduced what would become its most famous model. Still synonymous with the Auburn name, the AAC presented the speedster as part of the 115 line. The speedster fearlessly challenged Stutz's performance image. Both companies' speedsters represented an answer to a stock car racing problem: How does a driver keep the competition from drafting in the wake of a boxy sedan? The answer was simple: Create a streamlined stern that eliminates the air wake. While both the Stutz and Auburn speedsters accomplished this, aesthetically speaking, the Auburn was a better design.

An Auburn phaeton travels through a large California redwood.

OPPOSITE
The 1927 Duesenberg Model X speedster, which served as inspiration for the first generation of Auburn speedsters.

An early Auburn speedster rests on the grounds of the Auburn Automobile Company's complex.

The origins of the first Auburn speedsters are rooted in Duesenberg's Model X speedster. In his book, *Auburn Cord Duesenberg*, Don Butler published a drawing of a Duesenberg Model A speedster, rendered by John Tjaarda (who was later responsible for the Lincoln Zephyr, among others). The drawing has the stern lines that would find their way onto the 1927 Duesenberg Model X speedster. The design shows a windshield of similar rake and design as that of the Model X speedster, but the height proportions are smaller. Tjaarda's speedster also uses motorcycle fenders, something the Model X (or later Auburn speedsters) never offered. McFarlan manufactured the Model X speedster's coachwork. After its assembly, Harold Ames sold the Duesenberg Model X speedster to Chicago hotel owner Arnold Kirkeby, a friend of Cord's. The Auburn speedster, which continued the legacy of the Model X speedster, was and is sheer aesthetic genius, exuding speed even when parked. Perhaps it's the 25-degree rake of the hood louvers, or the door and storage-compartment door lines, or even the stern of the boattail itself.

While stunning, the steep rake of the doors made the car's ingress and egress something of a chore. The speedster's windshield sported an even steeper angle, so much so that it became a knuckle buster for larger hands that tried to swing the steering wheel past the windshield. No doubt, the early

continued on page 68

Auburn followed its attention-getting boattail speedster of 1928 with a cabin speedster. When he pursued aviation, Cord promoted cabin fuselages over open cockpits. The cabin speedster project was born when Cord became interested in applying this idea to an automotive design. The cabin speedster never became a production model; instead, it was a prototype in the same light as today's show cars. A Lycoming 4MD straight eight supplied power, and the chassis was assembled from two Auburn frames. The front half of the frame remained in its standard position, and the back half was actually the front half of another frame, flipped upside down and joined in the middle to create an underslung effect. This lowered the chassis some 6 inches and the overall height of the cabin speedster some 12 inches. The seats were made of wicker, and a compass and altimeter were part of the dash, to the left and right of the standard Auburn instrument cluster. The cabin speedster had teardrop hood screens on the side, an icon of Harry Miller. At the time, Harry Miller was on the AAC's payroll, the company employing his engineering talents for the L-29 project.

There is some contention as to how the cabin speedster project started. Although the Griswold Motor Body Company of Detroit made the body, Auburn had never called on Griswold before, and the company never used it again. So how did Griswold get the contract for building the cabin speedster's body? The sales brochure lists Wade Morton as the designer of the cabin speedster. A design patent even exists to back this claim. However, it's questionable whether Morton had the design skills to render from scratch such an automobile. His name, however, would go a long way to lending credence to the cabin speedster. Apparently, Cord issued a design contest of sorts, asking for a cabin speedster design from various

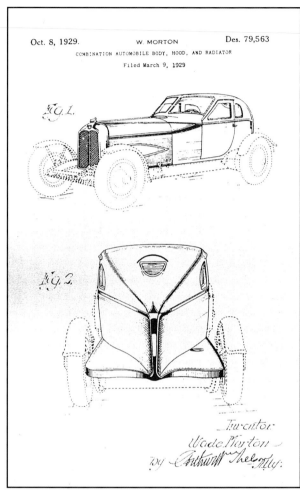

The patent drawings, bearing Wade Morton's name, as submitted to the U.S. Patent Office.

The early illustration submitted to the AAC by Griswold Motor Body suggesting the basic lines of the cabin speedster. Robert Grimshaw, who rendered this drawing, was not aware of Auburn's plans to install the cabin speedster onto an Auburn chassis, which this is not.

coachwork manufacturers. The winner would receive the contract to build the prototype body and ostensibly gain more business once the model was placed into production. Robert Grimshaw, a designer at Griswold during the late 1920s, designed the winning entry but placed it on a Duesenberg chassis since no stipulation had been made as to what kind of chassis the cabin speedster would be fitted with. Grimshaw's design did not use motorcycle fenders, instead relying on standard clamshell designs. He included a running board, too. The subsequent prototype, however, did not follow Grimshaw's lines with total dedication. It's likely that Morton, body draftsman Dick Robinson, or both may have modified the cabin speedster design as necessary.

The prototype Auburn cabin speedster shortly after its completion by Griswold Body. Headlights had not yet been attached when this photo was taken.

The prototype and 320 other cars burned out of existence on March 5, 1929, at the Los Angeles Automobile Show. The tent under which the cabin speedster was displayed caught fire after either a car backfired or an electrical short ignited the canvas. The question remained for some 50 years why the AAC had not continued to pursue the project. The answer was pro-vided when a fortunate set of circumstances allowed the cabin speedster to be faithfully recreated in the 1980s. As it turned out, the car's shortened leaf springs, reduced wheelbase, and rigid frame all conspired to produce a back-slamming ride. The wicker seats did nothing to alleviate the discomfort—they were simply a case of beauty over function.

The Auburn 115 speedster with which Wade Morton set new one-mile speed records for stock cars. The speedster was displayed in Daytona Beach, Florida, after the run. The speed painted across the door likely reflects a flying one-mile figure.

continued from page 64

speedsters were pushing form over function. The speedster—as with the rest of the Auburn models for 1928—utilized bold, 13-inch headlamps, some of the largest on the market. Adorned with Dayton wire wheels and exclusive knock-off hubs, the speedster's beauty nearly defies description.

The remainder of Auburn's offerings somewhat paled in comparison with the speedster. Ten-spoke artillery wheels remained standard on the rest of the line with wire wheels optional. The 8-88 line was now labeled simply 88. It, too, enjoyed a more powerful Lycoming, known as the GS. While displacing only 246.7 cubic inches, this straight-eight, at 88 horsepower at 3200 rpm, nevertheless surpassed the 8-88's power output. The GS mill shared the same bore and stroke as Auburn's new six-cylinder model, the 76, also built by Lycoming. The following body styles were offered for the 88: sedan, sport sedan, phaeton, roadster, cabriolet, and yes, even the speedster body.

The 76 used the same bore and stroke as the 6-66's Continental. Therefore, its displacement

remained unchanged at 185 cubic inches. Lycoming produced its engine (the WS), but output was up substantially, to 60 horsepower at 3400 rpm. Auburn offered the 76 with a sedan, sport sedan, roadster, or cabriolet body. Gone were the Wanderer sedan and 147-inch wheelbase models.

On February 20, 1928, Wade Morton traveled with two speedsters to Daytona Beach. He set a new AAA, one-mile stock car record of 104.347 miles per hour. By July 1, 1928, Morton and Miller were at it again, this time with Morton driving a fenderless 115 speedster using high-compression heads and a tall rear-axle ratio. Morton covered 2,107 miles in 24 hours, his average speed of 84.7354 miles per hour exceeding previous records by 226 miles and 9 miles per hour. Discounting the 18 minutes and 9 seconds Morton was in the pits, the average speed rose to some 86 miles per hour. On November 3, 1928, Morton traveled to Pike's Peak with a 115 speedster to compete in the stock car category of the climb. The challenging course was 12 miles in length, its 203 snow-, slush-, and freezing rain-covered sharp turns rising to a final altitude 14,109 feet above sea level.

Morton finished first, beating the stock car record by only 14.5 seconds, but his speedster outweighed the previous record holder by 1,000 pounds.

The public now equated Auburns with performance, and race car builders and drivers wanted to play the part. On June 20, 1928, newspapers announced that land-speed record holder (at 207.55 miles per hour) Ray Keech had purchased a 115 speedster. Other Auburn-owning racing personalities included Leon Duray, Harry Miller, and even Fred Duesenberg.

Herbert C. Snow joined Auburn in 1928 as its chief engineer, replacing James M. Crawford, who had left earlier that year. Snow had previously worked for Willys-Overland and Bay State and would remain at the AAC almost until its demise. Another major appointment for the year included Ellis W. Ryan, who Cord named vice president in charge of the Connersville operations. For 1928, Auburn sales dropped slightly, to 12,899 units. Regardless, net sales climbed to $23.8 million, and profits to $1.6 million (AAC's cash surplus dipped slightly to just under $887,000). There were 141,450 total outstanding common shares, trading in a range of 78 to 141-1/4 during the year.

The Cord Corporation Forms

By 1929, Auburn's lines were rather dated when compared to its larger siblings, the Duesenberg Model J and the new, front-drive Cord L-29 (chapter five). Both models were placed into production in 1929, outshining their lower-priced brother. Auburn sales literature put a positive spin on this situation by claiming its continuance of styling since 1925 kept resale values high. If one could detect few changes, why not drive a four-year-old Auburn? Despite trailing its corporate brethren aesthetically, Auburn remained the lifeblood of Cord and Duesenberg operations.

Once again, Auburn's 1928 models carried over to 1929. It's interesting to note that in 1927, 1928,

and 1929, the AAC turned in its new-model information in time to make *MoToR*'s annual listings of specifications. That a first and second model series existed during these years leads one to believe the AAC was merely trying to sell leftover models from the previous year before releasing the new offerings.

The 115 model graduated to the 120, its Lycoming MDA 298.6-cubic-inch straight eight now listed as producing 120 horsepower at 3300 rpm, an incredible rating for the period. And this from a 5.25:1 compression ratio (a 6.56:1 compression ratio was available with the optional head). Body styles for the 120 included the venerable speedster, cabriolet, sport sedan, sedan, phaeton, and a new offering, a Victoria. The Victoria was a two-door, four-passenger hardtop style. The 88 became the 8-90, representing a return to the hyphenated model nomenclature of the past. The 8-90's horsepower rating increased to 93 at 3300 rpm. Body style offerings for the 8-90 remained the same as these for the 120 line, but on a 125-inch wheelbase chassis. The 6-80 was the former 76 line, with Auburn offering the Victoria in the straight-six model along with the cabriolet, sedan, and sport sedan. The 6-80 bodies rode on a 120-inch wheelbase chassis, powered by Lycoming's 185-cubic-inch straight six WS now producing 65 horsepower at 3400 rpm. Auburn never skimped on features, and even the lower-priced 6-80 featured the amenities of the more expensive models, including the Bijur lubrication system, four-wheel hydraulic brakes, Lovejoy hydraulic shock absorbers, and more. Auburn offered no modesty in promoting the 6-80, "It is the most automobile for the least cost in the world."

The 6-80 also held the honor of being the first Auburn to roll off an assembly line in Connersville. In fact, it was the first Auburn built outside the city of Auburn, assembled January 15, 1929, on a 900-foot continuous assembly line engineered by Cord's production people. In its first year of operation, Connersville produced 73 percent of the AAC's total output, and the percentages would only increase. In fact, it was only a matter of time before Cord pulled all Auburn production from its namesake city.

As always, the AAC remained a supplier-dependent company with Auburn factories acting as final assembly lines. A partial listing of suppliers reveals a few names still operating today: Purolator (oil filter), Delco Remy (ignition), Raybestos (clutch), A. O. Smith (frame), Trico (windshield wipers), Firestone or Goodyear (tires), Federal (bearings), and Lockheed-Wagner Electric (brakes).

New for 1929 was the Auburn Caravan, a representative selection of Auburns that traversed the country. The caravan would stop at local Auburn dealers with a sales promotion arranged around the event. In most cities, the caravan succeeded in obtaining local newspaper coverage. Auburn dealers

An early Duesenberg Model J showing the front-end sheet metal as designed by Alan Leamy. Notice the absence of the Duesenberg eagle hood ornament and chrome shutters over the radiator, all later additions to the Model J.

sold 23,297 cars for the year, an all-time high and an 80-percent gain over 1928. Sales hit a staggering $37.5 million, an increase of 57 percent. Net profits rose to $3.9 million, and cash surplus almost tripled to $2.6 million. Outstanding shares rose again, this time to 169,686. In this incredibly heated atmosphere, AAC stock prices followed suit, trading from 120 to a dizzying 514, earnings per share turning in a performance of $21.23.

Cord's corporate buying spree had not slowed down, either. On April 1, 1929, Cord purchased the former McFarlan Motor Car Company plant, some five blocks south of the Central complex. The buildings were used primarily as a storage depot for raw materials and finished cars. In September 1929, he purchased the Limousine Body Company of Kalamazoo, Michigan. Henceforth, Limousine built all open bodies for the AAC, while Central was in charge of closed-body manufacturing. This dual body-manufacturing setup continued until December 1933, when Limousine's operations were shut down and open-body production moved to Connersville.

Cord's acquisitions were piling up. To create an umbrella company that covered these various endeavors, Cord announced the formation of the Cord Corporation on June 15, 1929, its offices at 120 South LaSalle Street, Chicago. The Cord Corporation was a holding company and an operating company.

OPPOSITE
Auburn openly boasted of its body lines' continuity, easily seen here in this photo showing four consecutive years of Auburns with only subtle changes to mark the years.

In 1929, Auburn introduced a short-lived body style known as the Victoria. In 1931, with the new Auburn body styles, this style segued into the brougham.

71

Auburn executives stand in front of an early Auburn speedster. From left: Roy Faulkner, E. O. Penry, Wade Morton, Herb Snow, and an unknown gentleman.

turing Company, Checker Cab Manufacturing Corporation, Parmelee Transport Company, Continental Air Lines, Inc., Embry-Riddle Corporation, and the Stinson Aircraft Corporation.

Auburn Survives the Crash

Auburn's design languished further in 1930, having to wait another year before a totally new body style hit the market. Likewise, sales suffered, although a post-Wall Street crash economy contributed to a lean year for everyone. The 120 became the 125, and yes, horsepower increased to 125 at 3600 rpm from the Lycoming eight (MDA). The 8-90 was now called the 8-95, with horsepower rising in the Lycoming GR straight eight to 100 horsepower at 3700 rpm. Finally, Auburn promoted the 6-80 to the 6-85, though its Lycoming WR straight six's 70 horsepower output did not match its model number. The body styles from 1929 carried over for each line, save for the speedster, which was pulled from the line-up at the last minute. The speedster had never sold well, and Auburn foisted the model onto dealers, a practice most disliked. No doubt the speedster was a showroom draw, but cash flow is cash flow, something the speedster didn't provide to dealers. First, despite its undeniable beauty, it simply wasn't a practical car. Two passengers, three in a squeeze, and that was it. Second, few felt the desire to drive a flashy car in an increasingly depressed economy.

Interestingly, Auburn opted to enter the pickup truck market in 1930, although in a limited way. A factory service bulletin listed the availability of a pickup body for the Auburn chassis as a dealer's choice. The pickup body could fit any Auburn from 1925 to 1930, but it was never offered directly to the public. How many pickups the Union City Body Company built is unknown, since Auburn provided it only on an as-ordered basis.

The AAC's business plan for 1930 called for a 50 percent increase in production over 1929. Despite this, unit sales dropped precipitously, to 13,627 (though the Cord front-drive L-29 enjoyed its sales peak this year at 3,449). Industrywide, unit sales dropped 47 percent, but Auburn suffered with a 71 percent decrease. Price cutting spread like wildfire. Auburn prices dropped $200 to $400 below the previous year's prices. Net sales totaled $24 million with net profits of $811,000, and the AAC's cash surplus plunged to less than $255,000. Auburn shares traded from 60-3/8 to 263-3/4 in 1930.

Racing Through the Depression

After the stock market crash and the ensuing depression, race teams found it difficult to secure sponsors. Sanctioning officials quickly recognized this and created a new set of rules for the Indianapolis 500. Known as the "junkyard formula," the rules allowed stock engine blocks to compete at Indy

Cord, naturally, was named president. Manning filled the vice president slot, Pruitt was named treasurer, and Hayden Hodges served as secretary. Directors for the new company included Cord, Manning, Pruitt, Fred Duesenberg (vice president, Duesenberg, Inc.), Peter Paul Willis (president, P. P. Willis Corporation), Roy Faulkner, Ellis W. Ryan, J. D. Bobb (president, Limousine Body Company), J. H. McCormick (president, Lycoming Manufacturing Company), E. H. Parkhurst (president, Columbia Axle Company), B. D. DeWeese (president, Saf-T-Cab Corporation), and Edward A. Stinson (president, Stinson Aircraft Corporation). The Cord Corporation was capitalized at $125 million with some 10 million shares authorized at $5 per share. Incorporated in Delaware, the Cord Corporation issued more than one million shares. Auburn shares climbed to $300 at the news of the Cord Corporation's formation. Before the year was out, Cord Corporation stocks had risen to $37.37 per share. Assets tallied almost $29 million. The corporation directly employed only about 24 people. (For posterity, it's worth noting here that the Cord Corporation never produced a Cord, or anything else for that matter. Over the ages, this has been a constant source of confusion for writers. Only the Auburn Automobile Company produced Auburns and Cords.) A few of the Cord Corporation's holdings included: Columbia Axle Company, LGS Devices Corporation, New York Shipbuilding Corporation, Auburn Automobile Company, Lycoming Manufac-

MARION TREXLER, Driver — Russell Griffith, Mech.
In 'TREXLER SPECIAL
Indianapolis Motor Speedway 1930.

2837#
KIRKPATRICK
619 W. WASH. ST
INDPLS.

and gave "wannabe" racers a better shot at racing at Indy. As a result, qualifying speeds for the pole plummeted from a high of 122.39 miles per hour in 1928, to 112.79 miles per hour in 1931.

The effects of the junkyard formula were predictable. Entrants tried to enter marginal engines and chassis, names and makes that would have been unthinkable at the Brickyard just a year earlier. Some racers tried to qualify Lycoming-powered cars in 1931, 1932, and 1933, though only one entrant ever succeeded in finding a spot in the starting field. That was in 1930, and the Lycoming used was one of the muscular 298.6-cubic-inch straight eights. M. M. Lain, Jr., entered the Auburn-chassised car, dubbed the "Trexler Special," and Marion Trexler drove it. Trexler qualified at 92.97 miles per hour,

but wrecked on lap 19 after Red Roberts' Duesenberg crashed into a wall, triggering a seven-car accident including Trexler's car.

The Shifting Sands at Auburn

In the wake of the stock market crash, Auburn shored up its internal management arrangements and braced for the lean years ahead. While the names were not new, the positions were, as the company created a number of vice president positions.

These personnel changes were announced at the annual stockholders meeting on February 3, 1931. Cord turned the AAC presidency over to Faulkner, while Cord became chairman of the board. Most of the newly appointed vice presidents took on no additional responsibilities, since the positions were

Marion Trexler drove this "Trexler Special," a 298.6-cubic-inch Lycoming straight-eight-powered Auburn chassis, in the 1930 running of the Indianapolis 500. The Trexler Special survived only 19 laps, after becoming involved in a seven-car accident.

Alan Huet Leamy

Alan Huet Leamy was born in Maryland in 1903. His father, Alan, Sr., moved his family to Columbus, Ohio, to accept a promotion when the younger Alan was three years old. It was around this time that Alan, Jr., was struck with polio, leaving his left leg crippled for life.

Though Leamy lacked a complete formal education, he nevertheless was well-rounded having an interest in many fields, including architecture, music, literature, science, medicine, and firearms. His studies in architecture in particular set him apart from the functional design engineers of the time. Leamy was one of the first to understand the importance of three-dimensional automotive design. This capability to see beyond flat, two-dimension paper designs and his incredible intrinsic talent helped him create some of the most fluid, recognizable, and distinctive designs of his era.

Leamy's father recognized Alan, Jr.'s, design talents, and contacted Thomas Little, Jr., a former coworker then employed with the Marmon Motor Company in Indianapolis. Marmon hired Leamy in March 1927, but he found the company's conservative design philosophy too confining. Leamy preferred the designs issuing forth from the European automakers, such as Isotta-Fraschini and Hispano-Suiza, and from such coachwork firms as Labourdette and Castagna. If Leamy wanted to emulate the lofty work from the finer European automobile design houses, he was in the wrong place, and he knew it.

By April 1928, Leamy had moved from Marmon by making a rather straightforward move: He wrote a letter directly to Errett Cord. Was it sheer coincidence, or did Leamy know Cord was looking for a new designer? One reasonable connection exists. Two freelance engineers working on a project for Cord, Earl Cooper and Reeves Dutton, also worked for Marmon. It is likely one or both of these gentlemen told Leamy, or their talk of Cord's front-drive project made its way through the grapevine at Marmon, thus tipping off Leamy. Regardless, Leamy was looking for a designer's position, and Cord was looking for a designer with flair.

Work on two new models was underway over at Duesenberg, Inc. Both would be placed in production by 1929: the Duesenberg Model J and the front-wheel drive Cord L-29. The Model J was the crème de la crème of Cord's automotive empire, and the L-29 was positioned between the pricey Duesenberg and the Auburn models. Although Leamy joined the development of these models late, there was nothing unusual in expecting him to turn out a design based on the Model J and L-29 chassis. At the time, engineering aspects were designed first, and then a sheet metal form was created to envelope the chassis in the very late stages of development. Cord liked the samples that Leamy sent along with his letter seeking employment. Cord, in turn, had Cornelius Van Ranst (chief consulting engineer of the L-29 project) contact Leamy via letter. Short and terse, the Van Ranst letter read: "Your letter to Mr. E. L. Cord has been brought to my attention, and I wish that you would call at the Duesenberg plant to see me at your earliest convenience." Van Ranst subsequently hired Leamy.

Leamy was only 25 years old when he started to design the lines for what would become the first mass-produced, front-wheel-drive car in America, the Cord L-29. His work on the Model J included the front-end sheet metal, (fenders, hood, and radiator shell). After his work at Duesenberg was finished, Leamy was sent north to Auburn's headquarters where his assignment was to create a completely new design for the 1931 Auburn line.

Alan Leamy sits behind the wheel of one of his creations, the 1931 Auburn speedster.

new to the AAC. These officers held positions with similar duties, but now gained the prestige of a loftier title. Neil McDarby was appointed vice president of sales; Herbert C. Snow vice president of engineering; E. O. Penry vice president of manufacturing; H. L. Dunn, vice president of purchasing; Arthur Landis, vice president of Connersville operations. With Snow's promotion, George H. Kublin was promoted to the position of chief engineer. The AAC directors in 1931 included Cord, Manning, Pruitt, Beal, and Penry.

The Auburn line sorely needed to catch up in 1931. In 1929, with the introductions of the Duesenberg Model J and the Cord front-drive L-29, Auburn's styling had been left behind. As an investment for the future, the AAC called upon Alan Huet Leamy (see sidebar) to ensure the company's return to preeminence in product design. With Leamy's assistance, the 1931 Auburn exuded the elegance of a luxury car and delivered sound performance, too. Yet, one could buy a part of the Auburn action for as little as $945. As with most early designers, Leamy started his body lines with the radiator shell, fenders, and hood. This acted as a foundation upon which an astute designer could base everything else. The 1931 Auburn was groundbreaking in that its

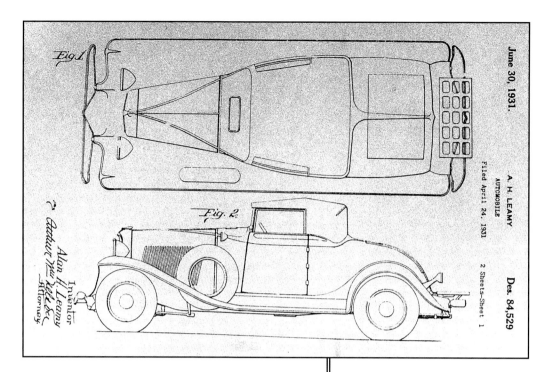

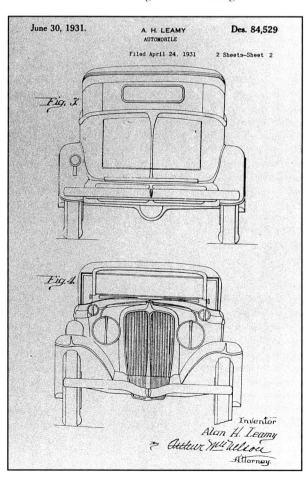

flat grille lost its identity, instead blending in with the hood line and painted in a matching body color rather than plated in chrome or nickel. The grille's visual impact may have lost its edge over the intervening years, but it was a compelling look back then. Its effect is akin to the rise of the monochrome look in recent years. The belt molding continued to sweep across and down the hood to meet the high waistline. The front bumper's drop matched the curve at the base of the radiator shell. The headlights and parking lights were divided by a thin, vertical chrome strip, a reflection of the radiator shell's treatment. The windshield carried an appropriate rake. The 1931 Auburn's styling is probably the most honest of the three (four, if one counts the retagged 1934 V-12 Auburns) years this shell was produced. By 1933, embellishments had washed out the elegant simplicity of the lines.

Although representing an advanced design for its day, few would guess that the AAC's Experimental Department had bothered to test the new Auburn's aerodynamics. As equipped for sale, an Auburn 8-98 turned in drag coefficients ranging from 0.47 at 25 miles per hour to 2.37 at 55 miles per hour. For comparison, many automobiles of the 1990s turn in coefficients of 0.28 to 0.32 at highway speeds. What was interesting about these tests is that the Experimental Department tested an 8-98's coefficient with an "under-chassis cover attached." This represents some very advanced thinking for its day, and only recently have automakers attached undercarriage covers on production models. On the 8-98, the cover dropped coefficients to 0.41 at 25 miles per hour and 2.16 at 55 miles per hour.

The design patent drawings filed by Alan Leamy.

Herb Snow was named as Auburn's vice president in charge of engineering in 1931. At the same time, others were promoted to the vice president level, including Neil McDarby, vice president in charge of sales; E. O. Penry, vice president of manufacturing; and Harry Leigh Dunn, vice president of purchasing.

Herb Snow

E.O. Penry

Neil McDarby

Harry Leigh Dunn

Auburn simplified its engine choices by offering only a 268.6-cubic-inch Lycoming GU straight eight, developing 98 horsepower at 3400 rpm. It wasn't as flashy as the 298.6, but the cost savings outweighed any loss in performance. For the first time in years, Auburn offered no six-cylinder to the public. There were no hydraulic brakes for Auburn this year either, reverting instead to a mechanical system dubbed "Steeldraulic." This simply was a circuit of steel cables running inside steel lines, providing the braking action to four 13-inch internal-acting drums. Seventeen-inch wood wheels were standard with wire wheels optional. The standard chassis was eight-inches deep and had a 127-inch wheelbase, while the seven-passenger sedan rode on a 136-inch wheelbase. Its muffler and exhaust were insulated with asbestos, and body mounts were made of rubber. The bodies were "sprayed with a semiplastic deadener material" according to Auburn literature. The doors were 42 inches wide, which meant passengers climbing into the rear seat of broughams and coupes did not have to flip the front seat forward, and the rear seats themselves spread 47 inches across the back. The cabriolet stood only 64-3/4 inches high. Open-body models sported a folding windshield, and all styles had adjustable front seats.

Auburn's features list continued to grow. Auburn's 8-98 custom models (denoted with an "A" suffix as in 8-98A) featured LGS Corporation's (recently acquired by the Cord Corporation) free-wheeling system which provided semi-automatic shifting. Inside the 8-98's transmission, the second and third gears were synchronized. This allowed, in the freewheeling mode, shifts from first to second and second to third without the clutch. Only when moving from a dead stop did a driver need to use the clutch. Freewheeling saved on gas by acting as a declutching device when a driver applied the brakes. Unfortunately, this did nothing to promote brake life. In addition to freewheeling, Auburn's custom models included trim and upholstery embellishments.

For 1931, Auburn offered the 8-98 in the following body styles (standard/custom prices): brougham ($945/$1,145), speedster ($945/$1,395), coupe ($995/$1,195), sedan ($995/$1,195), cabriolet ($1,045/$1,245), phaeton ($1,145/$1,345), and seven-passenger sedan ($1,195/$1,395). With such pricing, it's easy to see why Auburn was such a runaway hit in 1931. Auburn officials at the New York auto show took in some 4,000 orders. The automotive press reported that not a single Auburn dealer had a 1930 car on the showroom floor at the time of the auto show, as if Auburn was already on a roll. In truth, Auburn slowed its 1930 production lines early due to the sluggish sales year. Early in the 1931 model year, management anticipated production at 2,000 per month. By February, it had to be doubled. The Connersville and Auburn factories were working at capacity to keep up with demand. Despite blustery reports of booming sales in early 1931, a look at factory production records reveals the company wasn't ready for the onslaught.

Connersville produced only 48 8-98s in December 1930, the start-up for the new model. The Auburn plant didn't start 8-98 production until March. Connersville cranked out 804 of the 125 models in January, versus 436 of the new 8-98 and 634 of the 8-98A models. Albeit a 1930 model, another 126 of the 125 cabriolets were made in February before production finally ceased. This leads one to believe the AAC production lines lacked all the necessary materials to produce the 8-98 until February. The Auburn plant's contribution was limited mostly to the assembly of 8-98 phaetons and cabriolets. However, some closed-body 8-98s also rolled out of Auburn, including a good number of sedans and, starting in July, it was the only source for seven-passenger sedans. Only Auburn produced the speedster, but not until October and then only 56 were built for the month and another two in November. In 1931, April represented the peak production month at Connersville, with 5,326 8-98s built in 26 days, or an average of 205 cars per day. On April 10, the plant rolled out 240 cars. Employment at Connersville was up to 2,500, and almost overnight some 300 new workers were hired at the Auburn plants, bringing its employment to 592. Connersville also produced any number of phaetons and cabriolets. And whereas Auburn kept the speedster and seven-passenger 8-98 for itself, Connersville was the only source for coupes.

Auburn returned to offering the speedster after the 1931 body styles were released. Production, however, didn't commence until late in the year.

New equipment at the Auburn plant allowed 100 cars per day, but May peaked at an average of 61 cars per day, or 1,647 units for the month. By May 1931, registrations of Auburn products were up 122 percent over the same period from the previous year. McDarby noted dealer applications coming in at a rate of 10 per day. Auburn sales moved from 22nd to 13th place.

During November 1930, AAC shares were trading around 60. By January 1931, Auburn shares hovered in the low 80s, climbing to 191 in February. In April, share prices spiraled as high as 295-1/2. Outstanding shares amounted to 203,636, about half of which were held by the Cord Corporation. The total Auburn/Cord units sold for the year came to 34,045 (including 1,134 Cord L-29s). For fiscal 1931, net sales reached $37.2 million, profits climbed to $4.1 million, and Auburn enjoyed a cash surplus of $2.7 million.

A 1932 Auburn 8-100 speedster graces the front of the Roosevelt Theater at 110 North State Street in Chicago, a part of the Balaban & Katz Publix Theater chain. The chain helped Auburn promote the giveaway of 10 Auburn straight eights. Playing the summer night this photo was taken was MGM's latest release, *Night Court*, starring Walter Huston, Phillips Holmes, and Anita Page. Admission was 25 cents.

A line of 1931 Auburn seven-passenger sedans await taxi use for Century Air Lines, a part of the Cord empire when this photo was taken.

By April, the AAC had produced more cars than it had for all of 1930. AAC production was already at 6,203 units for March, 6,555 in April, and 6,007 in May. Yet the peak was short-lived, and production numbers declined steadily after this. Never again would the AAC factories hum with the sound of success.

After a heady year at Auburn, Faulkner resigned from that company's presidency on November 19, 1931, and headed to Pierce-Arrow. (Cord reassumed the post of Auburn's presidency one final time in Faulkner's absence, holding it for one year. It would be the last time Cord filled the position.) By December 23, 1931, Faulkner had been named vice president of the Studebaker Sales Corporation (Studebaker was Pierce-Arrow's parent company at that time). In June 1932, Studebaker merged its various sales organizations into a group known as SPAR, an acronym for Studebaker, Pierce-Arrow, and Rockne (another line owned by Studebaker). Faulkner was placed in charge of SPAR, overseeing 18 regional offices.

Rumors of the AAC merging with Pierce-Arrow surfaced. In its August 1934 issue, *MoTor* reported that "substantial progress has been made in negotiations for a merger of [the AAC] and Pierce Arrow Motor Car Company." The very next month, though, the magazine announced the merger talks were off. *MoTor* also reported that Reo, Hupp, and Graham-Paige had been invited to participate in the discussions; "Don Bates, Reo president, has stated that regardless of the outcome of the merger, his company might join Auburn and some of the other independents in a standardization of tools and dies which could affect large savings." Bates' remarks suggests that the independent automakers were concerned about their futures. Though the standardization of parts never came to pass, the demise of the independent automakers did.

Not long after 1931's wave of good fortune, the Cord Corporation decided to downplay its automotive operations. Although official reasons exist for this strategy and will be explored later in the book, there is, perhaps, an unofficial reason as well. After Helen Frische married Cord in 1914, she suffered alongside the entrepreneur during the hard times. When Cord needed it, Helen propped up his sagging spirits. With two sons, the family was close knit and apparently a cohesive unit. Cord always made time for his family. There were outings, picnics, and camping trips. This all came to a sudden halt late in 1929 when Helen took ill. Doctors struggled to pinpoint the problem until exploratory surgery revealed the answer the following year: terminal cancer. On September 13, 1930, Helen passed away.

There was no public grieving from Cord. Business had to go on. A wealthy and prominent person by this time, he was deluged by well-meaning friends who tried to arrange meetings with

appropriate, available women. Perhaps out of frustration over the fuss, Cord remarried very quickly, in January 1931. It certainly wasn't because he had forgotten Helen.

After Helen's death, everything slipped. The 1931 Auburn was an initial success, but that was achieved by previous momentum. Sales fell quickly for Auburn, Cord, and Duesenberg after 1931, and not only because of the ongoing Depression. Cord also pulled his support, and interest, from the automobile lines. He moved from the family home in Auburn, and spent less and less time at the AAC's administration building. From March 1934 to March 1935, Cord didn't even reside in the United States. Rather, he lived in England, ostensibly due to a kidnapping threat leveled at his two sons. Yet by September 1934, Cord returned the boys to the military academy they attended in Wisconsin, while he returned to England. With interest waning, management infighting broke out and the company's goals and vision suffered. Cord became more cynical in his business dealings. He bought into the Chicago taxi business, a metropolitan service that had all the airs of organized crime. He delved into aviation, attempting a hostile takeover of the Aviation Corporation. Cord started to play the stock market heavily, manipulating Auburn's stocks in particular. Of course, not all such activities were illegal at the time, but it does reflect a newfound callousness on

Cord's part. Along the way, Cord stepped on a few of the wrong toes, an action that wasn't easily forgotten. This recklessness became Cord's personal, and his automotive empire's, downfall.

After Helen's death, Cord married Virginia Kirk Tharpe (then 21 years old) on January 3, 1931, at the Presbyterian church on Wilshire Boulevard in Los Angeles.

The Horse Pulls the Cart: The Cord L-29

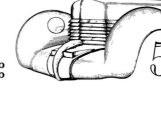

5

1927-1932

The idea of propelling an automobile by its front wheels was hardly a new one when E. L. Cord decided to pursue the technology in 1927. And when one considers the multitude of other companies whose front-drive projects didn't succeed, it's a miracle the AAC's efforts ever came to fruition at all. Yet, not only did the company eventually place a front-drive automobile in production, Auburn was the first American company to do so. The whole effort must have been propelled by sheer guts, determination, and Cord's own belief that if an automaker couldn't be big, it had to be different.

The idea of front drive was definitely different in 1927. The first "modern" front-drive vehicle—making a distinction from the primitive efforts that preceded it—appeared around 1904. Walter Christie applied the principle to racing cars, taxicabs, and tanks. In his earliest cars, Christie used an arrangement much like that of the later Austin/Morris designs of Alex Issigonis, with the engine mounted transversely over the front axle. This design is mirrored in the front-drive cars of today. But engineers in 1904 did not have the benefit of the metallurgy of almost a century later, and Christie's vehicles suffered from very heavy front ends. Still, the logical notion of pulling a car by the front wheels—of placing the horse before the cart, as AAC literature would later state—continued to draw the attention of automotive engineers. However, the seeds of the AAC's front-drive project wouldn't sprout until the early 1920s.

A successful approach to front drive was found in the crucible of racing, a forum in which many automotive technologies find their origins. In 1921, Jimmy Murphy won the French Gran Prix at Le Mans in a 183-cubic-inch Duesenberg race car. It was the first time an American ever won a Gran Prix, and Murphy's fame, at least in the United States, grew overnight from coast to coast. With the fame came the offers of better race cars. Murphy's mechanic, a fine engineer named Riley Brett, also worked from time-to-time for California-based race car builder Harry A. Miller. Interviewed by Borgeson in 1978, Brett recalled that in 1923 Miller approached Murphy with a proposal for a front-drive race car. The design utilized a front-drive mechanism that connected the front wheels with a DeDion-type solid axle.

This wasn't the first foray into front-drive technology for Miller. He had worked on at least one Christie machine, and Miller's shop once housed the Homer Laughlin Engineering Corporation, which had developed a practical universal joint and built a front-drive prototype as far back as 1918. He had also purchased front-drive patents from Ben Gregory in 1923. Murphy agreed with Miller that it seemed logical a car could be pulled around the turns at the Indianapolis speedway at higher speeds than conventional race cars could manage. Ironically, Brett was less convinced that front drive was the answer. In the end, however, it was Brett's input that made the front-drive race car possible.

Murphy and Brett teamed with Miller and his designer, Leo Goossen, on the design of a front-drive race car. They considered the Christie concept of a transverse engine, but front-end weight was still a

Auburn's Chicago dealership featured all of the Cord Corporation's products. Window displays take advantage of the Hayes-Sakhnoffsky coupe's awards. *National Photo and Advertising Company*

Miller's first front-drive race car was built for Jimmy Murphy but not completed until after his death. Unlike the later Miller cars, its front brakes were outboard. Pictured here at Indianapolis in 1925, it ran as the "Locomobile Junior 8."

One of Ben Gregory's 1920 patents for a front-drive system, purchased by Miller in 1923. Miller probably just wanted to avoid infringement issues; no part of this design was used in his race cars or in the Cord.

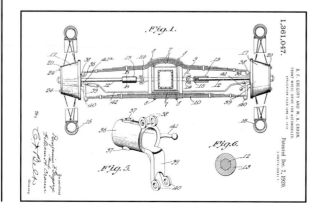

problem. Gregory's design, in which the differential, transmission, clutch, and engine were lined up front-to-back in that order, pushed the engine too far back for a race car. It was Brett who came up with the idea of a transverse transmission located in the drivetrain. As it was finally produced, the idea was a compromise in that the transmission was located after the ring gear. The ring gear, of course, multiplied the torque generated by the engine. This increased torque was then passed on to the transmission gears.

Construction of the car was well underway in 1924 when Murphy was killed in a Labor Day race in Syracuse, New York. When completed, Murphy's heirs sold the car to Cliff Durant, son of William Crapo Durant, the founder of General Motors. Cliff Durant entered the Miller in the 1925 Indianapolis 500 as the "Locomobile Junior 8"; the Locomobile firm was owned then by the Durant family. The 12 other Miller race cars entered in the 1925 Indy 500 (out of a field of 22) used conventional rear drive. One of these cars, driven by Bennett Hill, was forced to retire after suffering a broken rear spring on lap 69. Dave Lewis, who formerly drove for Duesenberg, piloted the Junior 8. He took over first place at 312 miles when Earl Cooper's Miller (also entered by Durant) hit the wall. Phil Shafer, driving a Duesenberg, was second. Ralph Miller in a Miller was third, and Pete DePaolo was fourth in another Duesenberg. By the 400-mile point, DePaolo had moved to second, but Lewis was still four laps ahead. On lap 173, Lewis pitted for a routine stop.

While changing wheels, a mechanic damaged the threads of the right front hub. By the time the pit crew filed the threads clean and got the Junior 8 back on the track, DePaolo was way ahead. Hill now took the wheel of the Junior 8 and managed to gain a lap and three-quarters on DePaolo, but it was too late. DePaolo crossed the finish line with Hill a half lap behind. The cars were only 50 seconds apart, the closest and fastest Indy 500 to date. DePaolo averaged 101.13 miles per hour in the Duesenberg. Lewis and Hill coaxed an average of 100.82 miles per hour out of the Junior 8. For the front-drive Miller, it was truly an exceptional performance for a brand new design.

Miller now created a series of front-drive race cars, driven by some of the country's best drivers. Motorsports was a popular subject with the public in the late 1920s, and Miller's record of successes created enormous interest in front-wheel drive. Automakers looked for ways to take advantage of the free publicity. General Motors bought two Millers. Cliff Durant pursued his own front-drive

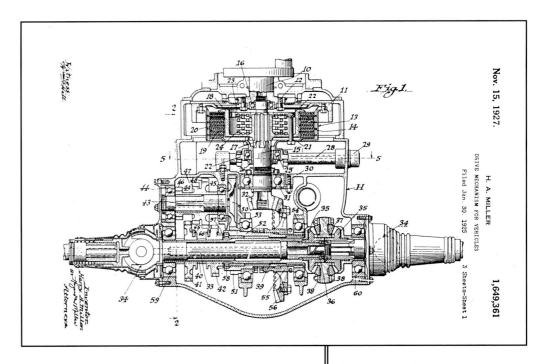

Miller's patent for the transverse gearbox of the race cars. Three shafts run inside each other to carry power to the gears and to the wheels.

The Detroit Special, designed by Cornelius Van Ranst and Tommy Milton and driven at Indianapolis in 1927. Milton is in the driver's seat. This car eventually influenced the engineering of the Cord L-29 more than the Miller race cars did. *Robert Fabris collection*

The prototype Cord Front Drive, with Auburn body and Miller-like radiator shell. It was photographed in the Duesenberg shops in Indianapolis. *Paul J. Bryant collection*

The great length of the L-29 drive unit is evident. This drawing was prepared for the 1929 catalog.

The bridgelike frame of the L-29. This was the first use of an X-member in the frame of an American car. It was designed by Snow, but patented by Van Ranst.

project. Packard signed a consultation contract with Miller. The Ruxton, using another front-drive system, was being rushed into production. It was only natural that Errett Cord would consider capitalizing on this publicity by applying Miller's front-drive principles to a passenger car.

Auburn Retains Harry Miller

The AAC decided to investigate the front-drive concept for a passenger car in June 1927. No one at Auburn knew how to build a front-drive car, so Cord sought the man whose name was now synonymous in the public's mind with front-wheel drive. Cord contracted with Miller for patent and manufacturing rights and also retained Miller as a consultant during the development of a front-drive automobile. As AAC

dealer literature put it, "In the fall of 1926 it was announced that the Auburn Automobile Company had purchased the right to use the front drive designs and patents, which had made Harry Miller of Indianapolis famous in racing car construction, for use on a passenger automobile to be built." (AAC literature claimed 1926 as the initiation date of its first front-drive project, but factory records show June/July of 1927 as the start-up date.)

The contract provided Miller with $1,000 per month, plus a royalty on each car sold. As previously mentioned, the Miller/Murphy/Brett transaxle design used in the race cars located the ring gear upstream of the transmission and magnified torque forces acting on the transmission gear teeth, making it difficult to shift gears at high speeds. The gears within the transmission were also very narrow due to space limitations. The front-drive Miller race cars were usually started in high gear by pushing them to avoid overloading the gear teeth. Such drawbacks were inconveniences in an oval-track race car. They would have been intolerable in a passenger car.

Of course, Miller didn't have a corner on front-drive technology. Other race car builders and drivers shared the growing interest in developing front-drive cars for racing. Tommy Milton and Cornelius Willett Van Ranst, the former an oval-track driver and the latter the chief engineer at Frontenac Motors, designed a race car for use at Indianapolis and on the road course in Monza, Italy. This car was built for Cliff Durant in the Hyatt Roller Bearing Lab at General Motors. It was powered by a 91-cubic-

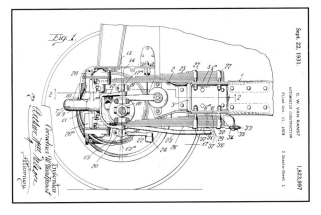

Hepburn drove the car to its eighth-place finish. So successful was the Detroit Special that it raced in various guises, though always with the Milton/Van Ranst front-drive unit, until 1947.

Leon Duray, a good friend of Cord's, met with the automobile entrepreneur in Chicago shortly after the race. Cord informed Duray of his intention to produce a passenger car based on the front-drive design of Miller, et al. It was important to Cord that the AAC's front-drive entry be the first to reach the passenger car market. Duray explained that the Miller design would not produce a satisfactory unit for a passenger car and that, if Cord was serious about this front-drive venture, he should get in touch with Van Ranst and discuss the possibilities of a different transmission design. Cord called Van Ranst and invited him to Chicago. At the subsequent meeting, which Harry Miller also attended, Van Ranst carefully explained why the Miller transaxle wouldn't work in a passenger car. He suggested instead a gear layout along the lines of the Detroit Special. Cord was impressed. Arrangements were made for Van Ranst to work with Miller as project engineer for the front-drive car. Van Ranst was to start development work in the building occupied by the Harry A. Miller Manufacturing Works. The shop was located on Long Beach Avenue near Vernon, California, then a dirt road parallel to the Pacific Electric tracks. All of Miller's facilities were placed at his disposal. Subsequent Auburn dealer literature chronicled the event in this fashion: "With Miller designs as a basis, the Auburn engineering

Van Ranst was granted multiple patents for the L-29's mechanical systems, including the front drive system, suspension, and universal joints.

inch Miller engine equipped with a two-stage centrifugal supercharger. Its transmission was located in the conventional position, namely, between the clutch and differential. High-speed shifting was practical, since gear tooth loading was no greater than in a conventional rear-drive powertrain. Milton and Van Ranst entered the car in the 1927 Indy 500 as the "Detroit Special." Durant was scheduled to drive the Detroit Special, but fell ill just prior to the race. Tommy Milton started at the wheel of the Detroit Special, and Leon Duray took over for a short time, which enabled him to compare the merits and performance of the Special and the front-drive Miller. Duray was impressed with the Special's transmission, allowing him to shift at almost any speed. Van Ranst also drove the car for some 40 miles until he was stopped by a fuel leak. Ralph

A sedan body, after being assembled on the second floor, is dropped onto the completed chassis by a system of pulleys. Each chassis rides on a dolly, guided by floor rails and propelled by a chain mechanism. *John McIntyre collection*

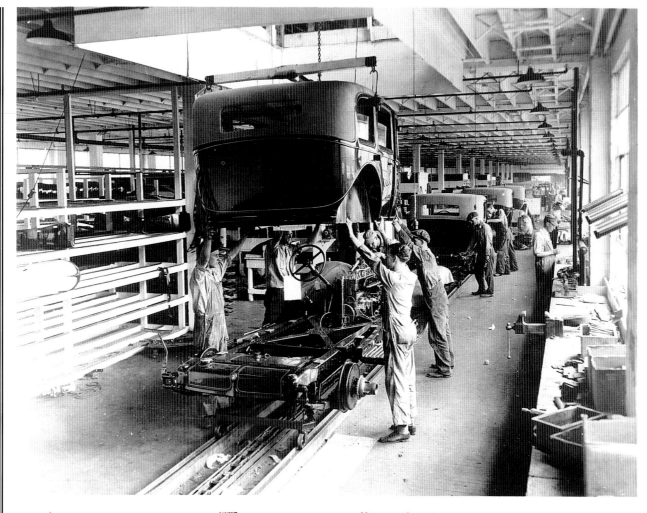

Driver's seat of a sedan. Instruments in the left grouping are temperature gauge, speedometer, and oil pressure gauge. The matching right grouping includes gas gauge, oil level gauge, and ammeter. Left controls are for spark, throttle, left windshield wiper, and instrument lights. Right group are choke, right wiper, and heat controls. Gearshift knob and lever protrude from the dash, right of center; the ignition lock is left of center. A locking glove box is above them. Below, the engine intrudes into the passenger space. *Don Howell collection*

staff immediately set to work—adding to its personnel several well-known experts along specialized engineering lines."

The AAC work order called the project L-27. Auburn and Cord historian Stan Gilliland determined that Auburn used the prefix "L" for chassis orders. It was a chassis that the Miller works was to build. The Auburn dealer in Los Angeles supplied a new 1927 Auburn sedan. The body and engine would be used for the new experimental car. The order was dated around July 1927.

Auburn's engineers studied earlier front-drive efforts in other countries. European front-drive cars were purchased, studied, and dismantled. (Herb Snow and his engineers followed this practice again when they designed the front-drive system for the later Cord 810.) Said AAC literature, "Engineers toured Europe and went clear to the bottom of the underlying fundamentals of all European Front Drive racers and trucks and a few of them were purchased and submitted to rigid tests to ascertain any frailties or faults."

The experimental design included standard Auburn parts as well as custom-designed

Technical Analysis of the Cord L-29

The cylinder-block casting, valves, rods, and pistons of the Cord L-29's Lycoming engine were the same as those used in the 298.6-cubic-inch Lycoming MD and MDA straight eights. A new crankshaft, camshaft, cylinder head, manifold, crankcase, and oil pan had to be specially made for the L-29. Because the block was installed in the opposite direction from the Auburn, the crankshaft rotates counter-clockwise as viewed from the front. Cars of this era still provided a manual crank to start the engine in the event of battery failure. Since the Cord's engine rotated "backwards," another set of gears was engaged by the crank handle allowing the operator to crank the engine by hand in the usual direction. The forward end of the accessory shaft drives the fan by means of a belt. After a while, the company started to use a double belt drive using matched belts. Both four- and six-blade fans were used. Auburn installed the Lycoming FDA 298.6-cubic-inch straight eight (3.25x4.50-inch bore and stroke) in more than 4,000 L-29s. The Lycoming FFA engine, as used in the last 700 L-29s, displaced 322.1 cubic inches by virtue of a bore increased to 3.375 inches. Five main bearings carried the crankshaft. A change in valve timing during the production run resulted in increased torque output.

The gearbox was built by Detroit Gear and Machine Company. In line with Cord's directive, as much of the existing tooling at Detroit Gear was utilized as possible. No radical changes in design were made, and no special machine tools had to be built. Detroit Gear added a separate line to make the transmission cases, but the gears and shafts were made on the regular production line. The gears were standard for the times, using straight cuts without synchromesh. Early gear ratios were 3.11 for first, 1.69 for second, and 1.00 for third; reverse was 3.78. Starting with engine number FD2177, ratios were higher. The gear case and clutch housing were a single casting to gain rigidity. Two arms bolted to the frame rails and formed the front engine mount. The transmission was shipped from Detroit to Columbia Axle in Cleveland, where it was mated to the differential. This unit was then shipped to Auburn where it was attached to a clutch from Detroit and a Lycoming engine from Williamsport, Pennsylvania, then dropped into an A. O. Smith frame from Milwaukee. The unique shift mechanism required by the front-mounted transmission entered the clutch housing vertically. The shifter rod ran above the engine to the driver's compartment, where it emerged from the dash panel. Shifting was done by swiveling the knob from side to side, then pushing or pulling it.

The sides of the differential case supported the front brake backing plates. The brakes were a substantial 12-inch diameter drum, with a 2.25-inch width. They were still too small for the car's weight. Ventilation of the brakes was inadequate, too. In late 1930, openings were cut in the aluminum housing, and louvered covers placed over the openings.

The frame was a massive affair, made up of 7x3x3/32-inch channel side rails and an X-cross-member. Four standard cross-members were also used; the forward one acted as the rear engine mount, the other stiffened the rear portion of the frame. The rear leaf springs were 61 inches long. The rear axle, an "I" beam, was dropped to pass under the springs. Houdaille shock absorbers were fitted all around, as were Wagner-Lockheed internal-expanding hydraulic brakes. The emergency brake lever operated the rear brakes mechanically.

Body construction of the factory cars was contemporary to the day, being sheet steel on a wooden frame. Aluminum was used by some custom builders, and at least one fabric-covered L-29 was built by Weymann American of Indianapolis, a technique Weymann was known for.

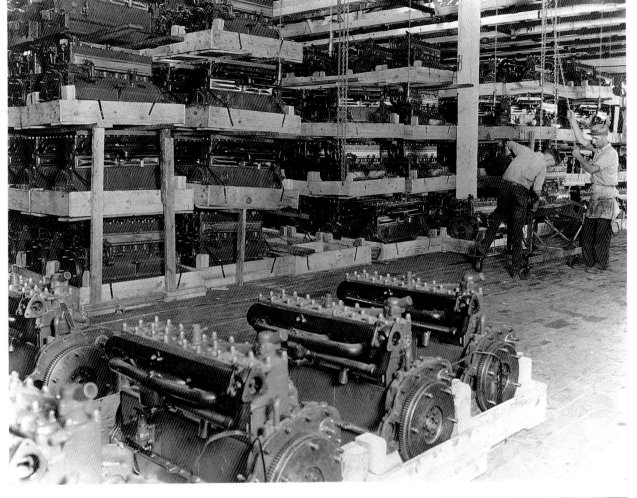

L-29 engines wait at Lycoming for shipment by rail. Accessories, clutch, and transmission were added in Auburn. *Al Light collection*

A Cord sedan poses in an elegant urban setting. Actor Warren William stands alongside. *Behring Auto Museum*

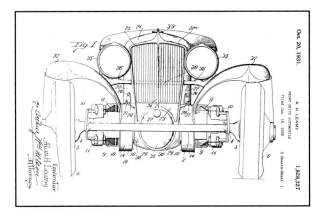

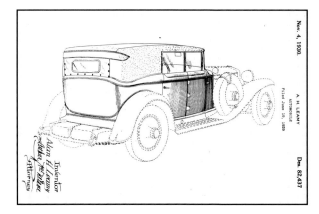

components. The engine had to be reversed to place the clutch at the front. Other modifications were needed, including the fan and accessory drives and cylinder head. A special gearbox casting accommodated a standard three-speed transmission and differential gears. Interviewed years later by historian Bob Fabris, Van Ranst gave a great portion of the design's credit to Leo Goossen. Goossen, modest man that he was, characteristically downplayed his role. A Miller-type front suspension was used, as was the method of mounting the brakes inboard. For economy's sake, a single Cardan-type of universal joint was used at the road wheel instead of the Rzeppa (pronounced "Sheppa") constant-velocity joint used by Miller.

The Auburn body shell basically remained in stock order, but a flat sill eliminated the kickup over the rear wheels, and the front and rear fenders were modified. Wellington Everett Miller—no relation to Harry—was employed by Miller as a draftsman. W. E. Miller did the layout drawings and chassis design for the front-drive prototype. In later interviews with historian Paul Bryant and with Dan Burger, at the time the staff writer for the Auburn-Cord-Duesenberg Museum, W. E. Miller confirmed that the project was based on an Auburn body and was to use the Auburn radiator. When the prototype was finally assembled, the radiator shell closely resembled those on Miller race cars. It's likely this look was the work of Goossen.

Five months were needed to complete the engineering and construction of this landmark car. Miller engineer Eddie Offutt headed the team that made the front-drive components and assembled the car. Myron Stevens, who would later become a race-car builder, created the sheet metal components. During the final stages of construction, Cord lodged near Miller's shop and visited the project daily. When the car was driveable, Van Ranst, Miller, and Duray joined Cord for the first ride. Cord was at the wheel, and he took the group through the hills and canyons of Beverly Hills, stopping after about an hour's ride at his home. He had already decided to go ahead with the project.

Van Ranst later noted that the car's performance was far from satisfactory. He felt a severe bucking caused by the single Cardan universal joint when the car made a sharp turn. Miller was less concerned; he thought the engine was missing. Years later, Offutt told historian Bryant that he rode in the car with Cord and Van Ranst and remembers that it ran well, the front-drive giving problems only at low speeds and with the steering at full lock. Van Ranst, however, was not satisfied. He felt that the public wouldn't stand for such an experience and that the problem would be solved only by a constant-velocity joint.

When E. L. Cord relinquished the presidency of Auburn in 1931, factory employees had this one-twelfth-scale model of an L-29 cabriolet constructed. Auburn's press release boasted that the job took six Swiss watchmakers six months to complete! Actually, it is believed that the work was done by Auburn's own model builders. Here, L. B. Manning inspects the model while Cord stands at right. *Automobile Topics*

The Four Marx Brothers, famous in "Animal Crackers" are shown in one of their four Cord cars.

ABOVE
The four Marx Brothers each owned an L-29. They're lounging here in a convertible sedan. Julius, with cigarette second from the left, became more famous as Groucho.

TOP RIGHT
Captain Cunningham of the *Leviathan*, docked in New York, supervises the loading of the first Cord to be exported. Destination: Coldwell S. Johnson, Auburn's agent in Paris. *Ralph W. Dwight collection*

RIGHT
Edgar Rice Burroughs, creator of "Tarzan," with his L-29 cabriolet. *Courtesy of the Edgar Rice Burroughs Foundation*

Whether to prove a point or just for the excitement of it, Offutt recollected that Cord and Van Ranst later drove the L-27 out of the Miller shop, intending to drive the prototype "all the way back East." Days later, the car arrived at the Duesenberg plant in Indianapolis. It seemed none the worse, except for its worn front tires. Here, in early 1928, the project continued.

Cord's instructions to Van Ranst were explicit. He was to use as many of the Miller features as practicality dictated, to use every possible standard Auburn part in the design, and to keep new tooling requirements to a minimum. Neither time nor a budget were given for the design of a new engine or other major components unless they became absolutely necessary. The first task at hand, after the project moved to the Duesenberg plant, was to design new constant-velocity joints for the outer universals. In August 1928, the experimental car was moved to Auburn. It is likely that Auburn's chief engineer Herb Snow and engineer Harry Weaver did not become involved in the project until it moved from Indianapolis. Arrangements were now made with other Cord Corporation companies to supply various components. Lycoming, Limousine, Central, and Columbia Axle supplied engines, bodies, differentials, and front axles. Other components came from Detroit Gear, Delco, Gemmer, Houdaille, A. O. Smith, Wagner-Lockheed, Long, and Dayton Wheel.

Although Van Ranst and his engineers tried to keep the nonstandard parts to a minimum, it was inevitable that special needs would arise. The unorthodox drivetrain called for a new and longer frame (and hood) than a standard Auburn chassis or body would allow. Thus an entirely new chassis and body, and consequently, the car's styling and looks, would emerge. Years after the development project, there arose a controversy over who was responsible for the magnificent lines of the front-drive production car. As covered in chapter four, Leamy was Auburn's chief body designer. Yet it was John Oswald, Auburn's body engineer, who later claimed that in early October 1928 he was approached by Cord while they were at the Auburn Country Club. Cord suggested some styling ideas and asked Oswald to make a full-size body layout on the blackboard for him to see that afternoon. It's

continued on page 94

Auburn's Work Was Never Done

A unique and endearing characteristic of the AAC was that the company never stopped improving its cars, even when they were already in production. This was true of the innovative L-29, and it was equally true of the later 810.

The Rzeppa constant-velocity joints, as used on the Miller race cars, were considered too expensive for the new Cord L-29. However, curiosity still existed as to how the Rzeppa joint would work on an L-29. The Gear Grinding Machine Company purchased an L-29 and installed Rzeppa joints at both the inner and outer locations. Engineers from both Gear Grinding and Auburn were involved. The engineers found no troubles with the joints, except for a noise problem that developed after several thousand miles of use. The Rzeppa joint was a superior design, but a great deal of development work would have been needed to reduce its cost to a competitive level.

Noise and vibration were always concerns. Engineers considered using a flexible clutch plate. Another plan under consideration was the use of rubber mounts for the engine. To improve the shifting of the unsynchronized gears, Detroit Gear was working on the design of a clutch brake. One design was installed in a factory car and successfully slowed the gears during shifting operations.

To combat the breakage of wheel spokes, spoke size was increased during the production run. Eventually all cars were equipped with a new, special tapered head spoke.

The original muffler location was along the right side of the oil pan, under the carburetor. A shield prevented leaking gasoline from striking the muffler and also served to deflect exhaust heat from the carburetor. It was soon discovered that moving the muffler back to a position within the X-cross-member would improve power output. Other advantages accruing from this move were the reduction of drumming sounds at speeds between 20 and 30 miles per hour, and the elimination of exhaust gas seepage through the floorboards and into the interior. Auburn engineers were never fully satisfied with the design of the exhaust system, and some tests were run to compare back pressure between the existing rectangular pipe and a round pipe.

Front axles were bent after heat treatment, inducing residual stresses. Caster and toe-in alignment settings would change during the first 1,000 miles of operation, as stresses within the axle tubes were relieved. Columbia Axle experimented with heat treatment after bending. Five axle sets were installed on factory cars and daily alignment records kept. Other Auburn engineers suspected that the tube diameter was not adequate. A car with a larger diameter axle tube and reinforced knuckles was also tested. Yet another car had a U-channel welded to the tube and knuckles for reinforcement. Few of these experiments resulted in changes to production parts, but all demonstrated the AAC's constant drive for a superior product.

Van Ranst's patent for the Cord gearshift. Before automatic transmissions, gearshifts for front-drive cars often had a Rube Goldberg air about them.

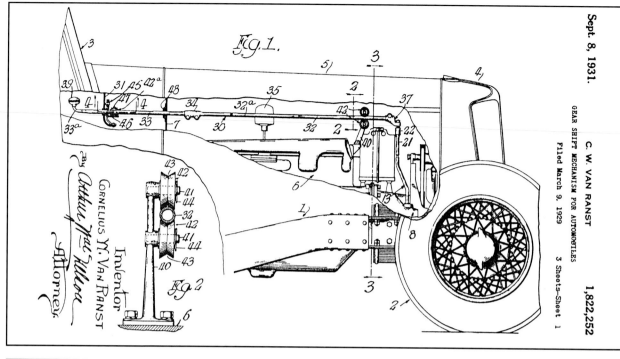

Sept. 8, 1931.

C. W. VAN RANST

1,822,252

GEAR SHIFT MECHANISM FOR AUTOMOBILES

Filed March 9, 1929   3 Sheets-Sheet 1

Leamy-patented sheet metal covers the Van Ranst-patented mechanism. The splayed front springs were a Cord innovation.

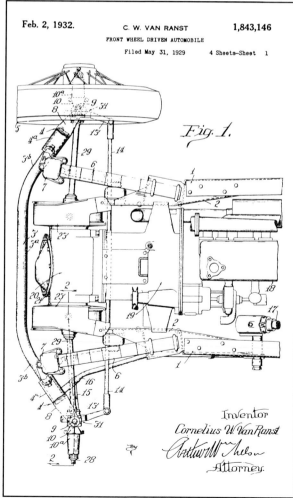

Feb. 2, 1932.   C. W. VAN RANST   1,843,146

FRONT WHEEL DRIVEN AUTOMOBILE

Filed May 31, 1929   4 Sheets-Sheet 1

Inventor
Cornelius W. Van Ranst

Attorney.

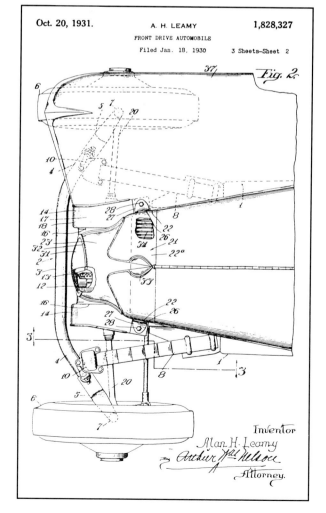

Oct. 20, 1931.   A. H. LEAMY   1,828,327

FRONT DRIVE AUTOMOBILE

Filed Jan. 18, 1930   3 Sheets-Sheet 2

Inventor
Alan H. Leamy

Attorney.

Cord Brougham

E.L.'s prediction that "Front Drive will generally be adopted by the industry" was right on the money. It took, however, 60 years longer than he thought it would! *Josh B. Malks collection*

continued from page 91

The Cord car creates a place for itself
no other car has ever occupied

CORD *FRONT DRIVE*

SEDAN $3095   BROUGHAM $3095

CABRIOLET $3295   PHAETON $3295

Prices F. O. B. Auburn, Indiana. *Equipment other than standard extra*

AUBURN   AUTOMOBILE   COMPANY   ·   AUBURN,   INDIANA

more likely Leamy developed the design concept and motifs in Indianapolis. All of the automobile's design patents bear Leamy's name, and surviving drawings by Leamy illustrate the car's basic lines. As body engineer, Oswald's role in the front-drive project included his execution of the full-size layout drawings after the project moved to Auburn. In turn, Cord, Van Ranst, and Leamy all approved. Cord originally preferred the Miller-like radiator treatment used on the L-27 experimental car. When it came time to assemble the production prototypes, Van Ranst convinced him to use one of several Leamy designs. Van Ranst authorized Oswald to develop the sheet metal parts. Oswald later claimed that he drew every working drawing, supervised the making, and assisted in the shaping of all die models and hammer forms.

The sedan body was built directly from the layouts, with Oswald assembling the parts as they were finished. This production prototype, today dubbed the L-29, was unveiled at a private showing for company personnel. In its day, the car was referred to as the L-29 only by personnel at the factory. Sales literature and publicity materials simply called the new model "The Cord Front Drive." Only years later did enthusiasts start to use the L-29 nomenclature. The Cord name was not attached to the new model until 1929. Perhaps this was deliberate, in case the project didn't come to fruition. But the addition of the entrepreneur's name to a new line of front-drive automobiles was only natural: Cord was the impetus behind the project since day one, and he remained keenly involved in it until completion.

Van Ranst ordered the construction of four more production prototypes, representing one prototype for each body style the company planned to offer. The production prototypes were used for testing and for publicity and advertising photos. A large part of the L-29's styling success is attributable to its long hood, mandated by the length of the drivetrain. Even at that, the combined length of the engine, clutch, transmission, and differential exceeded the space available forward of the cowl. It wasn't practical to make the hood even longer, so a full six inches of the engine—essentially the first cylinder—projected into the interior space in the center of the firewall.

There are conflicting stories about the testing of the production prototypes. Van Ranst recalled that Cord secretly flew to Auburn from California in January 1929, when the company's executives were in New York for the annual auto show. Upon his arrival in Auburn, Cord supposedly called for an around-the-clock team of mechanics to complete one of the four production prototypes, which were being built simultaneously. As soon as it was roadworthy, the story goes, Cord and a mechanic filled the rear seat area with 10-gallon gas cans and took off for a 2,000-mile trip to Phoenix, Arizona. They

A Smaller Cord Front Drive

In July 1929, Cord authorized preparation of a sample design for a front-drive Cord with a smaller straight eight. This model was to have been a slightly downsized version of the L-29 and had the experimental designation D-1. A model of the sedan with an L-29 body was set up for observation in the company's Experimental Engineering Department in October 1929. It was to have a 246.69-cubic-inch straight-eight engine riding in a chassis with a 132-inch wheelbase. The model was to use the same general body dimensions as

This photo is clearly a quarter-scale clay study of an alternate Cord Front Drive. It's possible that it was part of the L-30 design project. Some of its details—the vee windshield and the door belt line—are also seen in the full-size elsewhere in this chapter.

the proposed new Auburn for 1931. Entries from Snow's engineering design program notes of November 18, 1929, reveal that the maximum weight was restricted to 3,500 pounds. All effort was to be exerted to build the car at the lowest possible costs and to have a sample car built and running at the earliest possible date. Columbia Axle undertook design work on the axle, differential, and transmission. Nothing more is known of this project. The stock market disaster of the same month may have contributed to its demise.

stopped only to eat and refuel. Arriving at the Phoenix airport, Cord took a plane to New York, and the mechanic drove the prototype back to Auburn. According to Van Ranst's version, Cord joined the Auburn contingent at the show and made the startling announcement that he had just driven an L-29 nonstop from Auburn to Phoenix. The prototype returned to Auburn with only one mishap during the entire 4,000 miles. With only 15 miles to go, the prototype was struck a glancing blow by a drunken driver in a Dodge. The mechanic was unhurt, and the prototype continued on its way with little damage.

Snow's entries in his diary dispute the timing of this story, however. For January 6, 1929, Snow wrote, "Mr. Cord drove the new FWD car for the first time. Went to New York auto show with Cord and Faulkner." This hardly allows for Cord to make a trip west. A later entry mentions the mishap. "Feb 6 FWD car wrecked on return trip from West," Snow wrote. This places the trip west in the L-29 as occurring only after the New York auto show and doesn't confirm Cord's participation. The January 1932 issue of *World's Work* describes a trip taken during the 1929 New York auto show, but states that it covered 10,000 miles and that as a result, Cord made $500,000 worth of changes in comfort and appearance. This is likely an exaggeration on the episode.

Oswald related that he and Cord took the prototype out to the "proving grounds," in reality only a nearby cornfield, just after the private showing to Auburn employees. Inadequate torsional rigidity

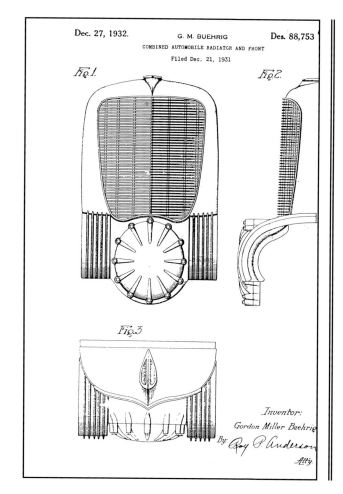

While Gordon Buehrig was chief stylist at Duesenberg he was summoned to Auburn and charged with the creation of a body design for a prototype, V-16-powered, front-wheel drive car. Buehrig told historian Paul Bryant that he was told that this car would be sold as a Duesenberg. There is no evidence that Duesenberg ever seriously considered a front-drive car. More likely this was a way for Auburn management to get an alternate styling approach for a new Cord without alienating Al Leamy, then AAC's chief stylist. In any event, Buehrig went no further than this radiator design, in which he deliberately retained the Miller influence in the radiator shell. He was granted this design patent in 1932. Carl Otto completed the brougham body design, patterned after a Buehrig-styled Duesenberg sedan. V-16 and V-12 Cord Front Drive prototypes were actually built and tested, but not with this front end design.

continued on page 99

Custom-Bodied Cords

About 50 Cord L-29 chassis were fitted with custom bodies by American and European coachbuilders. A sport touring phaeton was built by the Rollston Company in 1931 to a design by Rudolph Creteur. Rollston also built a Victoria and five-passenger Berline. In addition to the speedster, Union City Body Company built other "LaGrande" custom Cords including a Victoria, a town car, and a seven-passenger sedan. Custom bodies were built by European coachbuilders Proux, Gangloff, Freestone and Webb, and Million-Guiet. Designs have been found for additional bodies by some of these coachbuilders, as well as by Castagna and Sauotchik, but it isn't known if these were actually constructed.

Murphy also built at least one Hershey-styled sport sedan on the Cord chassis. The tops of the doors wrap into the roof, a detail this designer used in his Duesenberg sedans, too.

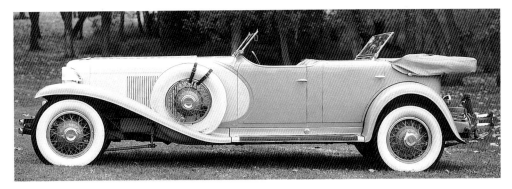

Staff designer Franklin Q. Hershey styled seven dual-cowl phaetons like this one for the Walter M. Murphy Company of Pasadena, California. An eighth phaeton was built by Murphy to a design by Philip O. Wright, another staff designer. *Dr. Frank Hayward*

Weymann-American was an Indianapolis coachbuilder who built fabric-covered bodies under patents held by its parent company in France. One fabric-bodied sport coupe was created by Weymann on the Cord chassis for orchestra leader Paul Whiteman. The car held three passengers, the third in a side-facing rear seat. The leatherette exterior was blue and gray, with leather interior to match.

Four Cord town cars are known to have been bodied by Murphy. Like this one, three were on an extended wheelbase, 15 inches longer than standard. Two of the town cars had spare tires mounted at the rear; the other two used sidemounts. Original owners were reputed to be screen stars John Barrymore, Dolores Del Rio, and Lola Montez; Errett Cord may have owned the fourth one. Another very formal town car body was built by LeBaron, to a design by its illustrator, Raymond Stickney.

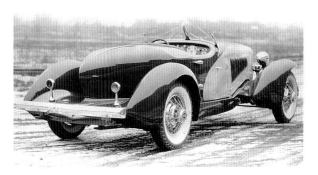

Twenty-three-year-old Phil Wright drew this speedster design for the Cord chassis while employed as a stylist with Murphy. He was seeking a new position in the East when his portfolio came to the attention of Roy Faulkner, then president of Auburn. Faulkner had the speedster executed by Union City Body Company as Cord's centerpiece for the annual New York auto show. In June 1931, the speedster was shipped to Europe to be exhibited and drum up sales. The AAC may have engaged actress Jean Harlow to appear with it at European concours. (Points were awarded for the appearance and proficiency of the female driver, too.) It's shown (left) at the Concours d'Elegance Femina l'Luter in Paris, further decorated by Harlow. In August 1931, the car was returned to North America and exhibited in Toronto, Canada. By November, it was back in Auburn (right). The stock round Cord headlights were replaced by stylish, aftermarket Woodlights during the winter of 1931–32. Here the trail ends; the Cord speedster was never seen again.

Alexis de Sakhnoffsky joined the Hayes Body Company of Grand Rapids, Michigan, in 1928. As designer for coachbuilder Vanden Plas of Brussels, he had won Grand Prix awards at the Concours d'Elegance at Monaco from 1925 through 1928. He now convinced Hayes to let him prepare an all-American entry on the Cord chassis for the 1929 Monaco Concours. When the beautiful coupe was shipped on the Ile de France, the generator wasn't charging. Sakhnoffsky sped off across France anyway. He arrived at the Riviera with a trunkful of dead batteries, a day late for the elimination contest for the concours; the sponsors permitted the car one day's grace. It won the Grand Prix the next day, the first such honor for a car with American-built chassis and coachwork. At the Beaulieu Concours a week later, the Cord coupe was awarded the Grand Prix d'Honneur. The Sakhnoffsky-Hayes coupe further exaggerated the Cord's low height and lengthy hood. Its total height of 54 inches was 6 inches lower than production models, and the new aluminum hood was 7 inches longer than standard. Conical aluminum wheel discs covered the wire wheels. Windshield wipers moved horizontally on a track under the visor; the mechanism was based on a Van Ranst patent for the L-29 (not used on the production cars). Body color was Mountain Mist Blue with gold trim; the raised moldings were done in Cicero Blue. The completed body cost $15,000.

This body shows substantial changes in form from the production L-29. The beltline drops smoothly downward along the length of the front door glass. An apron covering the gas tank blends into the rear fenders. The dashboard has been moved to a position in front of the driver, and large round instruments replace the small drum-type units used in the L-29. Headlights are mounted on castings fastened directly to the fenders. The characteristic Leamy "spears," as he used on the Auburn and Model J Duesenberg, have vanished from the front fenders. Striping studies were being conducted; one side of the body is striped, the other isn't.

continued from page 95

was immediately evident, as the car's doors popped open. The frame had to be reinforced. Hurried discussions with engineers from A. O. Smith of Milwaukee, frame builders for Auburn, resulted in their recommendation for a heavier frame. This idea was rejected. The engine was barely giving satisfactory performance with the existing design; the added weight would have only detracted from the car's effectiveness. Snow developed the idea of inserting an "X" within the frame, rather than relying solely on straight, transverse cross-members. Snow had two 3x12-inch scale models made. One duplicated the existing ladder-type frame; the other had an X-shaped cross-member inserted. The X-shaped cross-member was found to be far superior in resisting twist without significantly increasing frame weight. The models were shown to Cord and Van Ranst, and the design was approved. This was the first use of an X-cross-member frame in an American automobile (patent number 1,841,510).

Cord Front Drive Production Begins

When Central at Connersville started to produce Auburns in early 1929, this made room at the Auburn complex for production of the L-29. Auburn personnel put together the L-29 assembly line in February and March 1929. Hopes ran high, as sales literature reflected: "Through the ingenuity of AUBURN production men it is estimated that the quality CORD FRONT DRIVE will be produced at the rate of 6,000 cars for the balance of 1929, and by 1930 the Auburn, Indiana, plant should be turning at the rate of 15,000 or more C.F.D.'s per annum."

Limousine Body built the open bodies; Central manufactured the closed bodies. Both were shipped to the L-29 assembly line in Auburn. During March and April, Auburn sent four prototypes to California for a publicity photo shoot. It is easy to identify the phaeton-sedan as one of the prototypes in these early photos, since it bears three hinges per door. Production L-29 phaeton-sedans used only two hinges per door. The photo shoot reportedly occurred at Cord's Beverly Hills home and the surrounding neighborhood.

The first public announcement of the Cord Front-Drive appeared in the summer of 1929 in popular magazines and trade publications. The company decided to offer only four body styles, two open (cabriolet and phaeton-sedan) and two closed (brougham and sedan). Both closed models have four doors, but the sedan sports a rear quarter window. A prototype of a two-door brougham was built, but never placed in production. Initially, prices of the Cord L-29 were set at $3,295 for open-bodied models and $3,095 for closed-bodied models. In 1931, prices for all manufacturing goods plummeted. L-29 prices followed suit, with $2,595 for the cabriolet, $2,495 for the phaeton-sedan, and $2,395 for the closed-body models.

The L-29 chassis offered an excellent platform on which to place custom coachwork. The added attractions of low frame height and a long hood caused a stir among custom coachbuilders in the United States and in Europe. While many attractive designs were penned, only a few custom bodies were actually built on the L-29 chassis. Known coachworks that placed their creations on the L-29 frame include Murphy, Rollston, Weymann, Hayes, and Fuller in the United States, and Proux, Milion-Guiet, and Freestone and Webb in Europe. Renderings and sketches made by others are in existence, but with no record of any construction.

Production of the Cord L-29 began in June 1929. Twenty-four sedans were produced that month and 175 in July. Production increased in August and September, and by October, L-29 output averaged over 600 units per month. Dealers did not receive L-29s to sell until September. The company authorized dealers to register these cars as 1930 models; that's why the sales figure for 1929 L-29s is so small.

Internal memos indicate the company intended to build 5,000 L-29s, then move on to the L-30. The major improvement planned for the L-30 was its use of a larger straight-eight engine. This new engine was eventually used—installed in the last 700 L-29s—but no change was made to the model

This design demonstrates a new bumper and grille mounted on the same body shell as seen previously. The car's front-wheel drive is played down. Headlights are again mounted directly to the fenders, but with a bracket of different design. Lenses echo the vertical grille treatment.

Another body shell with sloping V-windshield and different belt molding and side window treatment. It's fitted with yet another radiator/differential/brake cover design. Hood side louvers are reshaped as well.

designation. There were 5,010 Cord L-29s produced when production ended in December 1931.

The L-29 Segues to the 810

The Cord L-29 has often been described as a passenger car that incorporated Harry Miller's racing car patents. That really isn't true. The quarter-elliptic front springs and the inboard brakes mimic the Miller, but these features were not covered in Miller patents. Neither was the DeDion-type tubular front axle, based on Ben Gregory's patent. When Auburn engineers borrowed the idea from Miller,

perhaps they didn't realize the design belonged to someone else. Miller had bought the rights to Gregory's design, but the AAC had not. Cord had to settle Gregory's lawsuit against the company for $3,600, essentially buying the rights to the design.

Cord was heavily involved in the conception, design, testing, and marketing of the first car to bear his name. During the creation of the L-29, the entrepreneur was young and more enthusiastic about building automobiles. He was energized by the idea of a car bearing his own name, and he was president of the AAC and directly affected by its financial fortunes. This would not prove to be the case when development work started on the second front-drive automobile from the AAC, which would arrive at Auburn dealers in 1936. An interesting footnote connects the Cord L-29 to this second front-drive model from Auburn. The last L-29 in stock at the factory wasn't sold until September 1933. During that very month, Harold Ames met with Gordon Buehrig in Indianapolis. Buehrig, an automotive designer formerly with Duesenberg and working at General Motors when his meeting with Ames occurred, would soon return to Duesenberg. And what was the subject of the discussion between Ames and Buehrig? The creation of a special body for a prospective new small Duesenberg, using a design concept that Buehrig had sketched. Buehrig and others at the AAC later developed that concept into the Cord 810.

Cornelius W. Van Ranst.

The Sun Sets on Auburn 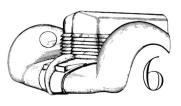 6

1932-1936

hile many have blamed the slogging pace of the Great Depression for the demise of the AAC, others have faulted the new management that took over the Cord Corporation in 1937 and its lack of interest in automotive production. In fact, Cord himself had lost interest. In Borgeson's Cord biography, he quotes a U.S. Board of Tax Appeals report from 1938, which is quite revealing: "The executive committee of Cord (Corporation) had determined prior to June 1, 1932, to liquidate a substantial part of its investment in the automobile industry and to increase its investment in the field of aviation." Aviation, as an industry, was still in its formative stages. There were no conglomerates stealing the show; the same couldn't be said for automobiles.

There were economies of scale to be had at Ford, General Motors, and Chrysler. Good cars were available at low prices. The AAC—like most independents—was being squeezed out of the car business. The company had to compete on price in the midst of the Depression, but didn't enjoy the previously mentioned economies of scale necessary to endure low profit margins. The Roaring Twenties could support an independent, boutique automaker; the Great Depression could not. The Cord Corporation at least had a chance in the aviation market.

By 1933, the Cord Corporation's annual report noted the company held less than 4,000 shares of AAC stock. Although the move to "liquidate a substantial part of its investment in the automobile industry" never completely came to pass, the fact that Cord Corporation management even entertained the idea is significant. By design or otherwise,

OPPOSITE
The story behind the short-lived 1934 Auburn is one of a company mired in mismanagement and a financial crisis. A Vultee rests behind the Auburn.

Auburn promoted the power behind its V-12 line without hesitation. Cord must have expressed to Willis his desire for ads that tied together the entrepreneur's endeavors in aviation and automobiles. Such a linkage is frequently found in company promotional materials.

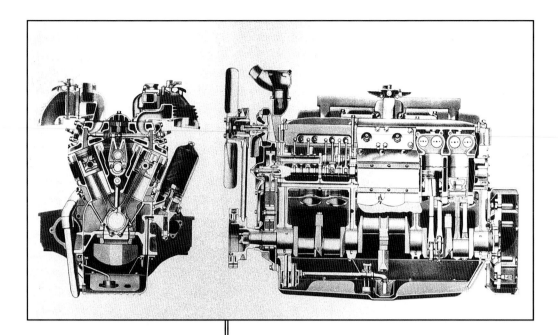

A cutaway drawing depicting the Lycoming V-12 as supplied to Auburn. The unusual valvetrain arrangement can be seen.

Dual-Ratio provided Auburn drivers with two sets of ratios throughout the three speeds offered, making Dual-Ratio models the earliest six-speeds automobiles. A driver selected high or low range via a lever on the steering wheel. The ratios can be changed while driving below 40 miles per hour. The lever is linked to a piston valve in a vacuum line via a Bowden cable. The line draws its vacuum from the intake manifold, operating the piston in a vacuum cylinder. This piston is found on the differential housing. Manifold vacuum pushes or pulls the piston forward or backward in the cylinder, depending on the lever setting. The piston moves a shifting clutch in the rear axle, either bringing a planetary gear set into operation for the high ratio, or locking it out for the low ratio. This gear set is an addition to the differential's ring and pinion gears, but housed within the same axle case.

the reality of the Depression-era auto market began to impact the AAC in 1932, though it took five years to complete the inevitable.

The 8-98 of 1931 segued into the 8-100 for 1932. The 8-100 used the Lycoming GU 268.6-cubic-inch straight eight from the previous year, the company now listing horsepower ratings for the engine at 100 at 3400 rpm. The standard line included many items from the previous year's custom line, including the LGS freewheeling system.

The biggest news for 1932 was the introduction of the Auburn 12-160. The 12-160 represented Auburn's entry into the V-12 market. The Lycoming BB 12 pack, displaced 391.2 cubic inches and produced 160 horsepower at 3500 rpm, the most ever for an Auburn. Two Stromberg 1.25-inch downdraft carburetors each supplied one bank of six-cylinders. The engine's 5.75:1 compression ratio meant a V-12 owner need not pump higher octane gasoline into the engine. The Lycoming V-12 used just four main bearings, like Packard and Cadillac, and could boast the best horsepower per cubic inch and pounds per horsepower on the market. The V-12's valvetrain design was particularly unusual. There were no pushrods, the rocker arms acting directly on the valves which laid nearly horizontal. This almost smacks of an overhead cam design, but the camshaft remained between the cylinder banks. The 12-160 enjoyed a wheelbase six inches longer than its eight-cylinder brother. Hydraulic, internal-expanding 14-inch drums provided the stopping power. Auburn also equipped the V-12 with LGS freewheeling, the Bijur lubrication system, a variable-ratio steering gear, and 17-inch wheels. Order a 12-160A, the custom model, and a customer also received a Dual-Ratio rear axle, ride control (which adjusted shock

rate), and a Startix system. The Dual-Ratio, in essence, provided an overdrive mode. However, it was available for use in all three forward speeds, not just in third gear. On the 12-160, the rear axle ratios included 4.54:1/3.00:1. For the 8-100, the ratios were 5.10:1/3.40:1. The Startix feature was a starting system that automatically turned over the engine simply by turning the key to the "on" position (it wasn't necessary to push a button or hold the key over). If the engine stalled for any reason, the Startix system would automatically try to start it again. A driver could bypass the Startix system, if so desired. The 12-160 even had a muffler bypass installed in its dual exhaust system in case one wanted to scare away stoplight competition. The most astounding feature of the Auburn V-12 was its price. A 12-160 coupe retailed for $1,425. By comparison its nearest competitor, the Cadillac V-12, brought $3,395 for a coupe. Later price slashing allowed Auburn's V-12 prices to drop even farther. Yet, if the 12-160 represented such a bargain, why was it necessary to discount prices? Bargain of the century or not, the market for $1,425-plus automobiles of any type was simply too narrow in the ongoing Depression. The V-12 entered the middle-priced market when it was receding, not expanding. The 12-160 would have been a great idea in the 1920s; it was a grave misstep in the 1930s. Although the AAC raised prices $100 across the board on April 15, by June the company slashed prices with a vengeance. The price of an 8-100 coupe

dropped $275; the 12-160 coupe price was cut $470. The AAC offered the 12-160 in the phaeton ($1,145 standard/$1,275 custom), brougham, ($1,025/$1,155), five-passenger sedan ($1,075/$1,205), cabriolet ($1,095/$1,225), coupe ($975/$1,105), and speedster ($1,145/$1,275). The 8-100 line included the phaeton ($845/$975), brougham ($725/$855), five-passenger sedan ($775/$905), cabriolet ($795/$925), coupe ($675/$805), seven-passenger sedan ($875/$1,005), and speedster ($845/$975).

Despite the deep cuts, Auburn's losses were staggering. By year's end, the company suffered a worse year than 1930. Net sales were only $12.9 million, profits turned into a loss of $1.1 million, and the company's cash surplus turned into a deficit, now at $2.6 million. Auburn/Cord unit sales totaled only 11,332 units (including a minuscule 157 Cord L-29s), and the company's stock ranged from 28-3/4 to 151-3/4. Merger discussions arose in late 1931 with Willys-Overland. Cord traveled to Toledo in January 1932 for talks, but nothing followed.

Miserable sales and a staggering company did not keep racer Eddie Miller from competing in an Auburn. This time he used two Auburn V-12s at Muroc Dry Lake in California to chase top-speed records. In July 1932, Miller pushed a V-12 speedster to 100.77 miles per hour in the flying one-mile category and obtained 88.95 miles per hour for 500 miles. This first mark represented the first time an American stock car had surpassed the 100-mile-per-hour mark. Miller also ran a V-12 brougham, grabbing a flying one-mile speed of 92.66 miles per hour and a 500-mile benchmark of 82.71 miles per hour. Although supervised by the AAA, records of Miller's run were not released until August 11.

Later in the year, Miller took a stripped 12-160 speedster with Dual-Ratio to Muroc. On December 27, 1932, he broke 31 American speed records from flying starts and nine international records from standing starts. Once again supervised by the AAA, Miller topped 118.32 miles per hour for the one-kilometer record, and chalked up an average of 113.57 miles per hour over 500 miles. Miller could have won at Indy with such a performance.

Auburn Introduces the Salon

On November 12, 1932, Cord handed over the AAC presidency to W. Hubert Beal. Beal had been a sales manager at Lycoming for a number of years, ascending to that company's presidency in 1931. Beal had also been appointed to Auburn's board in 1931. As a reflection of how little importance Cord now attached to Auburn, he allowed Beal to hold both Lycoming's and Auburn's presidential posts. Cord named Manning a vice president at Auburn, a position Manning disliked as he held little regard for the Cord Corporation's automotive operations. Tellingly, Manning dropped off the AAC's board of directors after 1934.

For 1933, the standard and custom 8s and 12s carried over from the previous year. The 8-100 became the 8-101; the 12-160 segued into the 12-161. However, the company did not change the horsepower ratings for either model. The new offerings from Auburn were the salon models, labeled the 8-105 and 12-165. The most notable features of the salons were the vee windshield of the closed-body models and the folding windshield of the open-bodied models. Chrome steel artillery wheels were available, and the eight-cylinder salons also featured hydraulic brakes. Otherwise, the salons enjoyed all the added features found on the custom models. In its 1933 sales literature, Auburn promoted its one-piece steel running boards as a safety feature "by acting as side bumpers." So side-impact safety beams are a new concept?

Prices for 1933 were higher. The 12-161/12-165 line included the sedan ($1,245 standard/$1,395 custom/$1,745 salon), brougham ($1,195/$1,345/$1,695), cabriolet ($1,295/$1,445/$1,795) phaeton ($1,345/$1,495/$1,845), coupe ($1,145/$1,295/no salon), and the speedster ($1,345/$1,495/$1,845). In the 8-101/8-105 line, the body

Eddie Miller emerging from his Auburn speedster after a speed record run at Muroc Dry Lake. The photo was likely posed, although some drivers did wear ties during their endurance runs.

RIGHT
James Cagney appears in the driver's seat of a 1933 Auburn 12-165 salon cabriolet. It's unknown if Cagney actually owned this car; movie stars were frequently called upon to pose with automobiles for promotional purposes. Hallmarks of the salon models are readily seen: rolled-over bumpers and a unique grille.

BELOW LEFT
Unlike Cords and Duesenbergs, not many Auburns had custom bodies installed by coachbuilders. This V-12 Auburn sports a custom body by an unknown European coachbuilder, but it was most likely created by a French firm. The V-12 was sold by the Parisian Auburn dealer E. Z. Sadovich, better known for his Duesenberg connections. The original owner of this model was Count Charles Simeon (Alain Dollfus).

BELOW RIGHT
Life on Auburn's assembly lines was a grueling proposition compared to today's work standards. Still, a sense of pride and accomplishment is reflected in the eyes of the Auburn factory worker.

styles included the brougham ($795/$945/$1,195), sedan ($845/$995/$1,245), cabriolet ($895/$1,095/$1,295), phaeton ($945/$1,095/$1,345), coupe ($745/$895/no salon), speedster ($945/$1,095/$1,345), and seven-passenger sedan ($945/$1,095/no salon).

In May 1933, wages at Auburn increased by 5 percent in accordance with the National Recovery Act. In August, wages increased another 15 percent. Looking back through 60 years of improvements in labor conditions, life on the Auburn factory line appears grueling. When the Auburn-Cord-

Duesenberg Museum interviewed former Auburn employees in the late 1970s and early 1980s, the project did not neglect to seek out factory laborers. Their comments were revealing: ". . . it was the worst work I ever did in my life, I mean to tell you that." "Some days it was long hours and then the next day we'd be laid off for two weeks or more." "At that time, anyone that worked was happy to have a job." Three line workers, who labored with fender production, remembered their jobs this way:

> Employee: "You would put the flat piece of metal in [the press], and the press would come down and form it in the rough shape of a fender, and then after that it still required a lot of hammer work and thinning."
>
> Interviewer: "How many [fenders] could you do, say, in an hour or in a day?"
>
> Employee: "I'm not sure. At least a hundred an hour."
>
> Interviewer: "One hundred an hour?"
>
> Employee: "Right. Sixty minutes out of the hour. We didn't have breaks at that time."
>
> Second employee: "It'd take one guy to push that fender on with a two-by-four, and the other guy had to screw it in tight before it popped back out."
>
> Third employee: "My God, we had . . . we had to give all we had to get that [fender] in there."

A standard day at the time consisted of 10 hours, 12 to 16 hours during a good sales season. Factory laborers worked six days a week. During 1933, Central Manufacturing was relatively idle. Cord decided to market its sheet metal stamping capabilities to nonautomotive companies.

Auburn continued to bleed red ink in 1933. Net sales dropped to $5.4 million, the company registered another loss of $2.5 million, and the deficit rose to $3 million. Unit sales dropped from 11,332 to 4,630 units. The AAC closed its factory operations in Auburn—though the administration and factory service departments remained there—leaving only the Connersville factory complex to produce Auburns after 1933. The AAC had a number of Lycoming V-12 engines (some 400 remained as late as 1935) and 1933 bodies left in inventory. Naturally, to clear out the old stock, Auburn sold the previous 12-165 (salon) models as "1934" Auburn V-12 salons—using the model number 1250—until the old stock was nearly depleted. The bigger news for 1934 was the all-new body styles.

Auburn photographed this side-by-side comparison of its 1934 model (left) versus a 1934 Studebaker. The company frequently shot these comparison photos, possibly for engineering purposes, on the south side of the administration building (in the background).

In Auburn advertising, Beal announced some $1 million had been spent on new tooling (others state $500,000). Snow switched to all-steel body construction, at roughly the same time as Chrysler and at least three years before General Motors. Snow correctly believed that all-steel bodies would be highly cost effective. Eliminating the wood sills allowed for a lighter Auburn, while lowering its profile for even better performance. Leamy designed the 1934 Auburn body amid management fighting over what direction a new Auburn style should take. In the end, the plunging hood molding, the drop in the front bumper, and split grille treatment of previous years remained, but that was all. The new Auburn eschewed the taut, lean, and angular look of earlier Auburns. Instead, the new design reflected the streamline trend of the day with a sloping front end, rounded fenders, and three sweeping openings in the side of the hood where once there had been a multitude of vertical louvers. Auburn dropped the hyphenated model designations forever. Instead, the AAC dubbed the straight eight model the 850X (standard) or 850Y (custom). A straight six returned to the model line, dubbed the 652X or 652Y. The 850 came equipped with the Dual-Ratio rear axle, LGS freewheeling, Bendix hydraulic brakes, and Bendix power assist on custom models. Wheel size dropped again, to 16 inches, with a wheelbase of 126 inches.

Auburn offered a simplified selection of body styles in 1934. In the 1250 line, this included the

The NEW AUBURN

6 and 8 cylinder *Models*

The world's Smartest low priced car
119-inch wheelbase Six, low as
$695

⊛*Car illustrated once is the 139-inch*
Wheelbase, Straight Six, 115 Horse-
Power, Lycoming 12 seems to list as $13-5

Not only does the new Auburn introduce a new high standard of quick acceleration, combined with quiet, smooth, flexible power—not only does it "hold the road" in a manner that makes it easier to drive and safer to ride in—not only does it run in an even, straight line with a minimized tendency to side-sway or roll— But climaxing all these performance-advantages are

the many ways in which the new Auburn takes the "work" out of driving. Auburn for 1934 makes automobile driving remarkably easy; more restful; more comfortable; requires less exertion and leaves you refreshed even after long drives. We invite you to ride in and drive the new Auburn models. If the car does not sell itself you will not be asked to buy.

6 CYLINDER MODELS $695 TO $945; 8 CYLINDER MODELS $945 TO $1225; SALON 12 MODELS $1575 TO $1945
All prices at the factory, subject to change without notice. Equipment other than standard, extra
AUBURN AUTOMOBILE COMPANY, AUBURN, INDIANA. *Division of Cord Corporation*

AUBURN

phaeton ($1,745), cabriolet ($1,695), brougham ($1,594), and sedan ($1,645). These prices represent a $100 drop from 1933 levels. By February, Auburn dropped the 1250's price yet again, by another $200 across the board. Although no literature listed a 1250 speedster, a few dealers apparently sold them, or called their leftover 1933 V-12 speedster as much. Prices for the sixes and eights remained the same, ostensibly due to the 1934 model's brief model year. Styles for the 652 included a sedan ($745 standard/$845 custom), brougham ($695/$795), cabriolet ($795/$895), and phaeton ($945 for the 652Y only). The 850 line offered the same styles: a sedan ($995/$1,125), brougham ($945/$1,075), cabriolet ($1,045/$1,175), and a phaeton ($1,225).

Powerplant changes accompanied the new body style. The Lycoming 279.9-cubic-inch straight eight now used evolved from the previous 268.6-cubic-inch GU block, but with a 1/16-inch increase in bore.

Lycoming dubbed these new eights the GF in the 850X where it was rated at 100 horsepower at 3400 rpm, and the GG in the 850Y where it made 115 horsepower at 3600 rpm. Power differences came on the top side of the engines. The GF used a 1-1/2-inch single-barrel carburetor, and the GG sported a 1-inch two-barrel carburetor. The GF used cast-iron cylinder heads and had a lower compression ratio of 5.30:1. The GG used aluminum heads with a higher 6.20:1 compression ratio. All of the 209.9-cubic-inch straight-six Lycoming engines carried the WF designation, regardless of whether they were installed in the standard or custom models. The bore and stroke of the six was the same as the eight; Lycoming essentially left off two cylinders to make the block. It, too, featured aluminum cylinder heads. Installed in the 652 (X or Y), the six produced 85 horsepower at 3500 rpm.

Financial difficulties notwithstanding, Auburn still strove to offer a quality product even in its low-priced 652. Standard 652s came with 17-inch

The Weymann-bodied Duesenberg Model J speedster designed by Gordon Buehrig. It later served as his inspiration when he created the Auburn speedsters for the 1935 model year.

tions on the Auburn somehow turned out better."

Four speedster prototypes were assembled by hand in time for the New York show. Deliveries of speedsters to dealers started in February 1935. "[The 1935 speedsters] were largely hand-made with only very cheap hardwood draw forms used on a hydraulic arch press to form the body tail end panels and the fenders," Buehrig wrote in his autobiography. Each speedster was equipped with a plate signed by Ab Jenkins and stating that the car had been driven to 100-plus miles per hour. For the record, Auburn did not have Jenkins drive each and every speedster to its maximum speed. In fact, Ames takes credit for the plate: "[When we] started putting that plate down there [stating Ab Jenkins] had driven this car—it was a gimmick that I

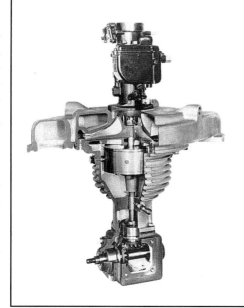

had." Dick Robinson remembered walking down the assembly line and watching a worker tack the plates onto the dash of bodies that had not yet been installed on a chassis!

Despite the speedster's desirability today, at the time dealers did not want them. In fact, Auburn usually forced its bigger dealers to take at least one speedster for the showroom. As previously discussed, the speedster simply wasn't a practical car. The 1935 speedsters were initially priced at $2,245. Estimates of the number of 1935-36 Auburn speedsters produced range from 150 to 500.

Auburn equipped all speedsters with its flagship product of the year, the supercharger. Augie Duesenberg (working as a contractor for Auburn) worked with Pearl Watson to adapt a supercharger developed by Kurt Beier at Schwitzer-Cummins to the

This cutaway view shows the Schwitzer-built centrifugal supercharger as adapted by Augie Duesenberg and Pearl Watson for use on Lycoming straight-eight engines.

113

A 1935 Auburn hearse.

Lycoming 279.9-cubic-inch straight eight. Augie and Watson had the speedster ready in time for the 1935 New York Auto Show. Lycoming labeled the engine the GH. The supercharger was driven via a timing chain case through a sprocket in a 1:1 bevel gear box, from which a vertical shaft terminated in a planetary friction drive. This planetary arrangement increased the rpm by a ratio of 5:1 and, coupled with the chain drive, allowed the supercharger to run six times the engine's crankshaft speed. Supercharged Auburns featured flexible stainless steel pipes that exited out of the side of the hood. The supercharged engine provided horsepower of 150 at 4000 rpm, and 232 foot-pounds of torque at 2800 rpm. Useful pressure kicked in at 2000 rpm. For comparison, the naturally aspirated straight eight produced 115

horsepower at 3500 rpm, and 210 foot-pounds of torque at 1800 rpm.

Offering less flash, but definitely selling better than the speedster, the 851 models included the sedan ($1,095 standard/$1,188 custom/$1,268 salon/$1,545 supercharged), phaeton ($1,275/$1,368/$1,448/$1,725), brougham ($995/$1,088/$1,168/$1,445), and cabriolet ($1,225/$1,313/$1,361/$1,675). Auburn added the previously mentioned speedster ($2,245, supercharged only) and a coupe ($1,085/$1,173/$1,221/$1,545) to the 1935 line-up. Auburn also offered the 653 line in the standard, custom, and salon series. This included the sedan ($845 standard/$952 custom/$1,032 salon), phaeton ($995/$1,102/$1,182), brougham ($745/$852/$932), cabriolet ($945/$1,052/$1,100), and the coupe ($835/$942/$990). It is difficult to establish 1935 model

year prices, since the company adjusted them almost continuously throughout the year (the above prices were in effect February 11, 1935). For example, dealers complained that the competition kept a price difference of $50 between its two-door and four-door models. In response, on April 6, 1935, Faulkner circulated a memo to dealers, announcing that Auburn had dropped the price of its sedans. Yet, by the time the 1936 models rolled out in the fall of 1935, some prices had increased.

When it comes to buying an automobile, few things have changed over the last 60 years save the price. In 1935, there were any number of options to the advertised price. An internal memo to dealers listed a typical retail transaction for an Auburn. For instance, a supercharged sedan sold for $1,595, with optional equipment adding $66. Include federal tax ($39.07), advertising ($18.00), loading ($3.00), handling ($13.50), and freight and decking ($2.00), and suddenly this Auburn tallied $1,736.57 at delivery. These charges were common for the day. The Dual-Ratio option listed for $70.00, an Auburn-Crosley radio $48.50. One could mount a wild set of air horns up front for $10.50, a tachometer for $13.00, and an electric clock for $13.00. A rumble seat for the coupe model was an additional $51.50. Auburn even offered option packages. For instance, Group A equipment for a standard 653 ($25.00) included an extra taillight, chrome running board molding, an extra windshield wiper, front door armrests, an extra sun visor on closed models, a robe rail in two-seat models, and Startix.

It's amazing that with all its economic problems, and its heavy involvement with the Cord 810, the company continued to turn out new Auburn models. In late 1935, the AAC introduced an ambulance ($1,950), hearse ($1,895), and nine-passenger limousine ($1,895), all based on the same 163-inch wheelbase extended chassis. In November 1935, Auburn offered the 655, a Cummins diesel-equipped model, but found few takers. Approximately seven 655s were built, including two nine-passenger lim-

ousines, one phaeton, and four sedans. Cummins had already experimented with a diesel Auburn phaeton prior to production. The six-cylinder 377-cubic-inch diesel used an aluminum head, but the motor still weighed 860 pounds and generated 85 horsepower at 2200 rpm. Its slow-turning engine spun at only 1400 rpm at 55 miles per hour, which certainly provided for a long engine life. Best of all, the diesel Auburn delivered 34 to 40 miles per gallon, an incredible figure for the day. Regardless, few drivers seemed very concerned about saving fuel.

For 1935, unit sales came to 6,553, for a total of 9,645 1935–1936 Auburns sold in 1934 and 1935. The year-end figures were starting to sound depressingly familiar. Net sales dropped to $9.3 million. Losses amounted to $2.8 million, and the company's deficit was $2.6 million. In fact, the 1935 Auburn never surpassed the 1934 Auburn on a monthly sales basis. From September 1934 (the month Auburn introduced its 1935 models) to December 1935, some 9,645 1935 and 1936 models (the two model years were exactly alike) were sold. This represents an average of only 603 1935s and 1936s sold per month, against 920 1934s sold per month.

Things continued to look up for Auburn where racing was concerned, however. In July 1935, Ab Jenkins ran a supercharged 851 speedster at Bonneville. He broke 70 new American and international records. Jenkins took the flying mile at 104.17 miles per hour and the 1,000-mile mark at 102.77 miles per hour. Jenkins' Auburn was the first American stock car to exceed 100 miles per hour (102.9 miles per hour, to be exact) for a 12-hour period.

In November, Chief Engineer George Kublin left Auburn for General Motors. Stanley Thomas took over Kublin's position, while Herb Snow remained vice president of engineering. Partial financial salvation came from an unlikely source when Montgomery Ward contracted with the AAC for a line of metal kitchen cabinets to be stamped at Central Manufacturing. The cabinets proved a popular product for the retailer. By summer 1935, the

A handful of Auburns had Cummins diesel engines installed and were officially known as 655 models. Although the engines were fuel efficient for the day, few takers were found as gas consumption was of little concern to anyone in 1935.

A pit crew works on Ab Jenkins' supercharged Auburn speedster during his endurance runs on the Bonneville Salt Flats in July 1935.

This 1934 Auburn ad promoted the spaciousness of Auburn interiors.

HOW DAD WON

He was respected for his analytical ability. He had inspected the 1934 Auburn's rigid frame. He was impressed with the fact that the chassis contains no untried experiments. He had had years of experience with Lycoming engines; in

passenger cars, airplanes, boats, and trucks. His business acumen convinced him Auburn offers the greatest value. But it would appear that the feminine influence predominated in his home. So, Daughter got behind the wheel. The ample room, luxurious interior, and ventilation control won Mother and Sister over instantly.

When they came home from a demonstration, amazed at Auburn's easy riding, the way the car clung to the road, the absence of side-sway, and the advantages of the Extra High gear of Dual-Ratio—well, the Auburn had sold itself

AVBURN

6 CYLINDER MODELS (119" WHEELBASE) $695 TO $945. 8 CYLINDER MODELS (126" WHEELBASE) $845 TO $1125. SALON 12 MODELS $1145 TO $2245
All prices at the factory, subject to change without notice • Equipment other than standard extra
AUBURN AUTOMOBILE COMPANY, AUBURN, INDIANA, Division of Cord Corporation

The Indiana State Police purchased two supercharged Auburn phaetons in 1936. The Auburns were no doubt bought for publicity purposes rather than day-to-day patrolling, as indicated by the inscription on the side of the car.

retailer had given AAC a $1 million contract for more cabinets. That December, the AAC issued $2.8 million in debenture notes and pooled the money with the revenues from the cabinets in order to finance the Cord 810. Suddenly, Central Manufacturing was prosperous, adding other customers including Sears Roebuck and General Electric to its roster. The Cord Corporation started buying AAC shares again, adding 37,619 shares to the pot. Unfortunately, Cord's renewed interest was motivated purely by monetary concerns and reflected no reborn dedication to the automobile field.

The 1936 model year started in September 1935; it would be Auburn's last, hence changes were superficial at best. The company updated the 851 and 653 designations to 852 and 654. The only badge on 1935 and 1936 Auburns that designated the model was attached to the grille. This made it simple for Auburn dealers to deal with leftover 1935 models: The company simply sent new 852 and 654 badges to replace the previous versions. Presto, new model.

Auburn prices were unchanged from the previous year. However, word was out that Auburn was struggling, and pricing fluctuated throughout the year. Dealers, not wanting to be stuck with an orphan, discounted heavily. Auburn dropped its nine-passenger limo, though the hearse and ambulance were retained, as was a hearse/ambulance combo. Interested parties could also order these extended-wheelbase models with the supercharged straight eight ($2,345, hearse; $2,400, ambulance; and $2,435, hearse/ambulance combo). Auburn offered a seven-passenger sedan in place of the nine-passenger version. It used the standard 127-inch wheelbase, but used stiffer springs to handle the added passenger capacity. It, too, was available in standard, custom, salon, and supercharged form ($1,595/$1,688/$1,768/$2,045). Unit sales totaled 3,061 Auburns and Cords (1,174 Cord 810s), providing net sales of $8.3 million, another loss of $1.6 million, and the year's deficit amounting to $1.5 million. Regardless of the dismal numbers, AAC shares were up, with the new Cord 810 taking the kudos but the kitchen cabinet business pulling the money in. Auburn shares traded from 26-5/8 to 54-1/4 during the year. The Security and Exchange Commission, however, felt there were other reasons why AAC shares rose in value. This would later come to haunt Cord.

In Auburn sales literature, the company depicted the factory spreads at Auburn and Connersville as if they were still rolling out Auburns on a massive basis. In reality, the Auburn plant sat idle, and Connersville automotive production was minimal in the last days. By 1937, some 146 Auburns remained in factory lots. No new Auburns emerged in 1937, although in June 1936, management instructed what remained of the Engineering Department to submit proposals. The idea was to make use of the Cord 810 body shell with new front end sheet metal and a rear-drive powertrain. Another assignment called for Auburn, Cord, and Duesenberg designs for the 1938 to 1940 model years. These design projects were canceled in November 1936.

In mid-May 1936, the few offices still at the administration building in Auburn left for Connersville. Only a parts and service depot remained. Herb Snow resigned and the vice president of engineering position was eliminated. Chassis engineer Louis R. Jones took over the chief engineer position upon Stanley Thomas' departure. Manning left the Cord Corporation presidency, and for the first time since its formation, he did not hold an office with the holding company. Auburn had finally run its course. To be sure, the cars held pizzazz, flair, and a sporting air about them. Or, as an Auburn ad stated: "Exclusive, Distinctive, Individual." They were part of the country club set, cars made for Hollywood. So what was wrong with this? Nothing, per se, except for the grim reality of the ongoing depression. Although Auburns may have been affordable to many more than those who purchased the cars during the economically

troubled times, they exuded a personality beyond their price range. As the Depression ground on, the atmosphere in the country became gritty, hard edged. Few wanted to be associated with the leisurely wealth. It was no longer classy to be classy. The AAC's product planners continued to bring out lofty automotive products as if the Roaring Twenties had never ended. Part of this can be attributed to Cord's lack of attention and the infighting and ineptitude that broke out in the upper management ranks. No one was paying attention to the market anymore, and those who held the financial strings no longer cared. Ironically, had Auburn responded to the depressed state of affairs with models that could have been sold at a reasonable price, it would have diminished Auburn's reputation, then and now. Without the flair, without the pizzazz, Auburns wouldn't have been Auburns, they would have been, well, just cars. Auburn had fought the good fight, but was ultimately left without a place to make a stand. There was nothing anyone could, or wanted to, do about it.

Auburn was well known for its "White Caravan," which consisted of all the Auburn models for a given model year, all painted white. The caravan served as a promotional tool for the company and traveled from dealer to dealer to promote the new Auburn line. The caravan usually generated some free publicity in the newspaper of whatever town it appeared in.

A 1935 Auburn nine-passenger sedan, used by limousine services. This model was retired in 1936 in favor of a seven-passenger sedan.

Grace Under Pressure: A New Cord

1933-1935

 uburn had continued to develop front-drive concepts even after production of the Cord L-29 had ceased. Herb Snow, who had joined the AAC as chief engineer in the middle of the L-29's development program, was now vice president of engineering. He was a strong advocate of front-wheel drive. So, too, was Snow's assistant, chief engineer George Kublin. Kublin had come to Auburn in 1930, fresh from his involvement with the front-drive Ruxton. As the first American front-drive production automobile to market, the L-29 had barely beat the Ruxton to market.

Snow and Kublin had learned from the weaknesses of the L-29 and were ready to do better. They especially wanted to avoid the concept of building a front-drive car using rear-drive parts. By late 1933, Snow, Kublin, and their engineering staff were designing a completely new front-drive chassis. As they had done with the L-29, Auburn's engineers bought and studied other front-drive automobiles. Auburn purchased, examined, and dismantled a French-built Citroën Traction Avant Model 11 as soon as it appeared on the market. So, too, for an Adler, a German front-drive automobile. From these studies came ideas that would be incorporated into a new Auburn front-drive chassis. Among the first of these was a radical, light, six-cylinder concept called Project E 278. This car's transaxle would follow the suggestions made by Van Ranst in 1928 and further developed by Citroën in 1934. It would position the transmission ahead of the differential, which avoided multiplying the torque to the transmission gears. This also reduced the length of the drivetrain as used in the L-29 and shifted more

weight toward the front driving wheels. The L-29's drivetrain was mostly to the rear of the front wheel's centerline. With body, fuel, and passengers in place, the E 278's front-to-rear weight distribution would be closer to the ideal 50/50 percent.

Auburn engineer Harry Weaver worked with Detroit Gear on the design for the E 278's three-speed transmission. They experimented with different gear ratios, especially third gear. Not one of these units was ever built, and no drawings exist. The engineering reports, however, managed to survive. The reports state the E 278's engine was to displace 220 cubic inches and develop between 71 and 77 horsepower. Engineers expected the 2,900-pound car to have a top speed of approximately 81 miles per hour. Factory memos show that the AAC planned to power the E 278 with a Continental engine. This is rather surprising, since Lycoming—not Continental—was a subsidiary of the AAC. It's likely that if the E 278 had ever gone into production, a Lycoming engine would have replaced the specified Continental.

The Citroën that Auburn engineers inspected used unit-body construction, still a unique manufacturing technique in the 1930s. With unit-body construction, there is no separate frame. The body is welded into a sturdy one-piece box shape, with the frame—such as it is—an integral part of it. Attachment points for the engine, transmission, suspension, and other mechanical parts are integrated into the body-chassis. In the early 1930s, Budd and other U.S.-based companies incorporated unit-body construction into prototype cars. Auburn engineers were a bit more cautious with the E 278 and decided on a unitized body from the cowl back, but with a

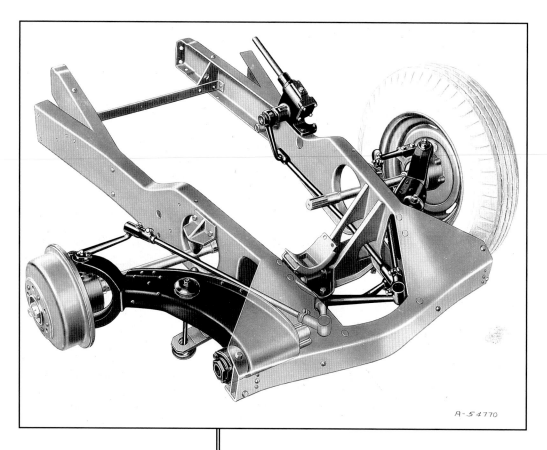

An airbrush rendering by AAC illustrator Paul Reuter-Lorenzen of the stub frame of the front-drive chassis, including suspension, steering, front motor mount, and drive axles. This layout was originally developed for Project E-278. *National Automotive History collection, Detroit Public Library*

A-54770

separate stub frame at the front, which would bolt onto the unitized body. This frame would carry the engine and drivetrain, radiator, steering linkage, front suspension and wheels, master cylinder and front brakes, and clutch and brake pedals. The AAC had been experimenting with independent suspension and had built at least one experimental Auburn with all four wheels independently suspended. Single trailing arms were used, a concept Snow borrowed from the French-built Harris-Léon-Laisne.

The engineers further refined their experimental Auburn design, using its ideas for the E 278. Bendix duo-servo brakes were specified, the latest in brake-system designs. The centerpoint geometry of the front end and steering linkage demonstrated Auburn's extensive experience with front-drive. So did the use of compact constant-velocity joints. Economic considerations had prevented the use of Rzeppa constant-velocity joints in the L-29. For the new design, the Gear Grinding Machine Company quickly made samples available for Auburn's consideration. So did the Bendix Aviation Corporation, licensee of a design patented by Carl W. Weiss. The engineers tested both joints and experimented with various seal arrangements to keep the joints from leaking.

In retrospect, it was fortunate that Auburn engineers had continued to experiment with front-drive systems. The AAC would once again offer a front-drive model, but this time the development project would be completed within an insanely short time frame. Without its earlier front-drive experience, the AAC might have never pulled it off.

Once it was decided to pursue a new front-drive model, it was inevitable the car would bear the Cord name, despite the automotive entrepreneur's lack of involvement with the project.

The "Baby" Duesenberg

The styling origins of the second front-drive automobile from the AAC can be traced to Duesenberg, Inc. As the Great Depression deepened, makers of expensive automobiles found it increasingly difficult to market their wares. Duesenberg, the most expensive make of all, was no exception. Other luxury carmakers were seeking salvation through the creation of less expensive models. Some used their own nameplate (such as Lincoln and Packard), others created a new nameplate (such as Cadillac's LaSalle) that the public would associate with its more expensive cousin. As president of Duesenberg, Harold Ames considered the same path. A smaller, lighter, less expensive Duesenberg might pull the company through hard times. An Auburn chassis modified by Duesenberg might be a starting point. It would need a powerful engine to uphold the Model J's reputation for performance, and a unique body might give it an edge in a crowded marketplace.

In September 1933, Ames met with Gordon Buehrig at Ames' home in Indianapolis. Buehrig was still serving his second stint at General Motors (he had left Duesenberg to again work for GM). Ames talked about his idea for a small, fast Duesenberg with what he called "a tricky body." Buehrig, in turn, talked of a design created for a contest among the stylists in GM's Art and Colour. Buehrig's group had submitted a rendering of a car with a sealed engine compartment, its radiators mounted in the space between the hood and fenders. The group's entry placed last with the judges, but first in an informal poll of peers. Buehrig showed Ames a sketch of the design. Buehrig's unusual concept fit Ames' plan for his "baby Duesenberg." At Ames' urging, Buehrig left GM again and returned to work at Duesenberg. J. Herbert Newport had taken Buehrig's position as chief designer at Duesenberg, but Buehrig was not usurping Newport, nor would Newport become involved in this secret project for a small Duesenberg.

Buehrig's work space was separated from the styling studio at Duesenberg. His only contact, other than Ames, was Phil Derham of the well-known Pennsylvania coachbuilding family who undertook the body engineering for Buehrig's proposal. By November, Buehrig had developed his concept into sketches for a workable body design. Ames approved. Buehrig turned the sketches into a 1/8 scale drawing, then built a clay model to the same scale. Derham prepared dimensional drawings for the coachwork builder.

With chassis by Auburn and his new "tricky body" by Buehrig, Ames now needed an engine to power the new car. He turned to Lycoming's chief engineer, Forrest S. "Bill" Baster, whose proposal for Auburn suggested a 90-degree V-8 to be cast in a single block. Lycoming designated the new engine the "FA" series. Lycoming's parts list for the V-8 is dated November 27, 1933, which coincides nicely with Ames' approval of the Buehrig sketches. The V-8 was an enormous undertaking for Lycoming. Ford had released its V-8 only two years earlier, and it planned to amortize the expensive tooling over millions of cylinder blocks. Lycoming was not likely to enjoy such an advantage in delivering what Ames needed.

The Lycoming V-8's counterbalanced crankshaft turned in three large main bearings. Cylinder heads and pistons were cast aluminum. A bore and stroke of 3.375x3.75 inches created a displacement of 269.4 cubic inches. Lycoming was still producing its first V-type engine, Auburn's BB series V-12, and many of the new V-8's design details were based on the V-12. Like the V-12, the new V-8 used a single camshaft mounted high in the block. Cam lobes met a solid rocker midway along its length, with valves actuated at the rocker's top end. This permitted the valves to lie nearly horizontal. As on the V-12, top-mounted exhaust ports allowed gases to exit without passing through the block, putting less strain on the engine's cooling capacity. The full-flow oil filtration system on the FA was also similar to that of the V-12. Borrowed, too, were the side access covers on the block and the use of a single thermostat. New were the aluminum cylinder heads, incorporating features patented by the vendor, Permold Manufacturing Company of Cleveland. Lycoming had no facilities for casting aluminum, so such fabrication was contracted to outside suppliers.

Meanwhile in Indianapolis, Derham placed an order for the new body with the A. H. Walker firm. The job, labeled "Auburn Stream-Lined Body," was ordered on January 19, 1934. An Auburn eight-cylinder chassis was ordered on February 5, 1934, and delivered to the Duesenberg factory in Indianapolis. Three weeks earlier, Ames had left Indianapolis to serve as executive vice president at Auburn. One of his immediate duties was

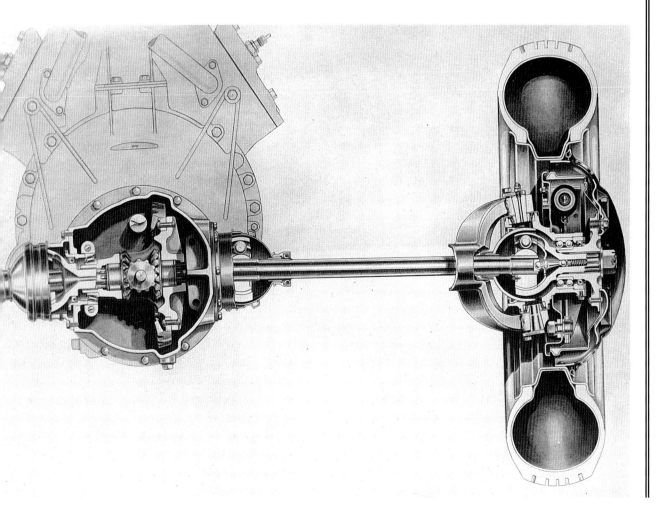

Lorenzen's illustration of the front-drive system. Lorenzen worked from photographs; when he executed these drawings and others, only the early prototype chassis—the Auburn-Cord E-294 hybrid and the E-306s—were available to be dismantled and photographed. The early developmental stage of some of the details shown in the various renderings—very small brake drums, pressed-in lower kingpins, lack of transmission lube pump, universal joints, and seals design—support this idea. *National Automotive History collection, Detroit Public Library*

These sketches have been oft identified as those that Gordon Buehrig showed to Harold Ames, later becoming the basis for the "baby Duesenberg." The identification is not correct, and the dates are misleading. Buehrig told the author that he drew these sketches in the 1950s, as reminiscences of the state of development of the design in 1933. He added the 1933 date only to commemorate the day when Harold Ames approved the actual drawings for the baby Duesenberg. Note the different stage of development of the front fenders in the two views. *Gordon M. Buehrig*

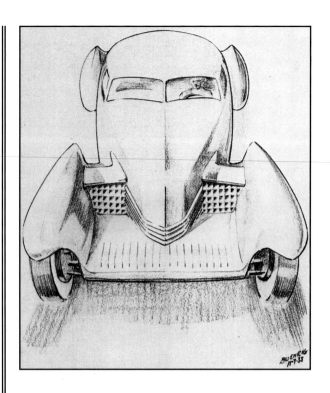

RIGHT
Lycoming's production FB engine used roller-equipped rocker arms to operate nearly horizontal valves.

installing the twin outboard radiators. The U.S. Patent Office later granted Augie a patent on the system. The completed prototype was carefully photographed, then sealed behind locked doors. Harold Ames now faced a dilemma. His brainchild, the baby Duesenberg, was now a three-dimensional reality. This prototype of an exciting new model might have been in a position to salvage the fortunes of Duesenberg, Inc. Still president of Duesenberg, Ames had to consider this. Yet, as executive vice president of the AAC, he was charged with saving that company, too. Ames knew that even Auburn's redesigned model line, with superchargers and speedsters, would not be enough to stave off disaster. This new prototype could equally improve the AAC's fortunes. Ames was certainly aware of the E 278 project, now a chassis looking for a body. Ames made the connection. The dramatic Duesenberg prototype would be turned over to the engineers and stylists at Auburn. They would adapt its modernistic design to Auburn's new front-drive chassis.

Buehrig and Denny Duesenberg, Fred's son, drove the erstwhile baby Duesenberg to Auburn late on a Saturday night in June 1934. The plan was to arrive under the cover of darkness. The outboard radiators, however, turned out to be less than effective, forcing the two to stop every 20 miles to allow the prototype car to cool down. Despite their stealthy plan, the sun was coming up by the time they reached Auburn and parked the car safely inside the factory garage.

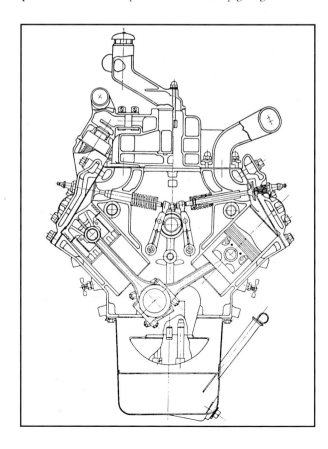

to facelift the 1934 Auburn and to introduce it as a 1935 model by the summer of 1934. Ames called for Buehrig to come to Auburn. Back in Indianapolis, Walker delivered the "Auburn Stream-Lined Body" to Duesenberg. Ames probably exhorted the coachbuilder to deliver the body as quickly as possible. Walker did just that and racked up enormous overtime charges. The body arrived in Indianapolis on April 3, 1934, only 74 days after the order had been placed. At $12,035, the bill was several times what Walker charged Duesenberg for custom Model J bodies.

In the Duesenberg factory, Augie Duesenberg started to work in secret on the rear-drive baby Duesenberg,

Lycoming was notified of the change in plans, as modifications would be needed to adapt the FA engine to power a front-drive car. The revised V-8 would be known as the FB series. The FB V-8 required pulleys at both ends of the camshaft; one drove the generator, the other end powered the water pump and fan. Lycoming engineers made other changes after testing of the prototype FA. For instance, the solid rocker was replaced by a roller when cam lobes were found to be scuffed. Lycoming experienced some problems with the FA and FB V-8s from the start. The sample engines experienced vapor lock while being tested on the dynamometer. August W. "Rick" Rickenbach, in charge of Lycoming's Experimental Department, redesigned the FA's exhaust-heated intake manifold, substituting heated water flowing through an aluminum manifold. Since the thermostats would control water flow, Rickenbach moved the water outlets (with a thermostat in each) to the center of each head to simplify the plumbing required. That offered the additional advantage of an interchangeable cylinder head, usable on either bank. The FB engine was fully pressure lubricated. Also among modern features of

the new V-8 was a rudimentary, valveless positive crankcase ventilation system. Full-flow oil filtration was a casualty of the switch to front-drive. With the block turned end-for-end, the oil filter would have interfered with the steering box and steering column. Lycoming proposed bypass oil filtration as a substitute. Cost considerations probably influenced the final decision to offer no oil filtration at all.

Auburn and Lycoming considered three different sizes of FB engines. All had the identical 3.75-inch stroke, like the FA's. The bore, however, varied, giving displacements of 249, 258.5, and 288.6 cubic inches. Lycoming horsepower and torque curves, dated May 1934, also show theoretical outputs from centrifugal-supercharged versions of each engine. The successful adaptation of the Schwitzer-Cummins supercharger to the straight-eight engine used by Auburn convinced Lycoming engineers to consider superchargers for all its new engines. From the beginning, the FB engine offered the possibility of supercharging. The camshaft came with a shoulder on which a bevel drive gear could be installed, and mounting bosses were cast in place in the block.

There's much to see in Auburn's Art and Body Drafting Department in early 1935. From the left, in the background: Behind cigar-smoking Paul Reuter-Lorenzen is a drawing of a "stretch" Auburn sedan. Richard Robinson and Gordon Buehrig work on a model of the Gentlemen's Speedster, a Harold Ames idea intended to use up leftover Auburn V-12s; a full-scale airbrush rendering of an experimental front-drive unit is on the wall behind Robinson. Vince Gardner is seated at the desk in the corner. Dale Cosper sculpts a convertible coupe body. A model of the convertible phaeton stands in the center of the room, showing rear windows shaped like those of the sedans. The front end of the clay model at right was later executed on race driver Ab Jenkins' personal Cord.

125

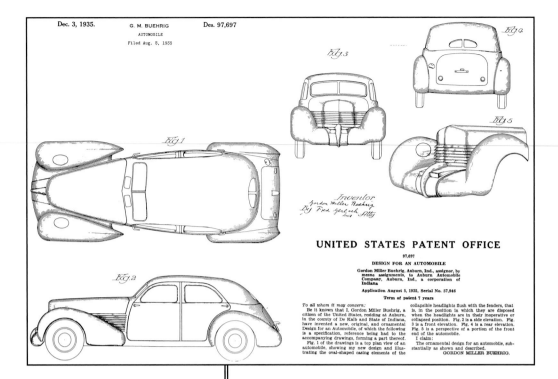

Fig.3

Fig.4

Fig.1

Fig.5

Fig.2

Inventor
Gordon Miller Buehrig
By Fred Gerlach
his Atty

UNITED STATES PATENT OFFICE

97,697

DESIGN FOR AN AUTOMOBILE

Gordon Miller Buehrig, Auburn, Ind., assignor, by
mesne assignments, to Auburn Automobile
Company, Auburn, Ind., a corporation of
Indiana

Application August 5, 1935, Serial No. 57,946

Term of patent 7 years

To all whom it may concern:

Be it known that I, Gordon Miller Buehrig, a
citizen of the United States, residing at Auburn,
in the county of De Kalb and State of Indiana,
have invented a new, original, and ornamental
Design for an Automobile, of which the following
is a specification, reference being had to the
accompanying drawings, forming a part thereof.

Fig. 1 of the drawings is a top plan view of an
automobile, showing my new design and illustrating the oval-shaped casing elements of the
collapsible headlights flush with the fenders, that
is, in the position in which they are disposed
when the headlights are in their inoperative or
collapsed position. Fig. 2 is a side elevation. Fig.
3 is a front elevation. Fig. 4 is a rear elevation.
Fig. 5 is a perspective of a portion of the front
end of the automobile.

I claim:

The ornamental design for an automobile, substantially as shown and described.

GORDON MILLER BUEHRIG.

The design patent for the Cord 810 body, in Gordon Buehrig's name. Drawings were done by an unknown draftsman from photographs of E 306 No. 2. The rear-view photo he was given was printed backward, so he placed the gas hatch on the wrong side. *Josh B. Malks collection*

OPPOSITE
The die model for the 810 sedan being crafted in the spring of 1934. Don Miller of Auburn, a high school senior who was hired to sweep up the showroom on Saturdays, remembers seeing the completed die model in the Experimental Wood and Metal Shop in the summer of 1934.

Buehrig was now formally in charge of Auburn's Body and Art Drafting Department. In July 1934, he was given the responsibility of creating a body for the front-drive car and authorized to hire the required personnel. Already on his staff were Dick Robinson, with whom he had worked on the Auburn redesign, and Paul Peter Reuter-Lorenzen, an illustrator immensely talented with the airbrush. Buehrig added others, including Dale Cosper, a recent graduate of Tri-State College in nearby Angola, Indiana. Cosper's degree was in chemical engineering, but he was a skilled modeler in clay and other media. To create three-dimensional automobile body styles, Buehrig trusted three-dimensional sculptures more than he did drawings and engineering layouts. He wanted one more modeler, and luck provided Vincent Edward Gardner who had graduated from high school in Duluth, Minnesota, in June 1934. Gardner was in Auburn for the summer, visiting an uncle. He showed a sample of his work to Buehrig and was promptly hired as the second model builder.

The body for the new front-drive car was to be based on the concept Buehrig developed for Ames at Duesenberg. It was not simply a revision of the baby Duesenberg, now carefully locked away on another level of the building. Buehrig said later that his team never referred to the earlier prototype. They simply began with the same germ of an idea that had resulted in the baby Duesenberg and developed it in a different direction. The E 278's chassis concept, a unitized body mated to a stub frame carrying most of the mechanical components up front, was an ideal

package for body designers to work with. Front drive meant that no provision would have to be made for a driveshaft, so the car had a lower stance. Unitized construction permitted frame rails to be built into the perimeter of the body. The result was a step-down design, much trumpeted by Hudson's marketers 14 years later, but a true first for Auburn. The young men of Auburn's design studios worked at the project well into each night during the summer of 1934. They listened to the radio, consumed soft drinks, and felt fortunate for the opportunity to do what they loved most, and to even be paid for it. By then, the front-drive chassis had evolved from project E 278 to E 286. The engineers informed the stylists that while all other parameters would remain unchanged, the wheelbase had increased 3 inches to 123 inches. Buehrig later said that while he worked for Auburn he never attended a committee meeting. This contributed to minimal interdepartmental communication. Even at an automaker as small as the AAC, with all the design work taking place in one building, there were many instances where one department didn't know what another was doing.

Working within the limitations of the mechanical components, Buehrig now drew the basic design lines that would guide the modelers in the creation of a quarter-scale clay model. Buehrig, Cosper, and Gardner were all modelers. To meet their specialized needs, Cosper and Gardner designed a bridge that traveled on tracks over the clay model. Holes in the top and side faces of the bridge allowed the tips of dowels to locate any point in space. That meant that after one side of a model was complete, the bridge could be used to make the other side identical. Since this principle holds true whether the model is to scale or full size, the bridge over a small-scale model could be used to translate the same point to a full-scale clay model standing under its own larger bridge. In the decades to come, every major automobile styling studio used this styling-bridge concept.

Gardner built a quarter-scale wood armature to which the clay would be applied. Buehrig now sculpted on one side of the armature the body design of what was to become the next front-drive model from Auburn. He was guided by his drawing, but even more by what *felt* right. Using the bridge, Cosper and Gardner repeated the shape in clay on the other side. The basic model now stood on the brink of greatness.

Though other studios would have invested their efforts in the construction of a full-size clay model, Buehrig used his resources differently. He set his design team to studying the quarter-scale model from all sides. Because of its small size, the team could examine it from fresh angles. Sculptors and artists all, they brought a variety of viewpoints to the task. Gardner, a firebrand even at the age of 19, no doubt enthusiastically offered suggestions. So

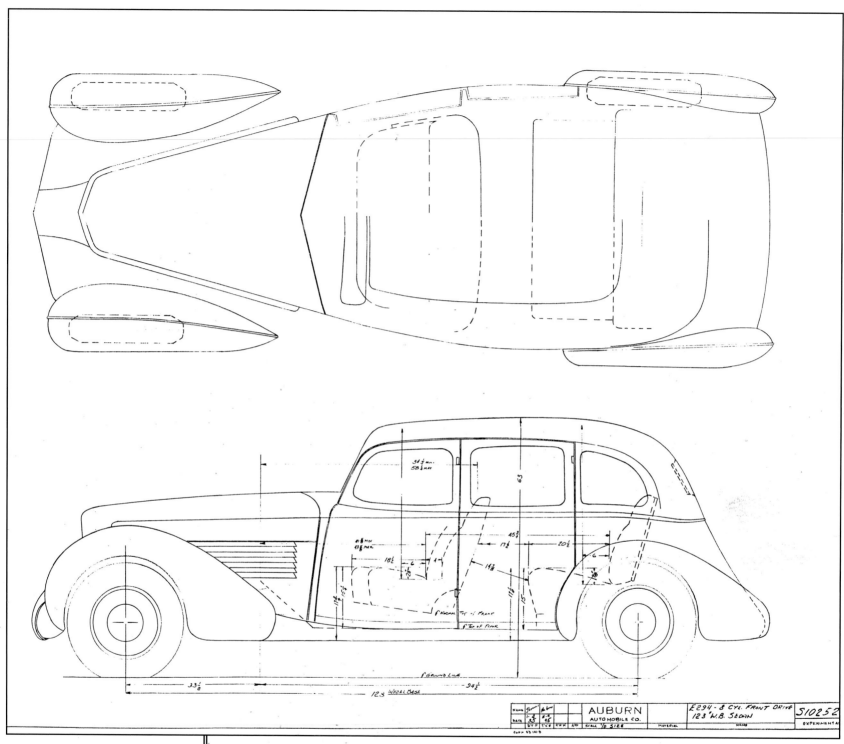

Stanley Thomas drew this layout for the hybrid E-294 on January 2, 1935, probably at Snow's instruction. Buehrig had not yet returned from his honeymoon. *Herbert C. Snow collection, Auburn Cord Duesenberg Club/redrawn by Robert Fabris*

did the others. Buehrig accepted some ideas and rejected others. When it was done, the completed clay model was painted with red lacquer.

Buehrig and his team now turned their attention to details, including the concept of disappearing headlights as found on the baby Duesenberg. It was Ames who suggested the original, using as inspiration the landing lights system used by several light-

plane makers, including the Cord Corporation's own Stinson. The baby Duesenberg prototype had hidden headlights located on the inboard surfaces of the fenders. It was felt that this design would make the fenders easier to fabricate. When craftsmen at Central demonstrated that the headlights could be located on the front of the fenders, this preferable location was adopted. Buehrig adapted the upholstery patterns from some of his own earlier work at Duesenberg. Stock instruments were purchased from Stewart-Warner and King-Seeley. Buehrig designed new matching faces, with some of the graphics silk-screened on the glass. Instruments were set in a glittering machine-turned dash panel. When combined with Magnavox's new edge-lighting concept, the green glow of the dashboard was positively enchanting.

The new car's striking beauty was in its shape, not its chrome decoration. The design team had succeeded in turning practical engineering into fine art. Doors hinged at the center pillar, offering an opportunity to save on scarce tooling dollars. The left front and right rear door were stamped from the same dies; ditto for the right front and left rear doors. An inexpensive trim die created the cutout in the rear doors to clear the rear fender.

Steadily, the front-drive car moved toward production. Draftsman Bart Cotter worked on the engineering drawings for the new body design. The E 286 was dubbed an "eight-cylinder special front drive." Stanley Menton, production body engineer at Central, prepared tooling estimates for the new front-drive car in November 1934. Although it had already been superseded by the E 286, the tooling estimate was based on the dimensions of the E 278! No full-size version of the E 278 or E 286 was ever built. Costs were worked out for six-cylinder and V-8 versions. Unit costs for the six-cylinder chassis were estimated at

$322.90, the eight-cylinder version at $407.29. Adding in the identical unitized body for both ($271.00), direct charged labor ($41.00) and freight costs brought the total to $656.04 for the six and $774.39 for the eight. By December 1934, engineers were able to offer management several options for obtaining tooling for this new car, including the alternative of farming out all prototype work to other companies.

In late November, Cord Corporation President Manning asked Buehrig to bring the red quarter-scale clay model to Chicago in preparation for the corporation's next board meeting. Manning and Cord Corporation and AAC Vice President W. Hubert Beal met with Buehrig and reviewed the model. If they had an opinion, they didn't share it with Buehrig. The clay model was not shown to the board at its next meeting.

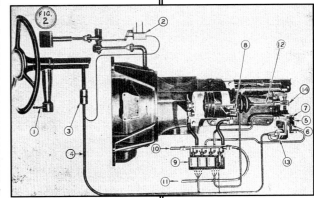

The project was on a roll during the late months of 1934. The final design for the all-new front-drive car was approved by AAC management. Numbered E 294, it differed from the E 286 only in a lengthening of the wheelbase to 125 inches. Full-size body drafts had been prepared for the sedan body, and wooden die models

There are nearly 100 feet of wire, 10 feet of vacuum tubing and hoses, and a multitude of switches and solenoids in the Cord's pre-selective gearshift. This phantom view provided by manufacturer Bragg-Kleisrath shows the location of all the components.

An early FB engine and drive unit, as used in the E-294 hybrid and the first E-306 prototypes. Production engines had different details. Fan, oil pan, fuel pump, air cleaner, and regulator were changed, as were exhaust manifold and cylinder head details. The breather seen here on the timing chain cover was eliminated. Rzeppa inner universal joints are pictured. When this drawing was done, the transmission oil pump had not yet been specified.

This retouched photo of the E 306 No. 2 was used in dealer ads well into 1936. The retoucher has removed the grooves in the front bumper and added a transmission emblem. Perhaps Auburn thought that no one would notice the inboard placement of the headlights!

were well along in construction. Auburn's Body and Art Drafting Department worked on a quarter-scale clay model of a convertible quarter-window Victoria. The next big auto shows were scheduled for January 1936, more than a year away. Auburn would be ready.

In late December 1934, the Cord Corporation's board met in Chicago. It's likely the important items on the agenda related to the Cord Corporation's aviation ventures and new acquisitions. Auburn was not a priority. Indeed, it had become something of an albatross. In later years, Cord's second wife, Virginia Cord, said that her husband mentioned to her in 1931 that he did not believe that the AAC could long survive on its automobile sales alone.

RIGHT
Two of the photographs of the red clay model that Buehrig and Cosper took on July 7, 1934. This is their original size. Directors of the Cord Corporation board passed these little snapshots around at their meeting on July 8, then made the momentous decision to advance Auburn the cash needed to purchase tooling for the new body. *Sally Cosper*

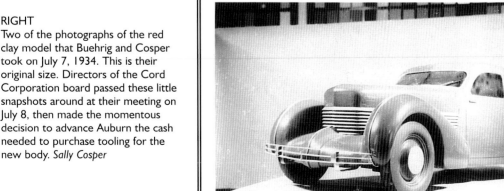

Cord made this pessimistic, though realistic, statement during Auburn's best sales year ever. Now the company was out of cash; net losses for 1934 alone were $3.9 million. The Cord Corporation board decided not to infuse the additional funds to create the tooling for an all-new unit body, and the board informed the AAC management as much. Still, the idea of a front-drive model for 1936 wasn't entirely out of the question. The board, however, was concerned about the AAC's rising deficits and didn't see any way clear to authorize expenditures for a model that had to be built from the ground up. However, if a new model could be introduced using mostly existing tooling, that would be another matter.

Auburn had now been working with front-drive cars since 1927. Snow desperately wanted to build another one and proposed a design compromise. The E 294 stub chassis could be mated to an Auburn frame and body. The board had ruled out funding tooling for the new unit body, but perhaps the Buehrig design's front-end sheet metal could be adapted. Tooling costs would then drop, and the board's demands for economy would be met. Work moved ahead on two fronts. The Auburn-bodied hybrid prototype was built in the experimental shop (Buehrig and team, under protest, produced a new quarter-scale model of the bastard design). Simultaneously, work on the styling and engineering of a new purebred design based entirely on the red quarter-scale clay model continued. To confuse future historians, both the hybrid and the new designs were referred to as E 294.

Acceleration and top speed calculations for E 294 were based on the midsize FB V-8 and a three-speed transmission. Performance was compared with that of a stock Auburn 851 sedan equipped with a supercharger and a Dual-Ratio rear axle. Results did not favor the new design. The stock Auburn easily out-accelerated the front-drive prototype and even reached a higher top speed. It's likely that Weaver was the one who worked with Detroit Gear to add a fourth speed to the transmission. It was also clear that the new car had to be powered by the largest of Lycoming's V-8 options. Auburn engineers explored alternate ideas for gearshift linkages. A choice had to be made between a mechanical system of rods and cranks or an electro-vacuum fingertip gearshift marketed by the Bragg-Kliesrath Division of Bendix Aviation Corporation. Hudson and Terraplane had offered the device on their 1935 models, calling it the "Electric Hand." Auburn engineers were concerned about the reliability of the Bendix system; but the unit was certainly easier to fit to the forward-mounted front-drive unit, and Bendix stood ready to adapt it to the new car and to deliver the finished product. The pressures of time won.

The design studio could now render the transmission cover. Designers built a wood mock-up of the right side of the Bendix unit, where mechanical parts pro-

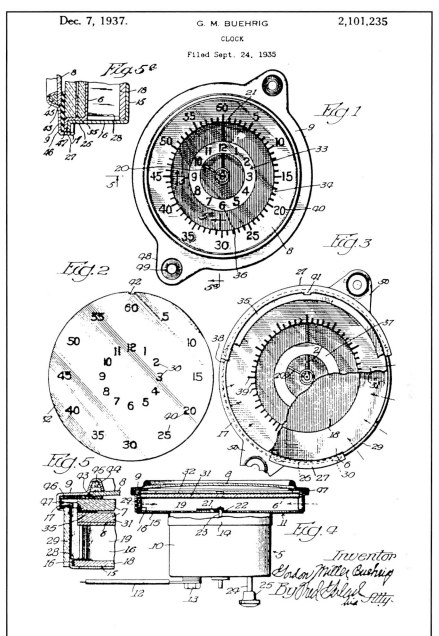

truded farthest. They laid slabs of hot clay over the wood and smoothed off the lines, then transferred this design to the other side to make it symmetrical. Other changes from the clay model to the prototype's design related to the state of manufacturing in 1935. The clay model's one-piece rear window would have required curved glass, something not readily available at the time. Instead, two small flat panes were used in the final design. Buehrig remembered the salesman who had left a sample bumper with Augie Duesenberg, which was installed on the baby Duesenberg prototype. The salesman's firm, the Buckeye Manufacturing Company of Springfield, Ohio, would later supply the bumpers for the production cars.

Auburn considered no detail too small for a patent application. Buehrig was also granted a design patent for the Cord clock face. This utility patent was far more important; it covered the multilayer glass dial also used on the Cord's other instruments.

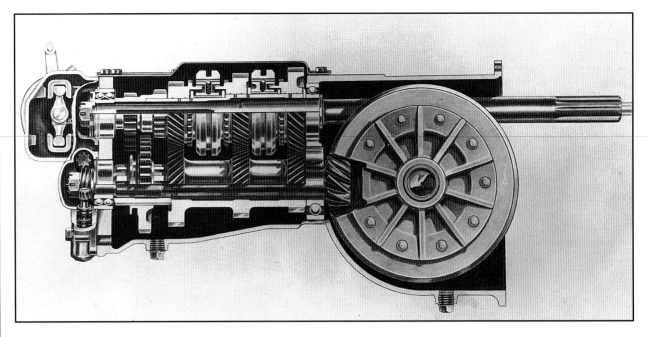

Until a decision was made about moving forward with one design or the other, the designers had time on their hands. So they worked on other projects, including the "Gentleman's Speedster." A body was designed for a two-passenger prototype, an Ames idea which would allow the company to liquidate leftover V-12 engines and possibly create another inexpensive Duesenberg alternative. The designers also drew plans for a front-drive model like the purebred E 294, but aimed at a wealthier clientele. The wheelbase was longer for more legroom, and a higher roofline provided more headroom.

The insularity at the AAC in those early months of 1935 was such that the designers were probably unaware that the other engineering workrooms at the company were humming with activity. Auburn engineers were submitting requests for proposals for tooling and parts from suppliers. Engineers moved forward with decisions as suppliers submitted their quotes. The initial orders were likely for parts sufficient to complete five sample cars. The first car to be completed, the hybrid E 294, used many of these parts. Performance tests began at the end of March. The hybrid E 294 was powered by the first Lycoming 288.6-cubic-inch V-8 delivered to Auburn, namely, engine FB 103 with Rickenbach's water-heated intake manifold. The hybrid E 294's four-speed transmission was the first of five experimental transaxles hastily assembled by Columbia Axle. The independent rear suspension of the E 278 and E 286 was replaced by a light tubular axle carried on conventional semi-elliptic springs.

Factory records show a major increase in hours in all departments in April 1935. Within a month nearly everyone in the engineering departments was on overtime. The project to which all efforts were focused was E 306: the construction of five prototype sedans. Parts now arrived at Auburn from vendors all over the Midwest. In the Experimental Wood and Metal Shop, metalworkers created the steel panels for five sedans. Columbia Axle completed five experimental transaxles, with Detroit Gear making the gears and shafts. At Auburn, these units were mated to the Lycoming engines and installed in the prototypes. While the first transmission had been installed in the hybrid E 294, it's likely engineers removed it and used it in one of the five prototypes. If the design team was unaware of any further activity on the front-drive project earlier, they were well aware of it now. Buehrig's men were working nine-hour days, six days a week. Their new tasks included final design and body engineering for two open-body models, a two-passenger convertible coupe with rumble seat, and a four-passenger convertible Victoria, later named "convertible phaeton sedan" by the sales department.

Buehrig realized that the only way the front-drive car would reach production was if initial outlays, including tooling costs, could be kept to a minimum. He chose a simple existing steering wheel pattern from which Sheller Manufacturing Company could cast wheels in Eastman Kodak's new Tenite plastic. The Auburn design team dressed it up with a cast bronze center, replaced with a button of Tenite in production cars. At the time, horn buttons in the center of the steering wheel were traditional. Buehrig, however, designed a chrome ring that could be operated from any position on the wheel without the driver removing his or her hands from the wheel. Tooling costs were avoided on the interior hardware, too. Obsolete window cranks were dressed up with bold Tenite knobs.

The already frantic pace now picked up even more. Auburn employees worked over 12,000 hours on the front-drive project in just the month of June 1935. By month's end, at least two of the five prototype E 306 sedans were completed, the other three nearly so. Engineers labeled the five prototypes numbers two through six (the hybrid E 294 was number one). The activity described above for the months of January through June 1935 contradicts the accepted version of what transpired during those months. According to lore, the AAC was supposed to have been all but idle for six months, rather than building prototypes and paying overtime. That "six-month delay" has even been blamed for the eventual failure of the new front-drive model as a marketable product. Surviving AAC memos indicate otherwise. In early January, as we've seen, the Cord Corporation's board ordered the cessation of development of the front-drive car as it was based on an all-new platform. Faulkner, with Ames as a reluctant co-conspirator, appears to have sought alternatives while not giving up the dream. Their hope, no doubt, was that in the year remaining until the next auto show season, the board could be induced to change its mind. Months of development lay ahead. Drawings and specifications had to be created and vendors approached for bids. All this was done by March 1935. Now prototypes had to be constructed and a plan developed to show the corporate board that funds would be available to tool up for actual production. No urgency was felt, since there were still nine months until the 1936 shows. Here, fate stepped in, in the form of the federal government.

Automobile sales, then as now, were a major engine of commerce. The national auto shows took place in all major cities in January, which resulted in large sales and increased employment in all automotive-related enterprises. Automotive sales, being very seasonal, tended to thin out by year's end, as did employment. Those who never lived through the Great Depression cannot remember how the federal government and corporations alike grasped at any straw that might improve the economy. One such straw was the idea that moving the national auto shows to the previous November would result in an earlier bulge in the economic statistics. President Franklin D. Roosevelt made such a request of the Automobile Manufacturers Association. In March 1935, the AMA agreed to this plan. Auburn suddenly had only seven months until the shows. If a new model wasn't at the shows, it might as well not exist. And prototypes could not be exhibited; the AMA required that 100 examples of a new model exist before qualifying as a production car. That was the bad news. The good news came from Connersville and from one of Auburn's production executives there, E. Roy Weisheit. As automotive production slowed at Central, Weisheit, as discussed in the previous chapter, developed a line of steel kitchen cabinets that could be manufactured on Auburn's stamping presses and welding fixtures. Styled by Paul Peter Reuter-Lorenzen, the stylish cabinets sold well and provided the AAC with the necessary cash to place an all-new front-drive model in production. Any further consideration of a hybrid was eliminated.

As president of the AAC, Faulkner had the authority to authorize design work and the construction of prototypes. Confident that the funds would be available, Faulkner did just that, and construction of the prototypes started in April 1935. Despite the antagonism between Faulkner and Ames, the potential of the Buehrig-styled front-drive model was one idea on which both could agree.

Weisheit's kitchen cabinets would reduce the AAC's immediate cash problem. But the board wouldn't meet again until July, and by that time it would be too late. Faulkner or Ames reached Cord in California, informing him of the cabinet income and plans for the front-drive model. Faulkner and Ames wanted to proceed with the prototypes without hesitation and to be ready to present the project to the board in July. Cord knew that Auburn needed something to keep it solvent. Perhaps that something was another front-drive Cord. Of course, Cord likely cautioned that production would require approval from the board, but there's no doubt that his wanting it to happen made such an approval a formality. (There is, however, a flip side to the story, which is the Securities and Exchange Commission's take on these events. Basically, the SEC accused Cord of seeing the new front-drive model as a means to manipulate Auburn's lagging stock prices.)

So Auburn engineers proceeded full speed with the construction of the prototypes. The board approved the project at its July 8 meeting in Chicago. The presentation to the board, however, didn't include the completed E 306 prototypes; officially, they were not supposed to exist. The day before the board meeting, Faulkner wanted some visual aids to help present the case for the all-new front-drive project. Faulkner recalled the red quarter-scale clay model. He asked Buehrig to have photos taken of the model to show at the meeting. Buehrig asked Cosper, an amateur photographer, to help. Cosper and Buehrig photographed the model, then developed the film and made prints in the basement darkroom at the home of Cosper's parents. The prints, barely dry, were rushed to the railroad station at Garrett and sent on their way to Chicago. Faulkner showed the board members a half-dozen poorly exposed snapshots. The board's approval was clearly *pro forma*. Cord had no doubt made his wishes known.

Three weeks later, E 306 No. 2 left its Auburn garage in the early hours of a Saturday morning with three engineers on board. They and the prototype were on their way to Los Angeles to a rendezvous with Cord and with automotive history.

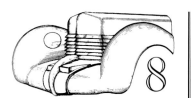

Kinetic Sculpture: The Cord 810 and 812

1935-1937

Herb Snow assigned George Kublin to head the three-man team driving the Cord prototype to California. For purposes of industrial security, the trip was scheduled for a weekend, when there might be fewer cars on the road. At 2:30 in the morning of Saturday, July 27, 1935, three weeks after the meeting of the corporate board, the odyssey of E 306 No. 2 began. There was no Cord emblem on the transmission cover of the prototype, nor even a space for one. The public, however, wasn't fooled. In a telegram to Faulkner from Evanston, Wyoming, Kublin wired: "EVERY EFFORT TO AVOID PUBLIC EYE IS FUTILE. THEY TRAIL US UP SIDE STREETS, COUNTRY WAYSIDE FILLING STATIONS AND LITERALLY STAMPEDE THE CAR. THEY GAZE IN WONDERMENT AT THIS SLEEK LOW CREATION. WE TELLEM ITS A SPECIAL, A FOREIGN MAKE, A BULGAT, A NAZI, A WHOSAT ETC FOR A PROMINENT HOLLYWOOD STAR ETC AND LOTS OF OTHER ANSWERS BUT IN SPITE OF IT DOZENS OF PEOPLE ALL WALKS OF LIFE, DOCTORS, FARMERS, MOUNTAINEERS, BUSINESS MEN ASSOCIATE THE CAR WITH CORD AND SOME WITH AUBURN." So indelible were the marques of Auburn and Cord etched in the public's collective mind as leaders in automotive design that even a prototype—so totally different from anything that preceded it—couldn't dissuade onlookers from associating it with the AAC.

The engineers followed U.S. Route 30 for most of the trip. The glitches typical of an untested experimental car appeared, as expected. Brakes proved too small. The transmission constantly jumped out of gear and the electric shift failed occasionally. The Bendix universal joints became noisy, and vapor lock was troublesome. The engine's high-compression ratio caused knocking even after the engineers started to pump high-octane Ethyl into it. Still, the prototype made fine time, completing the 2,300-mile trip on the mediocre roads of the day in only three and one-half days.

135

THE individuality of the New Cord is especially evident in the distinctive little niceties of interior finish; in the artistic use of garnish moldings and chromium bead; the D-shaped windows; the lacquered interior fittings; the engine-turned finish instrument panel with its unusually complete array of controls and dials. Broadcloth upholstering is in colors contrasting with body finish.

The Westchester Sedan

THE word comfort takes on an entirely new meaning when you ride in the New Cord. Both front and rear seat passengers ride in the same sumptuous comfort. Front Drive construction permits all seats to be between the axles and on the same level. You will be constantly amazed that a car so low in design should be so spacious — and provide so much head and leg room.

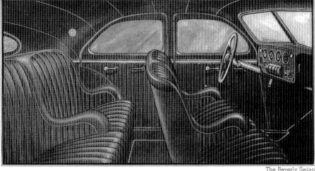

The Beverly Sedan

The style of the renderings in the color catalog distributed at the 1936 model shows is not that of Paul Reuter-Lorenzen. The authors believe them to be the work of J. Herbert Newport, on loan from his position as chief designer for Duesenberg. These illustrations of sedan interiors were clearly a rush job. In the upper drawing, several instruments are missing from the dash. They've been added to the lower drawing, in incorrect positions! *Josh B. Malks collection*

Behind the banjo steering wheel of E 306 No. 3, model Marjorie Stanley demonstrates the Bendix fingertip gear selector to newspaper photographers at the press preview for the Chicago auto show. The dashboard of these prototypes had no high-beam indicator; the rectangular water temperature gauge at the left side was replaced by a round one in production cars. The handle at lower right opens both inboard headlights together.

Ames was waiting when the team arrived. Some spare parts must have been flown to Los Angeles in advance; Auburn's L.A. dealership replaced one outer joint. New horns were installed, too. Personnel at the local Wagner brake service rebuilt the brakes; they also advised the engineering team that the brake hoses used on the prototype had been obsolete for two years. An electric fuel pump was installed to try to reduce the vapor lock.

Cord took his namesake out for a shakedown on L.A.-area roads. He was pleased with the new car, but made some suggestions to which the engineers responded with on-the-spot modifications. Six days later, after being extensively photographed for publicity use, E 306 No. 2 headed east again. More teething problems made themselves known on the way home. The rear end bottomed out on rough roads. Cord wanted a reduced stance, so lowering blocks had been installed. The engine ran warmer due to the small fan; this unit had been installed after Cord complained of the original and larger fan's noise level. The actuating cables for the troublesome inboard headlights broke. The engineers had to block the lids open at night. The *coup de grace* came only one day from home. In Dixon, Illinois, on August 9, the transmission jammed. Another of the five existing transmissions was brought from Auburn. E 306 No. 2 arrived back in Auburn at midnight on Friday, August 11.

Memos preserved by Herb Snow describe dozens of suggestions for necessary changes, large and small. The windshield and rear windows needed to be enlarged; visors had to be smaller. The brakes were too small, and so was the battery. Exhaust pipe

hangers had to be redesigned. The ignition key was inconveniently located. Several rattle points needed attention. And, of course, the transmission jumped out of gear and the engine vapor locked. Then there were those retractable headlights, which had been a problem since the hybrid E 294. A new design for a headlight mounted in the front of the fenders was prepared. E 306 No. 4 through 6 used this design, as did the production cars. According to Cosper, after trying a dozen alternatives a reliable manual crank-and-cable arrangement was chosen.

While E 306 No. 2 had been traveling between California and Indiana, those back at the AAC remained busy. Quotes had been received in the spring for most of the new model's tooling. Orders were placed right after the Cord Corporation board approved the all-new front-drive car for production. By now, the new front-drive model had been named "Cord" and tagged with the model number "810." This label was used within the factory and on the cover of the first owner's manual. Auburn also finalized the 810 model offerings and prices. The Westchester sedan represented the entry-level 810 ($1,995). The Beverly sedan was the plusher closed-body model ($2,095). Surprisingly, the convertible coupe ($2,145) and convertible phaeton ($2,195) sold for little more than the sedans.

Only 116 days remained until the New York and Los Angeles auto shows both opened on November 2. Most vendors would be able to deliver parts and assemblies before the shows. Lycoming would be ready to deliver new engines within 60 days. But the new transmissions were still in an early developmental stage. And tooling for major body panels would not be delivered until December, so the show models would have to have their bodies made and assembled by hand. Most body panels for the show cars were shaped on power hammers in Auburn. Panels and parts for the sedans were shipped to Connersville, where they were welded into complete bodies. There was enough variation between the body parts that each one fit only the car it had been

made for. Phaeton and convertible coupe body shells were completely assembled in Auburn and shipped to Central as they were completed. Final assembly, metal finishing, painting, and upholstering of all the show cars were done in Connersville. Some smaller body parts were fabricated in Connersville as well. So were all the wood parts. For other pieces, it was found that making permanent tooling in Connersville would take only a little longer than making the parts by hand, so the tooling was created first. Except for the engine, Columbia Axle assembled most of the mechanical parts for the show cars. To meet the show deadlines, Columbia fabricated some parts from scratch.

In most of the United States and around the world, men and women sought honest work in vain. In the cities of Auburn and Connersville, however, 60- to 70-hour work weeks were common for many AAC employees. Their pockets may have been full, but the workers were bone weary. In later years, AAC employee Don Merchanthouse remembered the foreman in charge of the power hammers, Ed Jaquet. Upon spotting a worker drowsing over a hammer, Jaquet would spit a wad of tobacco on the panel being worked. When the hammer came down again, the ensuing shower never failed to grab the drowsy worker's attention. The tyranny of the calendar drove the employees at both locations. Only 100 days remained, then 80, then 60. The five prototypes were driven hard over Indiana roads. Their weak points soon surfaced, most being in the experimental transmissions. Gears lost teeth, thrust washers broke, synchronizers jumped out of engagement. Engineers shipped transmissions and parts back to Detroit Gear and Columbia Axle, only to have replacements promptly fail again. Less than two weeks before the first cars were to be shipped to the shows, Snow faced the facts. One-hundred cars could not be ready in time. He prepared to settle for 25. And the transmission problems had still not found resolution. Friction and heat in the new unit were extraordinarily high. Testing went on, and no more units were ordered until a final design had been agreed upon. It was clear that the new cars would go to the shows without transmissions. It was equally clear to the AAC's management that delivery of cars to customers was months away.

Weeks before the shows even opened, they ordered 100 1/32-scale bronze models of the Cord sedan. Still, they instructed salespeople to promise delivery of the new Cord 810s by Christmas. What they intended to deliver were the bronze models. (In mid-December 1935, the bronze Cord 810 models were delivered to Auburn. There was just enough time to send them off to the first 100 customers who had placed deposits in the expectations of Christmas delivery. A note of apology accompanied the token. Later customers apparently received nothing at all.)

First showing of the new

CORD

at
The Automobile Shows
This Month

YOUR NAME AND ADDRESS
WILL BRING COMPLETE SPECIFICATIONS
AUBURN AUTOMOBILE CO.
AUBURN, INDIANA

It was probably in the early morning of October 27 when "Slim" Davidson inventoried the cars ready for the shows. Davidson, supervisor of Central's Experimental Garage and overseer of the show car project, quickly determined that 11 cars were close enough to completion for exhibition to the public. Auburn got

The coy ad that introduced the Cord 810 to the public and to the trade. (That's E 306 No. 2, retouched.) With variations in text, this ad appeared in *TIME, Esquire, The Saturday Evening Post,* and *Automobile Digest. Ronald B. Irwin*

The Convertible Phaeton Sedan's rear quarter windows were unique in this era; other convertibles had blind quarter panels. The windows pivoted down manually. This showcar was photographed in Beverly Hills in November 1935 at the home of a neighbor of the Cords. Standing next to it is Don Smith, Virginia Cord's brother-in-law. *Josh B. Malks collection*

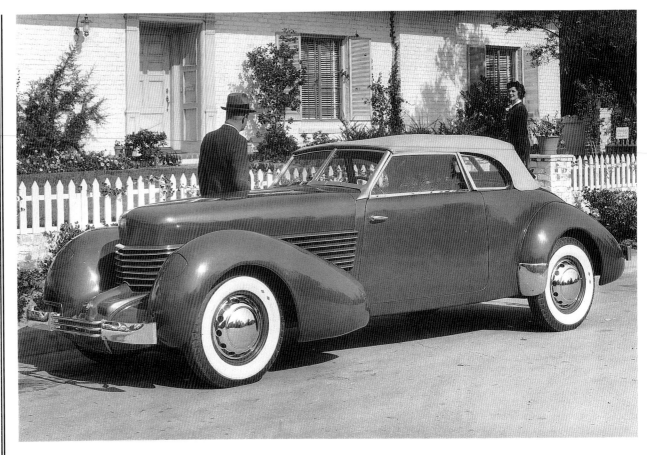

around the 100-model production figure requirement for the shows because the company was well established as an automaker. The rule basically applied to upstart companies, to prevent con artists from building a solitary prototype, selling stock in the company, and taking investors' funds. No one from the AMA would insist on counting the AAC's stock of Cord 810s. The shows in New York and Los Angeles both started on November 2, but the New York Auto Show would hold its press preview on October 30, and the new Cords simply had to be there. So while shipping times would be longer to the West Coast, both groups of cars probably left together. A Baltimore and Ohio way freight had already been waiting for hours. Tired workers pushed 11 show cars out of the plant, then up the hill to the rail siding. The way freight left shortly thereafter.

The auto shows were big news in 1935. Every major newspaper in New York and Los Angeles carried many pages of coverage. And a disproportionate amount of space sang the praises of the new front-drive Cord 810 from Indiana. The 810's startling styling, its dramatic interior, its innovative drivetrain, its exciting color schemes, all made it hot news for the reporters and exciting reading. Reviews referred to the dense crowds that surrounded the Cord exhibit. Papers reported that show attendees stood on the running boards and bumpers of competing cars to get a better look at the Cord 810. Color

brochures, prepared for the shows by the P. P. Willis firm, vanished quickly. The factory was deluged with requests for information, over 7,000 inquiries according to Faulkner.

The Prophets of General Motors

The General Motors Proving Grounds bought and tested an 810 Westchester as soon as they could lay hands on one. At the time they obtained their sample, only 88 Cords had been registered in the United States. Their report was issued in March 1936, and was very complimentary to the car's engineering and body design. The testers liked the ride; they called it a "roomy, comfortable cars, especially for four passengers". Quietness, steering, and stability were also praised. So was the Bendix finger-tip gear shift. The engineers were not pleased with the quality of construction. "The design appears to have been more carefully executed than the actual construction. The job actually impresses one as having been cheaply built".

Where the engineers hit the mark best was in their report summary, "This car attracts attention but we do not believe it will attract buyers to any extent."

The Convertible Coupe at Cordhaven after the Los Angeles show. Show models had rumble seats, production cars did not. On this showcar, matching T-handles open the rumble seat and the top lid. *Josh B. Malks collection*

The Chicago show opened November 16. Two weeks earlier, every manufacturer's models had been presented to the press in the lobby of the Merchandise Mart. That permitted newspaper and magazine photographers to snap photos unencumbered by crowds. All of the completed Cord 810s were still on exhibit in New York and Los Angeles, so the AAC sent prototype E 306 No. 3, to be photographed with models in formal attire. A news release from the Chicago show made special mention of the inboard headlights, although at the time no one outside the AAC knew the feature would not appear on production models. After the photo opportunity, the E 306 No. 3 returned to Auburn and obscurity. When the Chicago show opened, the Cord 810s were in place. The New York and Los Angeles stories repeated themselves, and attendees mobbed

the AAC's small 3,400-square-foot exhibit. Chicagoans, having read of the reception the new 810s received in New York and Los Angeles, wanted to see the new model for themselves. They were not disappointed. Every automotive trade publication featured the new Cord 810. Articles, straight from P. P. Willis' press kit, lauded the advantages of front-wheel drive. Accompanying the press kits were the now-familiar retouched photos of the E 306 No. 2. After the Los Angeles show, three of the transmissionless Cord show cars were sent via trailer to Cord's Beverly Hills home. Days were spent photographing them for future publicity.

While the new 810s basked in admiration at the shows, their Auburn creators wrestled with the problems of bringing them to production. Engineers tried to address the concerns raised on

the shakedown trip to Los Angeles, some fully, some less so. In late October, the engineers found that pressure lubrication by a small pump promised relief for the transmission's chronic heat problems. But the basic design was flawed, and some engineering decisions that needed thoughtful consideration had instead been made in haste. Perhaps most important, the gearbox had been modified from a three-speed to a four-speed unit, without the time to deal with the issues created by the modification.

Producing V-8s for the 810 was no problem for Lycoming; they had been building automobile engines since 1912. But now the AAC required its subsidiary to manufacture the complex drive unit, too. Spencer Heater cast the transmission, shifter, and bell housings; all were machined at Lycoming. Gears and shafts came from Detroit Gear. Lycoming workers assembled the transaxle, then bolted together the engine, clutch, and final drive units and shipped them to Central. The production FB

The Cord's concealed headlights captivated the auto world. Displaying one up and one down was especially titillating. This publicity photograph was taken by the Associated Press at the press preview for the New York auto show in 1935. *Ronald B. Irwin collection/Douglas Graham enhancement*

Bronze 1/32-scale models of the Cord sedan were sent by Auburn to the first 100 customers who had been expecting delivery of their new Cords for Christmas 1935. Two additional bronze miniatures were made into desk sets like this. One was given to Harold Ames, the other kept by the company that made the models.

engine was to be resplendent in polished aluminum, chrome, and black porcelain enamel. But even before production began, Auburn instructed Lycoming to cut costs on the finish of engines yet to be produced. So the aluminum cylinder heads and intake manifold were left unfinished, and most chrome plating was changed to cadmium. The cast-aluminum timing chain cases and oil pans of the show cars were replaced with stamped steel versions. Production FB V-8s were fed by a two-barrel

Stromberg EE-15 carburetor, with a new type of automatic choke. The choke had a bimetallic spring heated by a small element and was opened by an internal vacuum piston. A manual choke lever was still a part of the instrument panel and could be used by dealers to hook up an optional factory retrofit kit. Auto-Lite supplied the generator, starter, and distributor. Costs appeared to have played a role on the latter. The distributor had centrifugal advance only; other makes and models

Unit body shells roll down the assembly line, each on its own dolly, at Central Manufacturing Company in February 1936. Bodies were painted and upholstered before being mated with the stub frame which carried the drive train. Fenders, front end sheet metal, and bumpers were installed last. Every Cord produced until May 1936 was a sedan. *Ronald B. Irwin collection*

contemporary to the Cord 810 had a supplementary vacuum advance. The 810's third-brush generator design was in its last years of production. On the other hand, a touch of automation was supplied by the earlier-discussed Startix. The Eclipse Machine Division of Bendix provided these units to the AAC.

Advertising and press releases boasted of 125 horsepower for the new 810. Engineers at the AAC knew better; peak power shown on Lycoming's dynomometer charts was 117 horsepower. However, the last L-29 advertised 125 horsepower, and it wouldn't do to have a new Cord appear to have less power. Auburn's engineers couldn't decide between the Rzeppa and Bendix universal joints. Their internal memos indicate that they favored the Rzeppa principle, and production 810s used Rzeppa outer joints. It was a good choice; 60 years later, nearly every front-drive car would use this design. On the inner joints Auburn opted for the Bendix joints for the production models. The design of the Rzeppa inner joints would have required the removal of the transmission to service them.

Magazine road testers remarked on how quiet the 810 was at high speeds. Dramatically reduced wind noise was due to the model's shape and careful attention to windlacing (seals) around the doors. It was precisely this quiet that made other noises audible, from body squeaks to universal-joint knocks.

Auburn had committed itself to building 100 cars for the auto shows. As already noted, only a fraction of that number were actually ready in time for the shows. But mechanical parts and body panels for the waiting-to-be-built 810s had been ordered and delivered, so work on hand-assembled cars continued even as others prepared the production tooling. During November and December 1935, some 80 more hand-built 810s were assembled in Connersville. Production parts were now being delivered, and workers incorporated them into these hand-built Cords. The hand-built 810s were all sedans, because the open-bodied Cords were not marketable (lacking

The Model FC engine. The supercharger lies horizontally on top of the intake manifold. The relocated fuel pump, used on all engines for 1937, can be seen at lower left. Startix, the automatic starting device, is the box to the right of the fuel pump.

a top, their unit bodies twisted on rough roads). After the shows, reusable parts were removed from the show convertibles and the bodies hauled to the site of a federal flood-control project on the Whitewater River. The bodies were used to anchor the tons of rock and fill dirt that formed the new dam. Some of the early sedan show cars joined them. (One of the phaeton show cars, however, escaped burial when it was purchased by a dealer.) When time pressures were relieved a bit by the spring of 1936, surviving show car sedans were fitted with new drivetrains and sold to employees at reduced prices. Other unsold sedans from the shows stayed at the plant, cannibalized for mechanical and body parts.

The first Cord 810 came off the Connersville production line on January 31, 1936. Only 28 months had elapsed since Ames and Buehrig had first talked of Buehrig's unique styling idea and Ames' small Duesenberg. Yes, there were some bugs, and a few areas that weren't fully thought through. Still, the Cord 810 was a remarkable accomplishment for such a radical departure from the automotive norm, produced under such horrendous pressures of time and economics.

Service managers from Auburn/Cord dealerships attended training sessions in Connersville in February 1936, staged by Auburn's engineering staff. Cord 810 sedans, the Westchester and Beverly models, were now coming off the line at about 50 per day. The engineers continued to struggle to produce a serviceable open-bodied car. A heavy cage made of welded tubing was added to stiffen the cowl. More bracing was added even as production of open-bodied cars began in May. Later, engineers added more reinforcement to the front stub frame as well. Every effort helped, but even the later convertible coupes and phaetons were never as solid as the sedans.

810 Owners Encounter Troubles

Auburn's dealer network, painfully assembled by Cord in the 1920s, dwindled rapidly after the peak sales year of 1931. By 1935, only 499 Auburn dealers remained in the United States, but nearly half of these carried other makes as well. The AAC worked hard to help their remaining dealers. Sales contests were organized, and sales literature was provided in abundance. Quality and safety were major themes, and Cord 810 advertising touted front-wheel drive as a safety feature. It was an uphill battle. While many buyers admired the 810's mechanical innovation, most did not rush to lay down their money for the model, especially in the lingering wake of the Great Depression. The competition reminded customers of the Cord's well-known propensity for slipping out of gear. Vapor lock, often loosely addressed as overheating, was also discussed without hesitation.

About 10 percent of all Cord 810s produced were exported. Robert Wiley headed the AAC's active

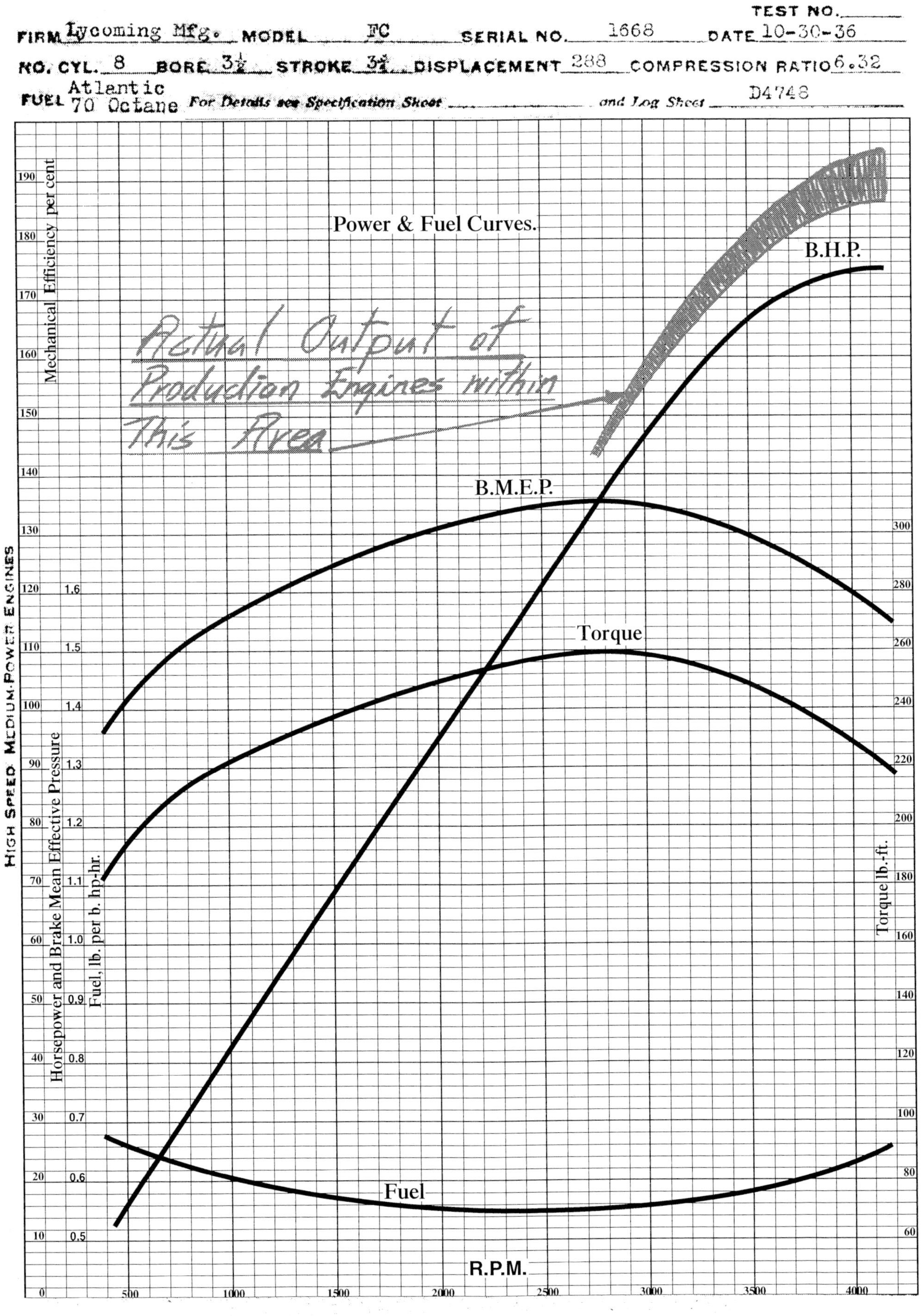

FIRM Lycoming Mfg. MODEL FC SERIAL NO. 1668 DATE 10-30-36 TEST NO._____

NO. CYL. 8 BORE 3¼ STROKE 3½ DISPLACEMENT 288 COMPRESSION RATIO 6.32

FUEL Atlantic 70 Octane For Details see Specification Sheet _____ and Log Sheet D4748

Power & Fuel Curves.

Actual Output of Production Engines within This Area

B.H.P.

B.M.E.P.

Torque

Fuel

Mechanical Efficiency per cent

HIGH SPEED MEDIUM POWER ENGINES

Horsepower and Brake Mean Effective Pressure

Fuel, lb. per b. hp.-hr.

Torque lb.-ft.

R.P.M.

This original Lycoming dynomometer chart for the supercharged engine shows the 175 peak brake horsepower developed by the first test engines. After cam and timing changes, production supercharged engines produced 185 to 196 brake horsepower, as shown by the penciled curves and legend. The penciled notations are in the hand of August Rickenbach, head of Lycoming's Experimental Engine Department from 1933 to 1939. He added them to the original chart in 1937. *August W. Rickenbach collection/Doug Graham enhancement*

143

The Yosemite Valley Economy Run sponsored by the Gilmore Oil Company in January 1937 was supervised by AAA's Contest Board. The event covered 352 miles through snow and freezing temperatures, from Los Angeles to Yosemite Lodge. A Cord sedan painted in the only stock two-tone combination—light and dark shades of Thrush Brown—won its class over a Packard and Chrysler Airflow. Weighing 5,000 pounds with five passengers, the Cord averaged 18.24 miles per gallon. It actually outpointed several smaller cars, including six-cylinder models by Chevrolet, Plymouth, Oldsmobile, and Nash. *Ronald B. Irwin collection/Doug Graham enhancement*

The Berline interior, as illustrated in the special Berline brochure. The elaborate vanity shown in the upper sketch was standard on supercharged cars, an extra-cost option on others. *Josh B. Malks collection*

export department. A substantial number of Cords, fitted with right-hand drive, went to British Commonwealth countries. Others went to Auburn dealers in Spain, France, and various points in South America and in the Middle East. The AAC received fan mail from happy customers and in turn circulated these letters to salesmen for use as testimonials. The company also received blistering demands for repairs and even refunds. These were kept quiet, and dealers coped as well as they could. The factory sent traveling troubleshooters to dealerships to solve problems the local service department couldn't handle. The major concern was the transmission. The propensity for the 810's transmission to slip out of gear was eventually stopped by an interlock device that locked the shift rails unless the clutch pedal was depressed, but not before more than 900 Cords were already on the road. The afterthought transmission pressure pump fell victim to metal particles scraped from the synchronizers by the brawny vacuum shift. Since there was no means by which the driver knew the pump was working, bushings scuffed and components overheated and failed.

Second only to gearbox difficulties were complaints about vapor lock in hot weather. Next in number were owners upset by the rain that seemed to leak into the car from every joint. Some owners complained of spotty paint work. Buehrig later recalled that the company used some leftover Auburn paints on the 810s, and the result was an uneven finish. Inadequate trunk space was another malady. The AAC, in turn, offered palliative accessories: a bustle-shaped accessory lid to replace the

original and a chrome fold-down trunk rack. Few were sold. After a few thousand miles of use, Cord 810s would begin to emit a clicking sound when the car turned corners. The noise was caused by wear in one component of the outer Rzeppa constant-velocity joints. The wear had no effect on the smooth operation of the car, but it irritated owners. Auburn supplied retrofit kits to dealers, replacing joints when owners complained. Yet, because the noise was endemic to the design of the Rzeppa joint, replacements by dealers were fruitless. The noise returned after some 2,500 miles.

Cord customers, alas, had become unwitting test drivers. As complaints and comments came in from the dealers, Auburn engineers worked at improving their product. Records of daily changes were dutifully typed and collected in small ring binders. Discovered years later by a Cord enthusiast, they reveal frantic efforts by the Auburn crew to perfect their car. They also reveal a commitment to excellence that does honor to their memory.

The AAC appears to have exhausted its human and financial energies getting the 810 to market. By May 1936, many of the top engineering staff—Snow, Kublin, and Thomas—had left. Cosper, Reuter-Lorenzen, Robinson, and Gardner took other jobs. By August, even Buehrig abandoned the AAC, this time for good. Young Alex Tremulis was hired as Auburn's stylist and became a one-man design department. Some 1,600 Cord 810s were produced

Two Cords set out on the 24-hour Stevens Trophy challenge. Car #1 broke a front hub 13 hours into the run. *Indianapolis Motor Speedway*

Jenkins switched to Car #2 to continue the run. *Indianapolis Motor Speedway*

through September 1936; about 1,100 were sold. By then, only 250 Auburn dealers remained.

In October, the AAC changed the model number (notching it up by two) and year of the Cord, from the 1936 Cord 810 to the 1937 Cord 812. The unsold 810s were renumbered and sold as 812s, much in the same manner as Auburn had done when renumbering the 1935 Auburn 851 into the 1936 Auburn 852.

With November came another auto show season. Externally, the Westchester sedan ($2,445), convertible phaeton sedan ($2,695), and the convertible coupe ($2,595) were all changed in small details only. The Beverly sedan ($2,545) underwent more serious changes. Despite price increases of more than 20 percent over 1936, Auburn continued to lose money on each Cord produced. The desperate price hike only served to reinforce the sales slide.

Tremulis redesigned the sheet metal of the unpopular accessory bustle trunk lid, blending it into the body. The 812 Beverly replaced the "armchair" seats of the 810 Beverly with pull-down armrests. Few mechanical changes were made for the new year. A state-of-the-art Auto-Lite shunt-type generator with an external three-unit regulator was fitted. The differential gear ratio was changed from 4.30:1 to 4.70:1, and a simpler shock absorber substituted. Bendix duo-servo brakes replaced the primitive Lockheed design. The noisy Rzeppa constant-velocity joint used on the 810 was superseded by the Bendix-Weiss joint. To combat vapor lock, the fuel pump on all 1937 engines was moved from the top front of the intake manifold to the lower rear corner of the block. Dealers were also provided with instructions for the installation of an optional Autopulse electric fuel pump.

Lycoming had always intended the FB V-8 to accommodate a supercharger at some point in the future. To that end, the Schwitzer-Cummins Corporation of Indianapolis adapted to the Cord's engine the centrifugal superchargers it had originally supplied for the Auburn models. Lycoming engineers designed the special parts needed to fit the blower to the Cord and dubbed the resulting V-8 the FC series. A larger Stromberg AA-25 carburetor replaced the EE-15 on FC engines. The engine firing order was revised, and the compression ratio slightly lowered. The most important change, however, was the

At customer requests, two hardtop coupes like this one were modified by the factory from stock convertible coupes. One was an 810, one an 812; neither was supercharged. A third hardtop coupe, a supercharged 812, sported a padded leather top, chrome Auburn headlamps, and other added decorations. *Henry Blommel collection*

The "official" photo of the winning Cord. On the right is Charlie Merz of AAA; at center, "Pop" Myers, manager of the Indianapolis Speedway. This photo accompanied Auburn's press releases. *Indianapolis Motor Speedway*

The photo of the real Stevens Trophy winner features Cord #2 and everyone who was part of the crew. Ab Jenkins leans on the door; to his left is Billy Winn, who was driving this car when the run began. Copies of this photo were distributed as mementos to those who posed for the picture. It was never circulated. *Otto Wolfer collection*

cam grind. Sample FC engines showed 175 horsepower on the dynomometer. Lycoming's Rickenbach remembers that his people felt they could do better. The cam in the production engines included considerably more overlap, and these produced between 186 to 195 horsepower. For whatever reason, Cord 812 advertising always used a figure of 170 horsepower. All of the supercharged models previously produced—the Auburn eights of 1935 and 1936 and the Duesenberg Model SJ—trumpeted their increased power with external exhaust pipes clad in flexible stainless-steel tubing. No such pipes had been fitted to the supercharged Cord 812s prepared for the shows for the 1937 model year, despite Tremulis' pleas to Faulkner for their addition. Tremulis later said that he cajoled Augie Duesenberg into so equipping three of the new supercharged 812s that were still at the factory. After being fitted with the pipes, the Cords sped down the highway for New York at the last moment; two of them arrived at the show and surprised Faulkner. Tremulis also recalled getting a raise as a result. Regardless of how they came to be, the supercharged 812s became a success with the buying public, relative to total Cord production for 1937. In all, the factory produced 688 supercharged 812s, nearly one-half of the total production of Cords in 1937. The option was available on all models and added $415 to the price.

The only Cord models that were truly new for 1937 were a line of long-wheelbase sedans. Their outline had been prepared by Buehrig and his team during a quiet time in early 1935. Buehrig later explained that the decision to add these models to the line was made by someone in management who felt that the standard Cord wasn't roomy enough for a car in its price class. It certainly wasn't Buehrig's idea. So opposed was he to the concept that he never voluntarily spoke of the long-wheelbase Cords during his many talks and writings later in life. The first long-wheelbase prototype included a crank-driven divider window. After some experimentation with proportions and experimental models cobbled together from 810 sedans, Buehrig settled on a 132-inch wheelbase with 2 inches of additional legroom for the front seat and 5 inches for the rear seat. This was to be the new Berline model ($3,060/$3,575 supercharged). A similar Beverly sedan ($2,960/$3,375 supercharged) would complete what was dubbed the Custom line. Few exterior parts interchanged between the standard and Custom Cords. Some were made especially for the Custom series, others modified from standard parts. The Custom's additional 1-1/2-inch height came from higher rocker panels. This created the need for a grille

Former championship race driver and engine builder Earl Cooper had been on Auburn's engineering staff when the L-29 was designed. He was working as a test engineer for Union Oil in 1937. When that company added a supercharged Cord Custom Beverly to its test fleet, Cooper picked it up in Connersville and drove it back to California. *Ronald B. Irwin collection*

Cords were used in movies of the era to suggest wealth and panache. A convertible phaeton here awaits the director's call for "action."

NO CAR at the New York Automobile Show next October will be as NEW as the new Cord you can get right now! What makes a car new? Not merely new model names, new bodies, or new gadgets. "Newness" goes much deeper! The Cord continues to be the newest car because it is designed and built on more advanced engineering principles. The Cord is Front Drive! This is newness in fact: not simply in name. It gives exclusive advantages, obtainable in no other car! The Cord continues to be the newest car in riding comfort. No other car offers a rear-seat ride, as comfortable as the front-seat ride! The Cord continues to be the newest car in ease of handling. No other car has the power applied to the front wheels. This makes it the easiest to steer! The Cord continues to be the newest car in performance. No other car offers the Cord's smooth, quiet, gliding ride that is like coasting! The Cord continues to be the newest car in Safety. No other car has the Cord's low center of gravity, balanced weight, ease of maneuverability, or its reserve power for emergencies! Those glistening chrome exhaust pipes of the Super-Charged Cord are the coat of arms of motoring royalty. As other drivers race alongside, they know they can pass the Cord driver only because he consents. The Cord owner does not need to drive fast to prove his car is the champion. Everyone knows it!

CORD

with one extra louver, eight instead of seven. The Custom cars were also much heavier. In addition to their greater size, more lead was used to cover additional seams. With the hectic pace in the spring of 1935, no further work was done on the Custom models until mid-1936. By then, Buehrig had left the company, so Tremulis completed the styling of the Custom models. He added the bustle trunk to these models, too. All Berlines include the divider window with the window crank located on the back of the front seat. Supercharged Berlines featured an elaborate rear vanity that included cosmetic compartments, an intercom with the chauffeur, and a radio speaker. These items were available at extra cost on unsupercharged Berlines. The upholstery was done in broadcloth, but leather was available by special-order for the chauffeur's seat. The interior of the companion Custom Beverly was virtually identical to that of the standard Cord Beverly sedan. Despite the addition of supercharged and Custom models, sales of Cords continued to decline. By May 1937, 812s were virtually being built to order; about five cars were coming off the line each day.

The 812's Last Hurrah

Customers valued speed records in those years. They saw such records as indicative of reliability, in addition to performance. In a vain effort to bolster business, the AAC turned loose its racing department, such as it was: Ab Jenkins and Augie Duesenberg. Jenkins, a native of Salt Lake City, had been instrumental in demonstrating the potential of the nearby salt flats at Bonneville, Utah. The expansive site made high speeds possible. Malcolm Campbell, George Eyston, John Cobb, and Jenkins himself all set world speed records there.

Auburn personnel knew the supercharged 812 was the fastest American model in production. Lycoming's chief engineer, Bill Baster, claimed to have driven his supercharged Westchester sedan in two directions on a measured mile, recording an average top speed of 113 miles per hour. Jenkins later wrote that he had driven Cords at over 120 miles per hour at Bonneville, "but nobody's stock tires would stay on the automobile even for 10 miles. . . ." As a warm-up to the speed record attempt, the AAC decided to go after the 10-year-old Stevens Trophy. Donated by Samuel B. Stevens of Rome, New York, "The Stevens Challenge Trophy for the Stock Closed Car 24-Hour World Record" was to be held by the manufacturer of the American car "to which is ascribed at any particular time the highest average speed for 24 hours over the Indianapolis Motor Speedway." The car had to be a "fully equipped standard closed-body stock car." Attempts were monitored by the American Automobile Association. A 16-cylinder Marmon held the trophy in 1937, having averaged 76.43 miles per hour in 1931. A Cord was about to change the standings.

Augie Duesenberg and Ab Jenkins brought two supercharged Cord 812 Beverly sedans to the speedway on June 17, 1937. Firestone provided the tires and pit crew supervision (Indy was still paved in brick and punished tires severely). The two 812s set out around the oval track at 5:30 a.m. on Monday, June 21. An ivory-colored 812 took the lead, with Jenkins behind the wheel. Billy Winn drove the second Cord 812, which wore a livery of Clay Rust, one-half a lap behind. The sedans circled the track while averaging more than 83 miles per hour, a comfortable margin over the Marmon record.

Thirteen hours into the run, disaster struck Jenkins' Cord 812. As Jenkins entered a turn, the right-front brake drum broke away from its hub. Jenkins guided the stricken Cord into the infield. Damage to the brakes and axle on the right side and to the right front fender was severe. Jenkins and Augie Duesenberg undoubtedly consulted briefly, then had a member of the pit crew flag Winn into the pits. Jenkins took control of the second Cord 812, and the run for the trophy resumed.

The following afternoon, a smiling Jenkins—along with speedway and AAA officials—posed for publicity photos with the now-repaired ivory-colored Cord and the Stevens Trophy. Close inspection of the photo reveals a new right front fender, devoid of any bugs or dirt. Press releases from the AAC included this photo, and it was to appear in magazines for decades to come.

So why was the first Cord so hastily repaired? Since the image of reliability had been one of the goals of this exercise, the public relations people probably thought that it would look better for the trophy-winning Cord to be wearing the number "1." A

The last ad for the Cord appeared in *Esquire* in August 1937. It wistfully pointed out that the 1937 Cord was a more advanced motorcar than any of the yet-to-appear 1938 models. Auburn was correct, but it was too late to convince the public. *Ronald B. Irwin collection*

Ames' notion of a smaller Duesenberg did not die when he sent Buehrig's modernistic prototype to Auburn in 1934. Alex Tremulis (who helped style the 1948 Tucker) and Phil Wright (best remembered for his design work on the Cord L-29 speedster and Pierce-Arrow Silver Arrow) started to work as designers for Duesenberg in 1935. Ames set them to developing body styles for a new, smaller series of Duesenbergs, modern in concept but traditional in execution. Power, Tremulis later remembered, was to have been delivered by a supercharged version of the Lycoming BB V-12.

The coachbuilder LeBaron delivered four aluminum body shells for this project: a fast-back sedan, a limousine with trunk, a convertible Berline, and a convertible coupe. By the time the bodies arrived, Duesenberg as a company could no longer entertain the idea of marketing a new line of cars. The bodies were stored in

The LeBaron limousine. E. L. and Virginia Cord chose this as their personal car. Before delivery, hood and grille were changed to the same one shown on the convertible sedan. *Henry Blommel collection*

Connersville. In July 1936, perhaps at the request of Cord himself, the project was completed. Auburn frames were scrounged from local junkyards, repaired, and welded to Cord 810 stub frames. Workers mounted the Duesenberg proto-type bodies on these customized frames. Tremulis designed hoods and radiator grilles (one grille—fit-ted to the limousine—came from Bohman and Schwartz. Tremulis later discarded this unit). The designer also used stock 810 front fenders, bumpers, and hubcaps; transmission covers and rear fenders were also adapted. All the prototypes sported a Tremulis-designed hood ornament. The prototypes were completed in late fall. It's known that the limousine, which Cord kept for himself, was supercharged; so was the convertible coupe. Perhaps all the cars were supercharged, but no out-side exhausts were fitted.

The LeBaron convertible sedan, one of four body styles mounted on used Auburn chassis, with supercharged Cord running gear. *Henry Blommel collection*

Vultee Airplane Development Corporation was a holding of the Cord Corporation, part of E.L.'s massive shift from automotive to aeronautical enterprises. This Cord 810 Westchester nestles next to Vultee V-1A #8 at the aircraft manufacturer's plant in Downey, California. The car was supplied by the Los Angeles dealership. *Jonathan Thompson collection*

souvenir photo of the real trophy winner—Cord No. 2—was given to all the members of the crew. The press never received this photo, and it would not be seen in print for another 58 years.

The next goal was to tackle Bonneville. In early July 1937, a small caravan left Connersville for the Bonneville Salt Flats. The group wanted to set new American stock car speed records under AAA supervision. Again headed by Jenkins and Augie Duesenberg, the crew also included Bill Oliver and Bert Updike (who would give Jenkins a break during the longer runs), Jenkins' son Marvin, and a Firestone tire team managed by Waldo Stein. With the crew went several supercharged Beverly sedans. Stein and Augie Duesenberg each drove to Utah in their personal Cord 810 sedans.

Rainstorms drenched the salt during July and August. The crew kept themselves busy by servicing Cords at the Auburn dealership in Salt Lake City . . . and waited. During the lull, the production lines in Connersville came to a halt. No new Cords were started after August 7, and 812s already in progress were half-heartedly completed over the next two weeks. If the crew's reason for traveling to Bonneville was to gather any number of speed records to bolster sales of the Cord 812, that reason now vanished. Still, the crew remained.

The speed-record runs finally took place on September 16 and 17 on a circular course with a 10-mile radius. The supercharged Cord 812 shattered class records for every distance and every time interval. It also redeemed itself after the Indianapolis debacle, traveling nearly 2,500 miles in 24 hours at an average speed of over 101 miles per hour, including all pit stops. Some controversy arose in later years when slide-rule engineers questioned the supercharged 812's ability to perform so mightily with an advertised horsepower rating of 170. In fact, as already discussed, all production FC engines developed 186 to 195 horsepower. An engine tuned by Augie Duesenberg would certainly have squeezed out several additional horses. It was too late for the record runs to bolster Cord 812 sales, but the favorable publicity probably helped dealers dispose of their remaining stock of Cord 812s. By the fall of 1937, that's all anyone could hope for.

An oil company photographer "just happened" to be standing by when Auburn test driver Ab Jenkins stopped for gas at an Amoco station in Yonkers, New York in 1937. The supercharged Custom Beverly is a relatively early example. The car isn't Ab's; it bears New York license plates, and Ab never lived in that state.

The Dismantling of Auburn 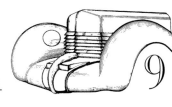 9

1937 Through the End

The AAC recorded revenues of $3.4 million in 1937, manufacturing only Cord 812s that year. However, the company continued to generate income with nonautomotive stampings. On the downside, it also racked up another deficit of $3.4 million. So bleak was Auburn's future that shares traded as low as 3-1/8, with the high of 36-3/4 obtained earlier in the year. Only an 11th-hour rescue could prevent the company from facing the inevitable, otherwise it was only a matter of time before the AAC disappeared.

Victor Emanuel undertook the rescue, but without any high-minded idealism as motivation. Seeking new challenges, Emanuel and partners went after the financially vulnerable Cord Corporation. To this day, why Emanuel pursued the Cord Corporation and how he managed to mount the takeover is still unclear. Borgeson, in his Cord biography, notes that Cord and President Franklin Roosevelt had a falling out. Perhaps that translated into a government vendetta against Cord. A long, lengthy, and complex takeover attempt of the Aviation Corporation may have also angered powerful interests in that company, another reason for revenge. Or perhaps it was simply that Emanuel, long a connoisseur of fine automobiles and a Duesenberg Model J owner, eyeballed the Cord Corporation because of its automotive reputation.

OPPOSITE
Milling machines were bolted to the terrazzo showroom floors of the former AAC administration building during the tenure of Winslow's Auburn Cord Duesenberg Company.

Victor Emanuel. *Archives collection, Roesch Library, University of Dayton*

153

Victor Emanuel

Victor Emanuel was born into the monied class in 1898; his father, Albert Emanuel, achieved his wealth within the public utilities field. Raised in Dayton, Ohio, Victor attended the prep school program at St. Mary's College (now the University of Dayton).

The Emanuels moved to New York in 1916, where Victor pursued a bachelor of arts program in economics at Cornell University. He quit during his junior year to serve as chief quartermaster of aviation in the U.S. Navy during World War I. During this time, Emanuel completed flying school at the Naval Air Station in Miami, Florida.

After the war, Emanuel returned to Cornell to finish his degree, then later transferred to Columbia. Shortly after resumption of his college career, Emanuel was called upon to take over his father's business. Emanuel never completed his college program, instead receiving a degree from Cornell in 1929 as a war alumnus. Regardless, Emanuel still managed to become president of his father's company by the age of 25. Within three short years, Emanuel joined forces with Arthur Cecil Allyn, a banker from Chicago, to buy out the elder Emanuel's business and form the National Electric Power Company (NEP). After NEP had bought 14 other utility companies, Emanuel and Allyn

sold it for $13 million. Emanuel was 28 at the time. By 30, he was purportedly worth $40 million.

After living a short while in aristocratic luxury in England, Emanuel and Allyn mounted another attack on the public utilities industry. The duo formed the U.S. Electric Power Company (USEPCO), and with the help of the New York investment banking firm of J. Henry Schroder and Company and $60 million, they went after the Standard Gas and Electric System conglomerate. H. M. Byllesby, of H. M. Byllesby and Company, controlled the lion's share of Standard Gas and Electric. Byllesby, however, had no interest in turning over his control of the company. Emanuel and his group uncovered alleged mismanagement and misappropriation of funds and threatened to file charges against Byllesby. Hog-tied, Byllesby capitulated, selling his shares of USEPCO.

Standard Gas and Electric was only the first victim. Emanuel and Allyn didn't stop until USEPCO had accumulated a public utilities powerhouse worth $1.1 billion, a staggering figure for the 1930s. The Public Utilities Holding Act of 1935 finally put an end to their utilities acquisitions. The brutal takeover tactics Emanuel learned during this period would serve him well when he later went after the Cord Corporation.

RIGHT
A Saf-T-Cab, circa 1925. Cord pursued any number of taxi ventures in the 1920s and 1930s, from operating companies to taxi manufacturers.

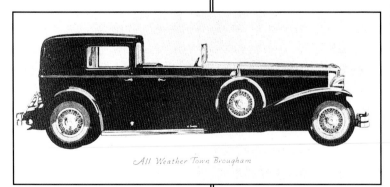

All Weather Town Brougham

This is an illustration of the Duesenberg Model J owned by Victor Emanuel, a town brougham produced by Brunn. In fact, it was the only town brougham made by Brunn for a Duesenberg chassis. The engine number, for Duesenberg fans, is J-398; chassis number is 2404.

But if the Cord Corporation's automobile line was the attraction, it wasn't the ultimate goal. When Emanuel and company moved in, the automotive lines were the first to go. The Emanuel group basically forced Cord to sell his holdings in the Cord Corporation for $2.6 million via intimations of mismanagement and other misdeeds. Not coincidentally, the Securities and Exchange Commission pushed Cord to sign a consent decree. The SEC had raised questions about, among other dealings, the role of the Cord 810 and how its announcement affected stock prices. The SEC inferred manipulation on the part of Cord, despite the agency's previous approval of the AAC's 4.75 percent bond issue, which helped finance the 810. (The SEC had also launched an investigation into Cord's takeover of Checker Cab, assisted by Checker Cab's president, Morris Markin. Within a 10-day period in 1933, Cord had garnered over 50 percent of Checker Cab's shares.)

Cord had suffered a number of nervous breakdowns by this time. One of the reasons for Cord's

weak state was the ongoing SEC investigations into his securities trading. Cord was unable or unwilling to appear in hearings. Cord's lawyers represented the industrialist before the commission on August 7, 1937, and, as Borgeson so eloquently put it in his Cord biography, "vouched that he would not do what he had not been doing." Cord's declining

health was further aggravated by the financial troubles of the various companies within his empire. Many of them were in dire financial straits, and his automotive holdings represented the worst of the lot. Unable to protect his stock holdings per a consent decree which prevented him from trading shares in the companies he owned, Cord had to sell out. Emanuel and company made Cord an offer that, quite literally, he couldn't refuse. It was as if the whole affair had been orchestrated. Driving a Lincoln Zephyr, Cord left Chicago with Ames and a suitcase containing Cord's $2.6 million and his personal holdings. He headed for his West Coast home in Los Angeles.

The announcement of the Cord Corporation sale hit the papers on the same day the SEC hearings came to a close on August 7. Those who backed Emanuel in his takeover effort included Gerald E. Donovan of Schroder, Rockefeller and Company; C. Coburn Darling of the Aviation Corporation; Henry Lockhart, Jr., of Shell Union Oil; Thomas Mercer Girdler of Republic Steel; and John Daniel Hertz, formerly of Hertz Drivurself and later of TWA; the Aviation Shares Company; and Lehman Brothers. All of these gentlemen became board members after the takeover. Other parties may have been behind the coup. What their motivation was for going after Cord remains a bit of a mystery. It is known that John T. Flynn, a New York attorney and formerly with the SEC, negotiated the buyout of the Cord Corporation for the group. Who better than an ex-SEC attorney to inform Cord of what could transpire if he didn't surrender? Manning took over the vice-chairmanship of the Cord Corporation, acting as front man for the Emanuel group. Emanuel emerged as chairman and president; Pruitt as secretary, general counsel, and a vice president; Faulkner and L. I. Hartmeyer as vice presidents; L. K. Grant as treasurer; and W. A. Mogensen as comptroller. Workers assembled the last Cord 812 during the week of August 21, 1937. It represented the end of automotive production for the AAC.

Faulkner remained president of the AAC until it was officially shut down on November 11, 1937. Those automotive operations still showing a profit—such as Central Manufacturing, LGS Devices, and Columbia Axle—remained. Initially, there was still some question as to whether automobile production would be pursued again. The press was rife with rumors concerning a new Auburn model. The Emanuel group, however, could quickly recover their investment in the Cord Corporation by liquidating its automotive operations. As the subsequent bankruptcy proceedings unfolded, it became clear that a return of the Auburn and Cord marques would not transpire.

The AAC filed for bankruptcy and protection from creditors on December 11, 1937, in U.S. District Court in Fort Wayne, Indiana. Judge Thomas W. Slick oversaw the proceedings for the next four years. During the bankruptcy proceedings, the SEC and the Debenture Holders Protective Committee (holders of debenture notes issued for the production of the Cord 810) suggested the possibility of filing a claim against Cord and the prior officers and

The AAC's official airplane, a Stinson. Stinson was a part of the Cord Corporation empire.

directors of the Cord Corporation for the reason of fulfilling the working capital needs of the AAC. This, however, never came to pass. Officers for the AAC during this time of reorganization included John MacGowan as chairman, G. G. Johnson as president, Albert H. McInnis as vice president, E. G. Meldrum as treasurer and secretary, and W. Moran as assistant treasurer and assistant secretary. The AAC's directors included Faulkner, MacGowan, Johnson, McInnis, Meldrum, and Moran.

On June 15, 1938, the bankruptcy court accepted a bid of $85,000 from Dallas E. Winslow, Inc., of Detroit for the remaining Auburn and Cord parts and tooling. For some years, Winslow was in the business of buying the remaining parts and tooling of automakers that had gone under. In addition to Auburn, Cord, and Duesenberg (the latter under a separate deal), Winslow continued to provide parts to owners of Franklins, Grahams, Hupmobiles, and others. For an additional $25,000, Winslow purchased the AAC's administration building, moving his operations there from Detroit. While Winslow can be credited with keeping many Auburns, Cords, and Duesenbergs alive until his business closed in the early 1960s, he also came close to irreversibly destroying the administration building. Many fixtures were removed and walls demolished. Winslow used the once beautiful art deco showroom as a room for his machine shop, bolting lathes and presses to the terrazzo floor. A coating of oil and shavings accumulated. To be fair, the preservation of such buildings was never in the forefront of anyone's mind in the late 1930s, but the citizens of Auburn, who 40 years later tackled the job of restoring the building as a museum for Auburns, Cords, and Duesenbergs, had an uphill battle on their hands.

The Auburn Automotive Heritage, Inc., the non-profit corporation that owns the Auburn-Cord-

Some of the studies in clay prepared by AAC designer Alex Tremulis for the company's 1938 models. It isn't known if the designs were slated to be Auburns or Cords. Fortunately for the image of either marque, none reached production. *William C. Kinsman collection*

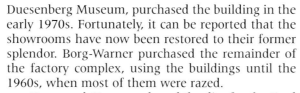

Duesenberg Museum, purchased the building in the early 1970s. Fortunately, it can be reported that the showrooms have now been restored to their former splendor. Borg-Warner purchased the remainder of the factory complex, using the buildings until the 1960s, when most of them were razed.

Norman deVaux purchased the dies for the Cord 810/812 body for $45,000 in 1938. His deals with Hupp Motor Car Company, and later with Graham-Paige, resulted in the short-lived rear-drive Hupp Skylark and Graham Hollywood.

The Cord Corporation Fades

Although an annual report for the Cord Corporation was released on November 30, 1937, the company's traditional fiscal year end, its annual meeting transpired on February 11, 1938, in Chicago. At that time, the Emanuel group voted to drop the Cord Corporation name, replacing it with the Aviation and Transportation Corporation, or ATCO for short.

On August 25, 1938, the AAC formed the Pak-Age-Car Corporation, a wholly owned subsidiary. The subsidiary had to be established since credit could not be secured by the AAC. The purpose of this subsidiary was to pursue production of the Pak-Age-Car, a small stand-up delivery van usually associated with milk delivery services. Faulkner was friends with C. A. Tilt, president of the Diamond-T company, manufacturer of various-sized trucks. The plan was for Auburn to produce the delivery van on a subcontract basis, and Diamond-T to market and service the vehicles.

In November 1938, ATCO moved its headquarters from Chicago to New York. In the process, Manning was dumped out of the company.

Auburn filed its reorganization plan with the bankruptcy court on July 28, 1939. Auburn's primary business was now subcontracting for the manufacture of such products as air conditioners, kitchen cabinets, sinks, refrigerator cabinets, and washing machines. Manufacturing car bodies also became part of the mix, with Auburn manufacturing them for GM, Packard, and International Harvester, and negotiating with Graham-Paige and Hudson.

On December 26, Auburn filed a revision covering its future financial policies. The court approved the plan on January 20, 1940. Henceforth, the Auburn Automobile Company would be known as the Auburn Central Manufacturing Corporation. The Emanuel group became the first board of directors of Auburn Central. On April 3, 1941, Judge Slick issued a final decree closing the bankruptcy proceedings. All assets of the AAC transferred to Auburn Central on June 12, 1941.

In 1942, Auburn Central renamed itself American Central. During the war years, the company manufactured aircraft wings and jeep bodies, a lucrative government contract by any measure. ATCO did well during the war, too. It held a backlog of $1 billion in government contracts by the end of 1941, and three years later passed the $4 billion benchmark. Only General Motors and Curtiss-Wright did better with war production contracts. In 1946, Emanuel decided to give ATCO the name of its subsidiary, Avco, short for the Aviation Corporation. It was Avco that had held the aviation operations of the former Cord Corporation, including Stinson, Lycoming Aviation (which separated from Lycoming Automotive), and Vultee.

American Central received a contract to build refrigerators for the Admiral Corporation in 1945. By 1946, the company produced kitchen cabinets marketed under the names of American Kitchens and Crosley Kitchens. On October 4, 1948, the company merged into its corporate parent and became known as the American Central division of Avco. In 1951, the Connersville operation was renamed the American Kitchens division, later simply reduced to the AK Division when Avco sold the business in December 1957. In 1959, Avco sold its dishwasher and sink businesses in Connersville to the Design and Manufacturing Corporation. The remainder of the buildings went to the architectural products division of H. H. Robertson Company in 1960. These descendants of the AAC were the last of the former automotive companies still within Avco. All ties between them and their former holding company were now cut. Emanuel was still at the helm of Avco when all this transpired.

In his Cord biography, Borgeson quotes ex-Avco treasurer Fred Larson to the effect that Emanuel made everyone rich but himself, and that he wasn't the boy wonder of finance that the press made him out to be. There are other sources that back up

Larson's remarks. In an old confidential memo from the University of Dayton's archives, it states that Emanuel had donated $200,000-plus in 1927 to build that institution's Albert Emanuel Library in tribute to his father. Years passed and Emanuel visited the university during World War II, promising to donate another $400,000 for a chemistry laboratory. This donation never came to pass. A memo, written shortly before Emanuel's death, stated that Emanuel "is now about 65 years old and is not wealthy, comparatively speaking." During World War II, Emanuel served as a director on the boards of Republic Steel Corporation, Consolidated Securities Corporation, Amberley Investment Trust, Ltd., Moffats, Ltd., the Cornell Aeronautical Laboratory, Inc., and the Aircraft War Production Commission during World War II. He also served on the Hoover Report Committee and on the advisory committee to the Senate Banking and Currency Committee. Emanuel died on November 26, 1960, at the age of 62.

Cord, as noted, headed west and remained there. All during his empire-building years, he had purchased real estate in and around Beverly Hills, long before values escalated. He also went on to pursue the broadcasting field in a small way and mining and off-shore drilling. Cord eventually built a ranch in Nevada, and Reno became his base until the end. He was elected a state senator in Nevada in the late 1950s, but returned to his business ventures soon after. Health problems including cancer caught up with Cord by the late 1960s, and he succumbed to a heart attack on January 2, 1974.

Although Cord's sale of his empire meant the disappearance of the AAC as an automaker in 1937, a core of enthusiasts have kept the marques of Auburn, Cord, and Duesenberg alive since then. Formed in 1952, the Auburn-Cord-Duesenberg Club's main goal is to preserve these makes. The organization's motto provides an insight as to why Auburns, Cords, and Duesenbergs continue to endear themselves to generation after generation: "For Those Who Have Never Relished the

Kitchen cabinets roll off the assembly lines in Connersville, Indiana, where once Auburns and Cords were produced. The cabinets brought in much-needed capital at a time when the AAC was struggling financially.

The Hupp Skylark and Graham Hollywood used the Cord unit body dies from the cowl back. Stylist John Tjaarda redesigned the front end to give a different look and to accommodate the 10-inch shorter wheelbase. *Robert Fabris collection*

Automotive Industries tracked the bankruptcy proceedings of the AAC for some time after the company ceased producing automobiles. Once World War II ended and the need for jeep bodies diminished, all ties to vehicle manufacturing were broken.

Commonplace." The club's first national meet at Auburn, Indiana, occurred in 1956. Faulkner, still living in Auburn and excited at the prospect of having Auburns, Cords, and Duesenbergs return to the city, helped with arrangements. The club scheduled the event for October 20 and 21. Unfortunately, Faulkner passed away just prior to that first meet. The meet, known today as the Auburn-Cord-Duesenberg Festival, is now held every Labor Day weekend. Tens of thousands attend yearly to catch a glimpse of the famous marques.

Gone But Never Forgotten

Almost a lifetime has passed since the Auburn Automobile Company closed its doors in 1937. Yet, a larger-than-life interest continues in the marques of Auburn and Cord.

By the 1930s, the independent automakers realized their days were numbered. Cord knew it. His management team probably knew it but certainly would never acknowledge the fact. But it is precisely because time was running out that the AAC went out on a limb to create such markedly different automobiles. Even when new, the AAC's cars were recognized as special; its reputation has only increased in the years since its demise. Driving an Auburn speedster or a front-drive Cord immediately put an owner in a different class. The makes bestowed individuality to the person behind the wheel. "This driver," the badge of Auburn and Cord whispers, "doesn't follow the crowd. He doesn't even *lead* the crowd. Instead, this driver follows a road of his own."

Cord at his desk in Cordhaven, Beverly Hills, California, 1953.

It's a bit of Thoreau, wrapped in steel, leather, glass, and chrome, and set in motion. And that's why the Auburn and Cord mystique has never faded.

A photo of the "Parade of Classics," part of the Auburn-Cord-Duesenberg Festival held every Labor Day weekend in Auburn, Indiana, to commemorate the marques of Auburn, Cord, and Duesenberg. This photo was taken during the 1958 event, only two years after the festival was established.

Index

Admiral Corporation, 157
Allyn, Arthur Cecil, 154
American Central, 157
Ames, Harold, 43, 54, 55, 64, 101, 109, 113, 122-124, 133
Ansted Engineering, 55, 60
Ashelman, Barbara Ellen, 10
Auburn Automotive Heritage, Inc., 155
Auburn Caravan, 69
Auburn Central Manufacturing Corporation, 157
Auburn-Cord-Duesenberg Club, 157
Auburn-Cord-Duesenberg Festival, 158, 159
Aviation and Transportation Corporation, 156
Aviation Corporation, 153, 157

Baby Duesenberg, 122, 124, 126, 128
Bard, Ralph, 28, 37, 40, 45
Barrymore, John, 96
Baster, Forrest S., 123
Beal, W. Hubert, 105, 107, 129
Beier, Kurt, 113
Bendix Aviation Corporation, 122
Brett, Riley, 81, 82
Buckeye Manufacturing Company, 131
Buehrig, Gordon, 95, 101, 109-113, 122, 124-126, 128, 129, 131, 132, 140, 144, 148
Burroughs, Edgar Rice, 90

Cagney, James, 106
Central Manufacturing Company, 50, 51, 61, 71, 99, 115, 116, 155
Chicago Gang, 28-31, 34, 37, 40, 44, 45, 54
Christie, Walter, 81
Columbia Axle, 26, 91, 132, 137, 155
Continental Motors, 19, 26
Cooper, Earl, 148
Cord Corporation, 71, 72, 78, 103, 109, 116, 133, 136, 151, 153-156
Cord, Charles William, 42
Cord, Errett Lobban, 14, 29, 33, 34, 39, 40-45, 47, 49, 50, 51, 54, 55, 57, 59, 60, 66, 69, 71-74, 78, 79, 81, 84, 85, 89, 91, 94-96, 103, 105, 110, 117, 131, 133, 136, 154, 155, 157, 158
Cord, Helen F., 42, 78, 79
Cord, Virginia K.T., 79, 130
Cosper, Dale, 125, 126, 133
Cotter, Bart, 110, 129
Crawford, James, M., 34, 69

Dallas E. Winslow, 155
Davidson, Lloyd "Slim", 137
Daytona Beach, 68
de Sakhnoffsky, Alexis, 97
DeKalb Company, 110
Del Rio, Dolores, 96
Denison, Wilson H., 29
DePaolo, Pete, 82, 83
Derham, Phil, 122, 123
Detroit Gear and Machine Company, 87, 119, 132
Detroit Special, 83, 85
deVaux, Norman, 156
DeWeese, B.D., 72
Duesenberg, Augie, 113, 124, 147, 149, 151
Duesenberg, Inc., 26, 44, 51, 55, 74, 124, 150
Duesenberg, Denny, 124
Duesenberg, Fred, 55, 69, 72
Duesenberg Model J, 69, 75
Duesenberg Model X, 64
Dunn, Harry, L., 50, 75
Durant, Cliff, 82-84
Duray, Leon, 69, 85, 89

Eckhart Carriage Company (ECC), 9, 10, 15, 22, 23, 26
Eckhart, Anne, 22
Eckhart, Charles, 9-11, 13, 19, 22, 23, 26, 42
Eckhart, Frank, 9, 11, 13, 16, 17, 19, 22, 25, 28
Eckhart, George, B., 9, 11, 13

Eckhart, Morris, 13, 19, 34
Eckhart, William, 22
Eclipse Machine Company, 142
Emanuel, Victor, 153-155, 157
Ermler, John, 110

F.B. Hitchcock and Company, 28-30
Farley, James Indus, 28, 34, 45
Faulkner, Roy, 34, 54, 72, 73, 78, 97, 109, 115, 133, 135, 155, 156, 158
Flynn, John T., 155

Gardner, Vince, 125, 126
Gear Grinding Machine Company, 91, 122
Goossen, Leo, 81, 89
Gregory, Ben, 81, 82, 100
Grinshaw, Robert, 66
Griswold Motor Body Company, 66

Harlow, Jean, 97
Hayes Body Company, 97
Hepburn, Ralph, 85
Hershey, Franklin Q., 96
Hilkey, C.E., 61
Hill, Bennett, 82
Hitchcock, F.B., 28
Hitchcock, H.H., 28

Issigonis, Alex, 81

Jaquet, Ed, 137
Jenkins, David Abbot "Ab", 115, 145, 147, 149, 151
Johnson, E.A., 22, 29, 34
Jones, Louis, R., 117
Junkyard formula, 72, 73

Keech, Ray, 69
Kemp, A.P., 28, 34
Kublin, George, 75, 115, 119, 135

Lain, M.M., 73
Landis, Arhtur, 61, 75
Larson, Fred, 157
Leamy, Alan Huet, 74, 75, 89, 91, 94, 95, 107
Leasure, Melvin E., 16
LeBaron, Inc., 150
Lewis, Dave, 82
LGS Corporation free-wheeling system, 77
LGS Devices, 155
Limousine Body Company, 71, 99
Lobban, Ida Lewis, 42
Lorenzen, Paul Peter Reuter, 110, 122, 123, 125, 126, 133
Lycoming Foundry and Machine Company, 50, 51, 60, 63, 123, 125, 136, 140, 143, 146

Manning, Lucius Bass , 39, 40, 45, 54, 72, 89, 105, 109, 129
Marx Brothers, 90
McCormick, J.H., 72
McDarby, Neil, 54, 75
McInnis, A.H., 30
Menton, Stanley, 129
Merchanthouse, Don, 137
Miller, Eddie, 59, 61, 105
Miller, Harry, 66, 69, 81-85, 89, 100
Miller, Wellington Everett, 89
Milton, Tommy, 83-85
Model Automobile Company, 14
Model Gas and Gasoline Engine Company, 14, 15
Model Gas Engine Works, 14
Model Z, 21
Montez, Lola, 96
Montgomery Ward, 115
Morton, Wade, 59, 60, 66, 68
Moyer, D. R., 10
Murphy, Jimmy, 81, 82

National Electric Power Company, 154
Newport, J. Herbert, 122

Offutt, Eddie, 89, 90
Oswald, John, 91, 94, 95
Otto, Carl, 95

Pak-Age-Car Corporation, 156
Parkhurst, E.H., 72
Penry, Emory Oscar, 16, 75
Permold Manufacturing Company, 123
Pierce-Arrow, 78
Pruitt, Raymond S., 54, 72

Rayfield, Charles, 12, 14
Rickenbach, August W., 125
Robinson, Richard, 66, 110, 113, 125, 126
Rollston Company, 96
Rooney, Tom, 59
Roosevelt, Franklin, D., 133, 153
Rose, James, H., 29, 45
Rutenber, 12, 15, 16, 18, 19
Ryan, Ellis, W., 69, 72
Rzeppa constant-velocity joints, 91, 142, 146

Schwitzer-Cummins Corporation, 146
Sheller Manufacturing Company, 132
Shugers Manufacturing Company, 22
Shugers, George W., 22
Smith, A.O., 99
Snepp, Blaine O., 31
Snow, Herbert C., 69, 75, 86, 95, 115, 117, 119, 122, 131, 135-137
SPAR (Studebaker, Pierce-Arrow, and Rockne), 78
Spencer Heater, 140
Startix, 104
Steeldraulic brakes, 77
Stein, Waldo, 151
Stevens Trophy, 145, 147, 149
Stickney, Raymond, 96
Stinson, Edward, A., 72
Straus, Simon, 15
Stutz Motors, 59, 112

Thomas, Stanley, 115, 128
Tilt, C.A., 156
Tjaarda, John, 64
Tremulis, Alex, 144, 146, 147, 150, 156
Trexler Special, 73
Trexler, Marion, 73

U.S. Electric Power Company, 154
Union Automobile Company, 23
Union City Body Company, 96, 97, 111
Updike, Bert, 151

Vaanden Plas, 97
Van Ranst, Cornelius W., 74, 83-85, 89, 91, 92, 94, 95, 101, 119
Vultee Airplane Development Corporation, 151

Walter M. Murphy Company, 96
Watson, Pearl, 26, 55, 113
Weaver, Harry, 119
Weidely engine, 35-37, 49
Weisheit, E. Roy, 133
Wexelberg, Clarence, 112
Weymann-American, 96
White Caravan, 117
Wiley, Robert S., 54, 142
William, Warren, 88
Willis, P.P., 59, 72, 138
Winn, Billy, 147
Winton automobile, 11
Wright, Philip O., 96, 97, 150
Wrigley, William K., Jr., 28

Zimmerman Manufacturing Company, 20, 23
Zimmerman, Elias, 20

Zimmerman, Franklin, 20
Zimmerman, John, 23

Auburn Models:
4-36, 23, 25
4-38, 25
4-40, 19, 23
4-44, 54, 57

6-38 Light Six, 25
6-38, 25
6-39, 31
6-39-B, 26
6-39C, 26
6-39 coupe, 30
6-39-E Chummy, 26
6-39H, 30
6-39-K, 30
6-39 Light six, 26
6-39M, 26
6-39-R, 30
6-39-sedan, 30
6-39 Sport, 26
6-40, 23
6-40A, 25
6-43, 34, 35, 37, 47
6-44, 26
6-45 coupe, 18
6-45 limousine, 18
6-45 touring, 18, 19
6-45B roadster, 18, 19
6-46, 17
6-47, 23
6-50, 19
6-50 touring, 18
6-51, 33, 34
6-51 Sport, 33
6-63, 34, 35, 37, 47, 49, 50
6-63 Sport, 37
6-66, 51, 52, 54, 57
6-80, 69
6-85, 72

8-88, 51, 52, 54, 57, 59, 60
8-98, 75, 77
8-100, 78, 104
8-101, 105
8-105, 105

12-160, 104
12-161, 105
12-165, 105, 106
30-L, 19
30-L touring, 18
30-M, 19
30-M roadster, 18

33-L, 19
33-L touring, 18
33-M, 19
33-M roadster, 18
35-L, 19
35-L touring, 18

37, 19
37-L touring, 18, 19

40, 16, 19
40-A, 19
40-H, 18
40-L, 19
40-M, 18
40-N touring, 18
40 town car, 18

76, 68

88, 68

115, 61, 63

652X, 107
652Y, 107
654, 116
655, 115

850X, 107
850Y, 107
851, 111, 114
852, 116

A, 13, 14
Auburn Model G, 9
Auburn Six, 19

B, 14, 15
Beauty Six, 30-32, 47

C, 14, 15
Cabin speedster, 63, 64, 66, 67, 68, 72

D, 14, 15

E, 14

F, 14, 15, 16

G, 15, 16

H, 15

I-20, 69
I-25, 72, 77

K, 15, 16

L, 16

M, 16

pickup truck, 72

R, 16

S, 16
Six-50, 18
Six Supreme, 25, 35, 37

T, 16

Wanderer sedan, 52

X, 16

Y, 16

Cord Models
810, 86, 91, 115, 117, 126, 136-140, 142, 144, 151, 154, 155, 157
812, 147, 149, 151, 153, 155

E 278 prototype, 119, 122, 124, 126
E 286 prototype, 126, 129
E 294 prototype, 129, 131, 132, 136
E 306 prototype, 126, 130, 133, 135, 136, 139

L-27, 86, 91, 94
L-29, 69, 72, 74, 75, 78, 84, 87-91, 94-96, 98-100, 119